Aristotle and Natural Law

Bloomsbury Studies in Ancient Philosophy

Also available from Bloomsbury

Happiness and Greek Ethical Thought, M. Andrew Holowchak
Ideas of Socrates, Matthew S. Linck
Socratic Method, Rebecca Bensen Cain

Aristotle and Natural Law

Tony Burns

BLOOMSBURY
LONDON • NEW DELHI • NEW YORK • SYDNEY

Bloomsbury Academic
An imprint of Bloomsbury Publishing Plc

50 Bedford Square
London
WC1B 3DP
UK

175 Fifth Avenue
New York
NY 10010
USA

www.bloomsbury.com

First published by Continuum International Publishing Group 2011
Paperback edition first published 2013

British Library Cataloguing-in-Publication Data
A catalogue record for this book is available from the British Library.

ISBN: HB: 978-1-8470-6555-1
PB: 978-1-4725-0660-3

Library of Congress Cataloging-in-Publication Data
Burns, Tony, 1953-
Aristotle and natural law / Tony Burns.
p. cm. – (Continuum studies in ancient philosophy)
Includes bibliographical references (p.).
ISBN 978-1-84706-555-1
1. Aristotle. 2. Natural law – Philosophy. I. Title.
K434.A7B87 2011
340′.112092–dc23
2011016511

Typeset by Newgen Imaging Systems Pvt Ltd, Chennai, India

Contents

Acknowledgements

Permission has been granted to re-use material from the following publications: 'Conceptual history and the philosophy of the later Wittgenstein: A critique of Quentin Skinner's contextualism', *Journal of the Philosophy of History*, 5 (1) (2011), 54–83; 'Interpreting and appropriating texts in the history of political thought: Quentin Skinner and poststructuralism', *Contemporary Political Theory*, 10, 4 (2011); 'Aristotle', in D. Boucher and P. Kelly eds., *Political Thinkers: A History of Western Political Thought*, 2nd ed. Oxford: Oxford University Press, 2009, 81–99; 'Sophocles' *Antigone* and the history of the concept of natural law', *Political Studies*, 50, 3 (2002), 545–57; 'The tragedy of slavery: Aristotle's *Rhetoric* and the history of the concept of natural law', *History of Political Thought*, 24, 1 (2003), 16–36 and 'Aristotle and natural law', *History of Political Thought*, 19, 2 (1998), 142–66.

Introduction

Terminology: Natural Justice, Natural Right or Natural Law

This book is devoted to a discussion of Aristotle and natural law. I emphasize at the outset that, unlike Leo Strauss, I employ the notions of 'natural justice' and 'natural law' interchangeably. Like a number of commentators who have written about the concept of natural law throughout its long history, Strauss maintains that the idea of law, in the strict sense of the term, ought to be associated with that of command, specifically the command of some superior who has the authority to make law. Strauss argues that these notions are alien to the life and times of the ancient Greeks, especially Aristotle. In his view, therefore, it is a mistake to employ the concept of natural law when discussing Aristotle's ethical and political thought. It is for this reason that Strauss prefers to employ the English term 'natural right', rather than 'natural law', as the translation for the Greek term φυσικον δικαιον (*physikon dikaion*), which is employed by Aristotle in the *Nicomachean Ethics* (Aristotle, 1995e: 1134b–1135a, 1790–91; Strauss, 1974 [1953]; 1983a [1968]: 140, 143).[1] According to Strauss, it is not Aristotle but St. Thomas Aquinas who provides us with 'natural law teaching', properly so called, in its 'classic form' (Strauss, 1983a [1968]: 143). Presumably, therefore, Strauss believed that for Aquinas the principles of natural law are at least in part a product of the divine commands of the Christian God. For only then could they be laws properly so called. This is necessary even if it is not sufficient for them to be (and to be correctly described as) 'laws' in the strict sense of the term.

I can see no decisive reason why the term 'law' ought to be associated only with moral rules or directive principles which come into being by a creative act of will on the part of some legislator or other. I have no problem at all, therefore, accepting the view of those who maintain that the moral rules which are usually associated with the concept of natural law might legitimately be said to be laws even if they were not the commands of any superior. Nor, therefore, do I have a problem with translating Aristotle's *physikon dikaion* into English by the expression 'natural law'. Something like this view is usually associated with the thought of Hugo Grotius. As Francisco Suarez points out, however, a similar view was held by a number of theologians in the medieval period prior to Grotius's formulation of it in his *De Jure Belli ac Pacis* in 1625

(Grotius, 2005 [1625]: Prolegomena, XI, 89; I, I, X, 5, 155). Moreover a similar view is also held by some commentators today. Anthony Lisska, for example, has recently offered what he refers to as a 'reconstruction' of the ethical thought of St. Thomas Aquinas, within which Aquinas's doctrine of natural law is detached from any associations which it formerly had with the notion that the principles of natural law derive their binding force from the fact that they are seen as the commands of the Christian God (Lisska, 1997: viii, 12, 41, 50, 109, 113, 116–20, 127, 132–3, 186, 195). According to Lisska, 'the existence of God' is 'neither a relevant concept nor a necessary condition for Aquinas's account of natural law' (Lisska, 1997: 120).

Key Themes and Issues

Having addressed this issue of terminology, let me return to summarizing the thesis advanced in this book. In brief, I attempt to do three things, which stand in a triangular relationship to one another. The first is to shed some light on a number of issues having to do with the concept of natural justice or law, understood in its ethical or juridical sense. Here I am interested in such questions as the following: does this concept have an essential or unitary meaning? When did this concept emerge in the history of Western political thought? Does this concept have a history? How, if at all, has its meaning altered over time? Is there such a thing as '*the* natural law tradition'? If there is, then how should we understand this expression? Who are the main figures who (rightly or wrongly) are thought to have contributed to it? The second thing I attempt to do is to relate a discussion of the concept of natural law to the ethical and political thought of Aristotle. Or rather, turning things around, I consider the issue of whether Aristotle's ethical and political thought can be related to what is usually referred to as 'the natural law tradition', and if so how might this be done. Here the questions in which I am interested include the following: was Aristotle a natural law theorist at all? Was Aristotle the first natural law theorist? How do Aristotle's views on natural law differ, if at all, from those of other natural law theorists? Is there a distinct Aristotelian natural law tradition? If so, what are the characteristic features which identify it? The third concern of the book touches on questions of method, or of hermeneutic understanding. Here I am interested in issues having to do with the elucidation of the meaning of concepts, on the one hand, and with the reading of texts on the other. The concept on which I focus is of course that of natural law. The texts in question are, not surprisingly, the writings of Aristotle, especially the *Nicomachean Ethics*, which I discuss in Chapter 1; the Politics, which is the subject of Chapter 2; and the *Rhetoric*, which I examine in Chapter 3.

It is arguable that in principle the first cluster of questions just mentioned could be addressed and answered quite independently of the second, or of an examination of the views of Aristotle. At the same time, however, these two sets of questions can also be connected to one another. For a consideration of each also sheds light on the other. Indeed, it might be suggested that the relationship between them is a reciprocal one – a 'dialectical' relationship in the sense in which Hegel understands the term. In my view one cannot develop an adequate understanding of Aristotle's ethical and political thought without relating it to the natural law tradition – without first having an understanding of the concept of natural law and its history. Equally, however, one cannot have an adequate understanding of the natural law tradition and of its history without first having understood Aristotle's ethical and political thought, and the place which it has within that history: the contribution which Aristotle made to it.

The circularity in this line of reasoning is readily apparent. Readers familiar with debates in contemporary philosophical hermeneutics will immediately recognize the allusion to the notion of the 'hermeneutic circle', which was first deployed by Martin Heidegger and later elaborated on by Hans Georg Gadamer (Heidegger, 1987 [1927]: 194–5; Gadamer, 1975a,b [1960]). Gadamer suggests that reading texts is an active and not a passive process. To some extent, readers add meaning to a text in the process of reading it. As Gadamer puts it, they read a text in the light of certain 'prejudices', or what Heidegger refers to as a certain 'foremeaning', which are given to them by the particular time and society in which they happen to live, its history, its culture and traditions (Gadamer, 1975a [1960]: 239–40, 242; Heidegger, 1987 [1927]: 62–3, 189–92, 194–5). This is inevitable, and therefore by no means a reprehensible thing. The meaning of the text in question, therefore, is at least in part a product of these initial prejudices. At the same time, however, readers can be led to revise their initial prejudices as a consequence of their engagement with a particular text. These revised prejudices can then be passed down to later generations of readers; and so the process is repeated, in what is perhaps more accurately referred to as an 'hermeneutic spiral' rather than an 'hermeneutic circle'. In Gadamer's view, it is by means of this process that the meaning which a certain text has for the members of a particular historical (and linguistic) community evolves historically over time.

It is not my intention to endorse wholeheartedly Gadamer's general approach to hermeneutic understanding. Indeed, this has been effectively criticized by a variety of commentators from a number of different points of view, not least because of what is considered to be its inherent conservatism. This criticism was made long ago by Jurgen Habermas (Habermas, 1982, 1988a), who is not the only person who has objected to Gadamer's hermeneutics on these grounds. Gadamer's approach can also be sharply contrasted with that of a number of French theorists whose ideas have been associated with Poststructuralism in the last few decades (Caputo, 1987; Michelfelder and Palmer, 1989; Schrift, 1990; Silverman, 1994; Silverman and Ihde, 1985). My point here is simply that, so far as the issue of Aristotle and the concept of natural law is concerned, the idea of the hermeneutic circle does possess some relevance.

My own experience has been, for example, that I initially approached the reading of Aristotle's texts with a particular idea in mind of what the concept of natural law means, and what it is that 'natural law theorists' think, or ought to think. In short, I had certain prejudices or starting assumptions associated with a particular way of thinking about natural law and natural law theory, which I now associate specifically with Stoicism and the Stoic conception of natural law, as this is classically represented by Cicero in the following passage from his *De Republica*, written two centuries or so after Aristotle:

> True law is right reason in agreement with nature; it is of universal application, unchanging and everlasting' it summons to duty by its commands, and averts from wrongdoing by its prohibitions . . . It is a sin to try to alter this law, nor is it allowable to attempt to repeal any part of it, and it is impossible to abolish it entirely. We cannot be freed from its obligations by senate or People, and we need not look outside ourselves for an expounder or interpreter of it. And there will not be different laws at Rome and at Athens, or different laws now and in the future, but one eternal and unchangeable law will be valid for all nations and all times (Cicero, 1966 [1928]: III, XXII, 33, 211).

Readers familiar with what Aristotle says in the *Rhetoric* about the 'universal law', which is also the 'law of nature', will recognize this account (Aristotle, 1995h: 1368b1–10, 2178; 1375a 25–35, 2190). It is not entirely clear whether Cicero presents it in his own name or simply as a depiction of the views of the Greek Stoic philosophers before him. It is often thought, however, that Cicero did himself endorse the beliefs expressed in this passage.

There are a number of features which Cicero associates with the concept of natural law and with natural law theory here. First, he states that natural law is said to be both universal in its application and also eternal or unchanging. Second, he says that it is a higher law to which the civil laws of all human societies ought to conform. Finally, he says that this law conforms with the demands of reason or 'right reason'. Cicero also suggests that any and all individual moral agents, who are assumed to be not citizens of Rome or Athens, but rather human beings generally, can come to an understanding of the requirements of this law by employing their faculty of reason alone. Cicero expressly states that according to the Stoics 'we need not look outside ourselves for an expounder or interpreter of it'. As we shall see, it is sometimes suggested that taken together these beliefs, or this way of thinking about the world of ethics and politics, is radically different from that of Greek thinkers of the classical age, specifically Plato and Aristotle. I propose to challenge that view.

Bringing this way of thinking about natural law and natural law theory with me to the study of Aristotle, an engagement with those of Aristotle's writings where he talks about natural justice or law led me to the opinion that what Aristotle says about natural justice or law, especially in the well-known passage which constitutes Book V, Chapter 7 of his *Nicomachean Ethics* (Aristotle, 1995e: 1134b–1135a, 1790–91), simply does not 'fit in' with the expectations which I had as a consequences of holding those prejudices. Although there is, of course, another way of resolving this conflict, in my case this led me to rethink my understanding of the concept of natural law, and of the natural law tradition, in such a way that Aristotle might be included rather than excluded from it. It was this that led me to the conclusion that it is wrong to identify the Stoic conception of natural law with the very idea of natural law and 'natural law theory' per se, and to recognize the existence of a distinct Aristotelian natural law tradition.

The Aristotelian Natural Law Tradition

This particular natural law tradition has a number of distinguishing characteristics, not least Aristotle's belief in Book II of the *Nicomachean Ethics* that there are certain actions which are essentially wrong or unjust in and of themselves, such as the acts of murder, theft and adultery. As Aristotle himself puts it, not every action 'admits of a mean; for some have names that already imply badness', for example 'adultery, theft, murder; for all these and suchlike things imply by their names that they are themselves bad, and not the excess or deficiencies of them. It is not possible, then, ever to be right with them; one must always be wrong'. Thus, 'simply to do any of them is to go wrong' (Aristotle, 1995e: 1107a9–14, 1748). In Aristotle's view, the laws which forbid the performance of these actions are valid for all societies and all times, and that is why they can be said to be 'natural' laws. These laws ought, therefore, to be (and are) incorporated within the systems of civil law of all societies everywhere. It is conceded, however, that this can legitimately be done in different ways. It is for this reason that the principles of natural justice or law might be said to be in one sense at least 'changeable'.

It is clear that this reading of Aristotle brings me into conflict not only with those commentators who read Aristotle as a 'conventionalist' or ethical relativist, but also with some of those who argue that he is not. Fred Miller Jr., for example, has presented a natural law reading of the political thought of Aristotle (Miller Jr., 1997). Miller Jr. emphasizes the importance of Aristotle's suggestion in the *Ethics* and in the *Politics* that some political constitutions are 'perverted' or 'unjust', and therefore in a sense 'unnatural', because 'there is but one which is everywhere and by nature the best' (Aristotle, 1995e: 1135a4–5, 1791; Aristotle, 1995f: 1287b; 1325b). In his view, passages like this support a natural law reading of Aristotle. According to Miller Jr., in the great 'naturalism versus conventionalism' debate which took place in classical Athens, and which is the subject of discussion in Chapter 4 of this book, Aristotle took the former side. He was an advocate of the principle of 'naturalism'. In itself there is nothing objectionable about Miller Jr.'s suggestion that Aristotle was some kind of naturalist. Indeed, I argue along such lines myself throughout the present work. Miller Jr., however, identifies naturalism in ethics and politics with the outlook which I have associated with the Stoic conception of natural law. Thus he attributes to Aristotle the view that natural justice or law is a higher standard of justice which might be used by individuals to evaluate the laws of the society in which they live. His version of a natural law reading of Aristotle's political thought is in consequence very different from my own.

Perhaps the most important of these distinguishing characteristics is the Aristotelian tradition's implicit or explicit denial of the Stoic view that the principles of natural law do not require any external, authoritative interpretation by positive law, but can be interpreted and applied by the faculty of reason of the individual moral agent. For once the logical implications of this denial have been worked out, it then becomes clear that for those working within the Aristotelian tradition natural law cannot serve the function of being a higher standard of justice which might be used by individuals for the critical evaluation of the laws and institutions of the society in which they live, which Aristotle refers to as the principles of 'political justice' of a *polis*, and later Aristotelians term the 'civil law'. Rather, on the contrary, the function of natural law is that of providing a theoretical justification or legitimating for those laws and institutions, especially of course (and notoriously) the institution of slavery.

The difficulties associated with any natural law reading of Aristotle, as this idea is usually understood, are readily apparent to anyone who reads what Aristotle has to say about justice in Book V of the *Nicomachean Ethics*, an important source for the ideas which underpin much of the argument of Aristotle's *Politics*, especially the classification of the various different types of political constitution which he offers there. From this point of view, to act unjustly is simply to do that which 'is contrary to law' (Aristotle, 1995f, 1129b1–25, 1782), or that which conflicts with the requirements of what Aristotle refers to as the principles of 'political justice' (Aristotle, 1995f: 1134b18, 1790) of one's own *polis*. But it follows from this that for Aristotle there is no independent standard of justice or morality which stands above the system of political justice of any *polis*. There are no higher principles of justice which might be used as a measure or yardstick for evaluating the laws of a *polis* from the standpoint of their justice or injustice.

It is obvious that these beliefs of Aristotle present a problem for anyone seeking to defend the view that Aristotle is the founding father of the natural law tradition, or indeed that he might be considered to be a natural law theorist at all, in any sense of the term. For such beliefs are usually associated, not with natural law theory, but with its antithesis, the doctrine known as 'legal positivism'. And as Aristotle did hold the beliefs in question, it will need to be carefully explained why Hans Kelsen's conclusion that Aristotle was a distant forerunner of that doctrine does not automatically follow from the fact that he held them. It must be shown how it is possible in principle for Aristotle to be considered as some kind of natural law theorist despite the fact that he held such beliefs. This problem is an insuperable one for those who think that the Stoic conception of natural law is the only possible one. Those who think of natural law theory in that way can only deal with these remarks which Aristotle makes in his *Ethics* either by ignoring them or by downgrading their significance in some way. In my view the best way of dealing with this problem is not to ignore them or argue that they are unimportant but, rather, to revise our understanding of the concept of natural law, and of natural law theory. We need to reconsider the beliefs which we think must be held before we are justified in claiming that a particular thinker, whether this is Aristotle or anyone else, is a natural law theorist.

Interpreted in this way, because of its peculiar understanding of the nature of the relationship which exists between natural law, positive law and civil law, Aristotle's political thought is fundamentally 'conservative' in terms of its political implications. Aristotle is the founding father of a distinctively conservative natural law tradition. I share A. E. Taylor's view that so far as existing laws and institutions were concerned, Aristotle was almost 'entirely devoid of the spirit of the social reformer' (Taylor, 1955: 105). Indeed, even Fred D. Miller Jr., despite his commitment to a natural law interpretation of Aristotle, has conceded that Aristotle's attitude towards political change 'is, on the whole, very conservative' (Miller Jr., 1997: 186). Again I agree entirely with this judgment. It seems to me, however, that it is not consistent with Miller Jr.'s own version of a natural law reading of Aristotle. I accept Miller Jr.'s claim that Aristotle subscribes to a doctrine of natural law in *some* sense of the term. Nevertheless I find it difficult to also accept his suggestion that the principal reason why this is so is because Aristotle has a vision of an ideal or 'best' constitution which he presumed to be 'natural', and hence universally valid, which might serve as a critical yardstick for evaluating existing laws and institutions. In my view, Miller Jr. attaches too much importance, not only to Aristotle's remarks on natural law in the *Rhetoric*, but also to Aristotle's assertion in the *Nicomachean Ethics* that 'there is only one constitution that is everywhere and by nature the best' (Aristotle, 1995e: 1135a5, 1791). By focusing on these aspects of Aristotle's thinking, Miller Jr. seems to me to give Aristotle's (admittedly inconsistent) political thought much more of a radical hue than is indicated elsewhere in Aristotle's writings. He transforms Aristotle from a conservative into a radical thinker (Miller Jr. 1997: vii, 15, 67, 74–5, 187–8).

H. Jackson has argued that, like Plato, Aristotle can also be associated with the utopian political tradition (Jackson, 2001). This reading of Aristotle is completely alien to the spirit of Aristotle's approach to questions of ethics and politics as I understand it, even though I accept that Aristotle's political thought is best seen as some kind of natural law theory. Against Jackson I would argue that Aristotle is an arch-critic of all utopian speculation, and of course of the views of the utopian tradition's first great exponent, Plato. This is so despite the fact that Aristotle endorses the concept of natural law and incorporates it within his own system of political thought. For Aristotle's way of thinking about natural law and its relation to positive law is quite different from that of Plato and, later, of the Stoics. From Aristotle's point of view, natural justice or law is very far from being what Corbett refers to as 'perfect law' (Corbett, 2009: 243).

The 'Natural Law Passages' in Aristotle's Writings and Their Significance

One point which is of obvious relevance to any discussion of Aristotle and natural law is the fact that Aristotle says so little about the concept of natural justice or law in his writings. The passages in which he does this, which I shall refer to as 'the natural law passages', are relatively few and far between. There is the passage in which he talks about the 'changeability' of natural justice or law (φυσικον δικαιον, *physikon dikaion*) in Book V, Chapter 7 of the *Nicomachean Ethics* (Aristotle,1995e: 1134b18–1135a5, 1790–91). There are the passages in the *Rhetoric* where he discusses the idea of a 'universal law' (νομος κοινος, *nomos koinos*), which he states is commonly thought to be the 'law of nature' (Aristotle, 1995h: 1368b1–10, 2178; 1375a25–35, 2190). And there are some scattered marks in the *Politics* in which he suggests that to act unjustly is to act 'contrary to nature', and that for this reason 'corrupt' or 'perverted' constitutions are unnatural and run counter to the requirements of natural law or the law of nature (Aristotle, 1995h: 1325b7–10, 2103–4). The interpretation of his ethical and political thought offered here relies heavily, therefore, on a relatively limited number of passages which, in the view of some commentators, are not that significant and are, indeed, extraneous to Aristotle's authentic thought properly understood.

In the view of these commentators, to attach too much importance to these passages, as arguably St. Thomas Aquinas did in his *Summa Theologiae*, is to go seriously wrong. Indeed, on some accounts to attach any importance at all to them would be to commit an interpretive blunder. As we shall see, thinking of this kind can be associated with the advocates of what is usually referred to as the 'virtue ethics' reading of Aristotle, where the expression 'virtue ethics' is understood to refer to a morality without rules or laws. In my view, such a reading is clearly incompatible with any kind of natural law reading, as all natural law readings are based on the view that Aristotle's ethics rests on the idea that a virtuous or ethical life involves obedience to certain moral rules or laws, especially those which Aristotle deems to be natural. It must be conceded, however, that not all commentators agree with me with respect to this issue. Leo Strauss's account of what he refers to as Aristotle's doctrine of 'natural right' is a case in point (see Burns, 2010b). Strauss insists that the idea of following universal rules, or indeed any moral rules at all, is alien to the spirit of Aristotle's thinking. At the same time, however, he insists that it is still legitimate to refer to Aristotle's ethical thought as a specific type of doctrine of natural right. Strauss, therefore, employs the expression 'natural right', on some occasions at least, in a very specific sense which, in my view, goes beyond the limits laid down by the linguistic convention which currently regulates its use.

According to advocates of the 'virtue ethics' reading of Aristotle and others, any natural law reading of Aristotle will rely far too heavily on certain passages in the key texts in which Aristotle says things which do not reflect the true spirit of his own thinking – where Aristotle stands in contradiction with himself. As examples of commentators who argue in this way we may take Hans Kelsen and John McDowell. As we shall see in Chapter 1, Kelsen offers a reading of Aristotle which presents him as a 'conventionalist' or an ethical relativist pure and simple, and therefore as somebody for whom the notion of natural law has no significance at all. The passages where Aristotle refers with apparent approval to the notion of natural justice or law in his *Nicomachean Ethics,* or to the 'law of nature' in his *Rhetoric,* are therefore problematic for Kelsen. This is so for the obvious reason that they provide evidence which counts against his proposed interpretation of Aristotle. In order to strengthen his own thesis, Kelsen has to find some way of rebutting this evidence. How does Kelsen do this? His general strategy is to suggest that the passages in question can and should be associated with the corruption of the original Aristotelian texts. In Kelsen's view they are not in spirit 'Aristotelian', as he understands that notion. Consequently Kelsen argues that they must have been inserted into the text of the *Ethics,* not by Aristotle himself, but by a later commentator, who evidently misunderstood Aristotle's authentic thought. Thus, for example, when commenting on Aristotle's suggestion in the *Ethics* and in the *Politics* that some political constitutions are 'perverted' or 'unjust', and therefore in a sense 'unnatural', because 'there is but one which is everywhere and by nature the best' (Aristotle, 1995e: 1135a4–5, 1791; Aristotle, 1995f: 1287b; 1325b), Kelsen argues that the passages in the *Politics* when Aristotle makes this claim, upon which Fred Miller Jr.'s version of a natural law reading of Aristotle is heavily reliant, stand 'in open contradiction to one of the main theses of Aristotle's political theory, regarding the natural givenneness of all states'. He claims, on these grounds, that it is 'more than doubtful' that these remarks are authentic, seeing that they contradict 'everything that Aristotle otherwise says about the nature of the state'. For Kelsen the line of reasoning in these passages, which evidently do support some kind of natural law reading of his political thought, are 'at variance with the intellectual scheme of the whole Aristotelian theory' (Kelsen, 1973b: 147). It is, Kelsen argues, difficult to avoid supposing that these passages, which are 'so crucial' to the 'alleged natural law theory of Aristotle' are 'not corrupt' (Kelsen, 1973b: 134–5).

I am in partial agreement with the broad thrust of Kelsen's argument against the kind of natural law reading of Aristotle which is advanced by Fred Miller Jr. In my view Kelsen is right to suggest that, in the very passages upon which Miller Jr. rests his claim that Aristotle is a natural law theorist, the views expressed by Aristotle do appear to be (and perhaps in some cases are) inconsistent with what he says elsewhere about questions of ethics and politics. In my opinion, though, this is *not* a reason for concluding that Aristotle is not a natural law theorist at all. Rather, it is a reason for changing the way we think about natural law theory. Moreover I find Kelsen's strategy for dealing with the passages in question unconvincing. It is true that the existence of such passages points to an apparent contradiction in Aristotle's thinking. However, in my view, to set these passages aside, or simply to dismiss them as being corruptions of the original Aristotelian texts, is not the best solution to this problem. After all, as Werner Jaeger has argued, Aristotle might simply have changed his mind about this issue. According to Jaeger, Aristotle moved from an earlier Platonic position in which he has an interest in problems of political theory, especially in establishing the nature of an 'ideal' constitution, which provides the subject matter of Books I–II and VII–VIII of his *Politics*, to a later position in which he adopts the standpoint of a 'political scientist' and undertakes his empirical study of the different types of constitutions, the results of which he presents in Books IV–VI (Jaeger, 1948; see also Grene, 1998 [1963]: 13–37).

John McDowell also deals with these natural law passages in a somewhat cavalier fashion. McDowell objects to any reading of Aristotle which attributes to him the view that the idea of virtuous conduct is something which 'can be spelled out as a set of rules of conduct'. He also notes that 'many commentators', including of course the advocates of natural law readings, 'equip' Aristotle 'with a kind of practical thinking' of this kind, and which 'applies rules to cases' (McDowell, 1998b: 26). McDowell insists, though, that this is not acceptable as account of the 'deliberative structure' that Aristotle 'must have' had 'in mind' (McDowell, 1998b: 26–7). McDowell does not deny that the passages upon which the 'natural law' interpretations of Aristotle rely exist. He does, however, that their importance. For example, in a footnote (which is all that he thinks discussion of this issue merits) McDowell concedes that Aristotle 'does seem (reasonably enough) to envisage universal prohibitions on, for instance, adultery or murder'; and he also concedes that 'if we formulated universal rules in such terms' then 'the sort of specificatory problem that 'rule'-'case' thinking is supposed to address' would then 'show up, on occasion, in the form of questions about the applicability of the key terms in the rules' (McDowell, 1998b: 27). McDowell insists, however, that 'it is hardly plausible that a conception of how a human being should live could be fully captured in terms of these universal prohibitions'. Consequently, he suggests that it is undesirable that such a view should be attributed to Aristotle. In other words, those seeking to understand Aristotle can afford to ignore those passages in his writings which appear to support a natural law reading of his ethical thought. McDowell seems to think that neither the idea of following universal rules, such as those forbidding acts such as murder and theft, nor that of applying such rules to the circumstances of particular cases, are sufficient alone or together for an adequate understanding of Aristotle's notion of an ethical or virtuous life. Nor, however, are they even necessary. Consequently he comes to the conclusion that the passages where Aristotle appears to endorse the notion of natural justice or natural law can simply be set aside.

My own view is that even if the idea of following universal rules and of applying such rules to the circumstances of particular cases are not sufficient for an adequate understanding of Aristotle's thinking on this subject, they are at least necessary. The natural law passages in Aristotle's writings cannot and should not, therefore, be dismissed so lightly. Rather we need to consider how the ideas contained within them can be integrated into a comprehensive account of Aristotle's views. These passages are not peripheral but rather central for any adequate understanding of Aristotle's ethical and political thought as a whole. The sentiments expressed by Aristotle within them are not extraneous to, but entirely consistent with, Aristotle's fundamental thought regarding the question of what is involved in the idea of a life devoted to virtue. With respect to this issue, then, I am in agreement with Aquinas's reading of Aristotle. In short Aquinas did not in my view anachronistically 'read into' the writings of Aristotle ideas which were not already there beforehand, especially the idea that leading a virtuous life is in part a matter of rule following (Burns, 2002a).

So far as the concept of law is concerned, a number of commentators have noted that there is a difference between asking the question 'what is the nature of law?' and asking the question 'what is the law of nature?' (del Vecchio, 1921: 19–20, 86–9, 120–1; 1952: 248; Kelsen, 1957b: 133–34, 1972 [1961]: 416–17, 439–40; Perelman, 1963: 37–40; Stammler, 1969 [1925]: 75–6, 85–91). Georgio del Vecchio, for example, has argued that the 'need for a logical determination of law' must be kept 'distinctly separate from the deduction of a system of natural or rational law' (del Vecchio, 1921: 19–20). In his opinion, there is a persistent tendency in the history of political thought for certain authors to confuse 'logical and ethical or deontological demands', or 'the purely logical concept of law' with 'other elements' of the theory of law. The authors guilty of this confusion or conflation have tried to solve these two distinct problems by a single doctrine'. Hence in seeking 'the logical qualities of law' they have at the same time attempted 'to establish its ideal paradigm', or what R. J. Corbett refers to as 'perfect law' (del Vecchio, 1921: 86–7; Corbett, 2009: 243).

Similar remarks might also be made about the concept of justice. It is arguable that there has been a persistent tendency in the history of political thought, from Plato onwards, to assume that an examination of the nature of justice, or a logical analysis of the concept of justice, can in del Vecchio's words provide us with a substantive 'ideal of justice' which is assumed to have a universal validity, and which is in consequence considered to be a principle of 'natural' justice (del Vecchio, 1921: 88–9). In my view, this observation certainly applies to Plato. As Glenn R. Morrow has observed, according to Plato natural justice and the nature of justice, or the idea of justice, are one and the same thing. As Morrow puts it, for Plato 'natural justice *is* the Idea Justice'. Thus in Plato's political thought '"justice itself" and "natural justice" mean the same thing' (Morrow, 1948: 31). More to the point for present purposes, however, is that this is also true of Aristotle's analysis of the concept of justice in Book V of the *Nicomachean Ethics*. Aristotle held, as did Plato before him, that to talk about the nature of justice and to talk about natural justice, or about that justice which is natural, is to talk about the same thing. For in Aristotle's view *all* justice is in a sense natural justice. One important implication of this is that, considered from this standpoint, Aristotle's remarks in Book 1 of the *Politics* about man being by nature a 'social and political animal' who is destined to live a life of justice together with others in a *polis* under a system of law are entirely consistent with a certain type of natural law reading of his ethical and political thought. They can, therefore, be legitimately claimed as offering support for such a reading.

Questions of Method

We have already seen that an examination of Aristotle's ideas in relation to the concept of natural law, and the natural law tradition in the history of political thought raises certain questions of method. Hence the references to Gadamer and the 'hermeneutic circle' above. In the remainder of this Introduction, I would like to say a little more about this issue and to introduce the reader to the theoretical framework, and the vocabulary associated with it, that I deploy when reading Aristotle's writings throughout the remainder of the book. In order to do this I shall make a distinction between those problems which are associated with establishing the meaning of concepts, especially of course the concept of natural law, and those which are associated with the reading of texts.

These two issues are related to one another, or rather they can be related to one another, as the meaning of text is closely related to that of the concepts which are deployed by its author within it. However, they are not identical. For it is not only in texts that concepts are employed. Nor of course are concepts employed only by the authors of texts, who always inherit them from the 'linguistic community' of which they are members, and who may or may not significantly alter their meaning by employing them in a new or different (and politically significant) way. I shall discuss these two topics in turn, starting with texts.

Issues Surrounding the Reading of Texts

So far as texts are concerned, the key issue is that of establishing their meaning. This is done by offering what I shall refer to as a 'reading' of them. Here the word 'reading' is employed as a generic term which covers three particular species, which I shall refer to by the notions of 'interpretation', 'appropriation' and 'negotiation', respectively. I shall assume that there are three basic approaches to this problem of how to read texts associated with each of these types of activity. I shall also say something about the notion of the 'reconstruction' of texts. Whether or not this can legitimately be thought of as a fourth approach to the reading of texts in its own right is open to debate. I should emphasize that the point of introducing the reader to this terminology is because I think it will help us to get to grips with our broad theme, that of Aristotle and natural law.

According to the three approaches to reading texts just mentioned, the meaning of a text is some thing which is

(1) created by and given to a text by its author and which is then later discovered by the reader of that text, in and through an act of 'interpretation';
(2) created by and given to a text, not by its author, but solely and exclusively by the reader of that text, in and through an act of 'appropriation';
(3) produced by an erstwhile dialogue between the reader of a text and its author, in and through a process of 'negotiation'.

The first of these three approaches to the reading of texts can be associated with the work of Quentin Skinner. The second is usually associated with Poststructuralism, as exemplified by a figure such as Jacques Derrida, Michel Foucault and Gilles Deleuze (wrongly in the case of Derrida). The third might be associated with the work of Hans Georg Gadamer.

Here the concept of a 'reading' is the most general and operates at a higher level than the others, which must be thought of as operating on the same level as one another. In other words, interpretations, appropriations and negotiations are all 'readings' in the sense in which that term is used here. By a reading I have in mind what is usually meant by the word 'interpretation'. A reading is an attempt by someone to understand a text, it being assumed that the text in question be, and often will be, understood in different ways. A reading may or may not pay attention to the intentions of the authors of texts, or the meaning which texts, and the ideas which they contain, have for the persons who wrote them.

Establishing Meaning by Interpretation

By an interpretation I mean a specific type of reading. Readings of this kind can be associated with the first of the three approaches to hermeneutic understanding referred to above. Interpretations, in this technical sense of the term 'interpretation', aim to 'get at' the intentions of the author of a text and/or the meaning which the text had for its author. The point of offering an interpretation is that it is an attempt to understand a particular text as the author of that text understood it herself or himself. On this view the aim of an interpretation of a text is to attempt to understand the ideas in a text in their own terms, or as the author of the text in question understands or understood them, quite irrespective of the use to which these ideas might possibly be put by the reader of the text in question. Rightly or wrongly, then, someone who attempts to offer an interpretation of the ideas of another can be thought of as someone who (some would say naively) seeks the 'truth' in relation to the meaning of the text in question. Interpretations of texts can be thought of as being either true or false, correct or incorrect. They can be evaluated on the basis of an appeal to relevant empirical evidence (e.g. an explicit statement by the author of a text relating to its meaning, or to the author's intentions when writing it, in diaries, correspondence, and the like; or the assumed to be reliable testimony of others relating to conversations had with the author; and so on). Moreover, on this view, disputes between interpreters can in principle be resolved by means of rational argument and debate, in which both parties appeal to relevant evidence in support of their own interpretation and in an attempt to demonstrate the falsity or implausibility of the interpretation which is offered by their opponent. There are of course problems with these 'realist' assumptions, which have often been discussed by those interested questions of philosophical hermeneutics.

Some readers of this book may think that this use of the word 'interpretation' is an unusual one, as the notion of an interpretation is sometimes associated with the principle of relativism, and hence the idea that all interpretations are equally valid or equally true. However, it is not clear to me that it is so rare to find hermeneuticists who are 'objectivists' rather than relativists. Quentin Skinner, for example, has argued that what he refers to as 'the traditional goal of interpretation' is that of 'grasping an alien action, utterance or text 'objectively' in its own terms' (Skinner, 1985a: 7). According to Skinner, thought of in this way the activity of 'interpretation' is again 'traditionally' considered to be a 'method of attaining truths', that is to say, objective truths, relating to the meaning of texts (Skinner, 1985a: 7). So it is far from clear, I think, that all advocates of hermeneutics are relativists. But in any case, the understanding of the concept of hermeneutic interpretation employed here is the one that focuses on those supposed rarities, namely hermeneuticists who are committed to the notion of objective truth so far as the interpretation of texts is concerned.

The claim that 'there are no facts, only interpretations', which is usually attributed to Nietzsche (1968: 267), reflects very well what is perhaps the most basic assumption of 'interpretivism' as again it is often understood today. Indeed this principle is associated with interpretivism, both by interpretivists themselves, who approve of it, and by the 'realist' critics of interpretivism who do not. On this view, the idea of a 'factual interpretation' or an interpretation which might be said to be, if not objectively true, at least an attempt to get at an objective truth, or the truth relating to the meaning of a text, a truth which subsists in some way independently of the reader (who does *not* therefore create it) is a contradiction in terms. According to the meaning of the term interpretation as it is used here, however, this is precisely what an interpretation, in the strict sense of the term, attempts to do. Perhaps the best way to think about this is to employ an analogy taken from the discipline of medicine. The images on an X-ray photograph, or the symptoms of a disease, do not speak for themselves. They do not directly and transparently indicate which disease it is that they are the symptoms of. They require interpretation. Different doctors, depending on their experience, might interpret these images or symptoms in different ways. But these interpretations are not all equally valid or true. Mistakes can be made, wrong diagnoses offered, and so on. This is the sense of the word 'interpretation' which is being used here.

The reader may or may not have noticed that one item which is missing from the above list is 'deconstruction', a term which is usually associated with the work of Jacques Derrida, and with Poststructuralism. The reason for this is that, as I argue elsewhere (Burns, 2011b), I consider deconstructive readings of texts to be interpretations of them in the sense just indicated. Thus, for example, if we consider what I have referred to as 'the natural law passages' in Aristotle's writings, then it might be said of them, employing Derrida's terminology, that for critics of natural law readings of Aristotle's ethics these passages in Aristotle's are of peripheral importance. Far from being central to Aristotle's thought, they are best seen as lying within the 'margins' of the texts (Derrida, 1982 [1972]). In their opinion, of course, this is a reason for dismissing them. Against this judgment it is tempting to follow Derrida, whose views on the subject of reading of texts have in my opinion often been misunderstood. Derrida's own approach to the interpretation of texts, which may be associated with the notion of deconstruction or a deconstructive reading, relies on the assumption that there are occasions when an author may say extremely significant things in the margins of a text, perhaps in a footnote or in a casual aside which, suitably interpreted, can provide the reader with a deeper insight into the meaning of the text in question. These statements may contradict (or appear to contradict) what the author says elsewhere, either in the same or other texts, about the issue they address; and it may well be that the author in question is not consciously aware of their significance. This can, however, be revealed by the interpreter, who is engaged in what might be referred to as a 'psychoanalytics of reading' (Eagleton, 1994a [1983]; Wright, 1995 [1982]). According to this view the intentions of the author of a text should not simply be ignored or set aside. At the same time, however, they are susceptible to critical scrutiny by the reader, who must focus as much on what the author actually achieved as on what he or she intended to achieve.

Derrida is generally considered to be a Poststructuralist, and his approach to the reading of texts as being typical of Poststructuralism. At the same time, however, it is also thought that Poststructuralists subscribe to the principle of 'the death of the author', and hold the view that when reading a text 'anything goes!' In my view, this understanding of Derrida itself involves an error of interpretation (Burns, 2011b). Derrida's approach to the reading of texts, properly understood, seems to me to have a possible application to the reading of Aristotle, and especially to those 'marginal' passages in the corpus of his writings in which he discusses the subject of natural justice or law.

Establishing Meaning by Appropriation

I associate the word 'appropriation' with the second of the three approaches to hermeneutic understanding referred to above. The notion of an interpretation as it is used here is associated with three key features. The first is that such a reading has a practical or political relevance for the person who produces it. In such readings the ideas of an author are taken up and used by the reader for purposes of their own. Such readings reflect the interest and concerns of the reader, who is situated within a socio-historical context which might be quite different from that of the original author of the text in question. The person who appropriates a text, or the ideas which it contains, is not motivated by the desire to offer a truthful interpretation of the text in the sense indicated earlier. The second feature is that those readings of texts which I call appropriations seriously distort the meaning of a text as we may presume it was understood by its author. They radically alter the meaning of the concepts contained within a text, and therefore the meaning of the text itself. If an appropriation of a text were presented as an interpretation of it then it would be rejected by the vast majority of scholars working within the field, or even all of them, as being false or invalid. The third feature is that the act of appropriation, like all other actions properly so called, is intentional. It is not possible, therefore, for a reader to appropriate the ideas of a text or of its author by accident, unconsciously or unintentionally. Strictly speaking, all three of the abovementioned features must be present if a reading of a text is to be correctly described as an 'appropriation' of it. It should be noted, in particular, that there is a significant difference between the idea of an appropriation and that of a false interpretation of a text. It is possible of course that in hard cases, not all three of these features will be present. It will not then be clear how a given reading ought to be classified – as a deeply flawed interpretation or as an appropriation of a text.

For those who make the conceptual distinction between the notion of interpretation and that of appropriation, appropriators of the ideas of others are prepared to plunder a text for ideas which they themselves find useful, and to present those ideas to the world, either in their own name or in the name of the author of the text in question, even if at the same time they seriously distort the meaning of these ideas, and of the text which contains them, by ignoring completely the way in which those ideas are used by the author of that text. Appropriators have no interest in the intentions of the author of a text, or the meaning and the ideas it contains have for the person who wrote it. They have no interest at all in the 'truth', so far as the meaning of texts is concerned. It is therefore incorrect to call their readings 'interpretations' of the text in question, in the sense of that term indicated earlier. Nevertheless, it is arguable that the appropriation of texts and of the ideas contained within them is an important activity in the history of political thought, and also therefore something which ought to be of interest to historians of ideas. The appropriative reading at a later time of a text written by an author at an earlier one is something which can and should be of interest to the historian. Moreover, the fact that a later reading of an important text might be an appropriation of it, rather than an interpretation, does not affect the historical or political significance of that reading in the specific context within which it is presented to the world. What really matters here is how the ideas associated with a particular reading are taken up and acted on at the time rather than any authenticity they might or might not be thought to possess in relation to the original text and its meaning. The later appropriations of texts, then, are just as much legitimate objects of study for the historian as are the texts themselves, and the issue of their interpretation. Interpretation and appropriation, and the study of them by the intellectual historian, are two separate and mutually compatible activities, neither one of which should be thought of as being superior to the other.

This way of thinking about the notion of appropriation has some interesting implications. One of these is that a reading of a text which most or even all commentators would accept is wildly implausible if it is thought of as an interpretation should not for that reason alone be classified as an appropriation. For even an interpretation which is unanimously considered to be false of invalid could, nonetheless, justifiably be said to be an 'interpretation' properly speaking, provided the person who offered it intended it to be one. It is not clear, however, that this argument 'works in reverse', as it were. For example it might be asked: what is the status of readings which most or even all commentators would accept as being plausible if they were offered as 'interpretations' of a text, but which in fact are not offered for this reason at all? If we assume that these readings reflect the interests and concerns of the reader in much the same way that appropriations do, then is there not a case for arguing that such readings, also, should be thought of as appropriations rather than interpretations? However, from the standpoint of my own understanding of the notion of appropriation, it would not be correct to describe such a reading as an 'appropriation', because in such cases condition two above is not satisfied, given that readings of this kind do not seriously distort the meaning of the original text or concepts.

Another implication of this understanding of the notion of appropriation is that in principle a particular reading of a text could be either an interpretation (a flawed one) or an appropriation of it, and which of the two it actually is will depend on the intentions of the person who presents it. It is worth referring to the work of Mark Bevir at this point. Bevir has drawn a conceptual distinction between what he refers to as 'texts' and 'works' (Bevir, 1999: 57–59, 74, 122). Texts, he says, have a 'semantic meaning' and can be associated with a variety of different possible intentions on the part of their authors. Works, on the other hand, have an 'hermeneutic meaning', which Bevir associates with the specific intentions of the author who wrote them. Like Quentin Skinner, Bevir attaches importance here to the principle of intentionality. Following J. L. Austin, both Skinner and Bevir maintain that language users generally, including the authors of works of political theory, 'do things with words'. They perform certain speech acts. And it is these which ought to be of interest to historians of ideas. On this view, in order to understand any 'speech act' it is necessary to be familiar with the intentions of the person who performed it, who in this case is presumed to be the author of a work. Bevir argues, therefore, that intellectual historians should be interested in works rather than in texts. Bevir does not acknowledge any debt to the work of Roland Barthes here. However, the affinity between his views and those of Barthes is readily apparent (see Barthes, 1977).

To illustrate his distinction between 'texts' and 'works' Bevir uses the interesting example of 'two essays, one written in the eighteenth century and one written in the twentieth century, containing exactly the same words and punctuation in exactly the same order' (Bevir, 1999: 59). He suggests that these essays can be thought of either as texts or as works. Not surprisingly, Bevir says that intellectual historians ought to be interested in these two essays, not in so far as they are texts, or perhaps two different productions of the same text, but only insofar as they are works (Bevir, 1999: 58). They must seek to establish what their authors were attempting to do when they wrote them. If, for example, the intentions of the two authors were different, perhaps because one intended the work to be a satire and the other did not, then according to Bevir it makes sense to say in this situation that there are two different works even though there is only one text. It is fruitful to think of the distinction that I have made between readings, interpretations and appropriations along similar lines. A reading in my schema is the equivalent of Bevir's text. If one thinks of this reading as being either an interpretation or an appropriation then one is thinking of it as a particular work, in Bevir's sense of the term, and not just as a text. From this point of view all readings of texts should be thought of as being works of some kind. The crucial question here however, in the case of any given reading, which is itself a 'text' in Bevir's sense, is of what kind? Is it a work in the sense of being an interpretation, or is it a work in the sense that it is an appropriation?

It should be emphasized that my distinction between those who interpret and those who appropriate the ideas of others is not intended as a criticism of the latter, or to be associated with the opinion that the *only* legitimate activity here is the interpretation rather than the appropriation of texts – just as I do not think that the only legitimate activity is the appropriation as opposed to the interpretation of texts, or the study of such appropriations. In my view these are two different and, depending upon one's concerns, equally legitimate activities. However, I do think that they ought to be kept conceptually separate from one another. Moreover I am reluctant to accept that there are no interpretations of texts in the sense in which I have used the term; and that all readings of texts are necessarily appropriations of them. In my view, then, the readers of texts should be clear in their own minds which of these activities they are performing – interpreting or appropriating.

Not all of those who have discussed these issues make a distinction between interpreting and appropriating texts and the ideas contained within them. For example, Martin Heidegger does not. In his view, 'in every case' an act of interpretation is 'grounded in something we have in advance' in a 'fore having' or a 'fore conception'. According to Heidegger, by means of an act of interpretation something which is hidden 'becomes unveiled by an act of appropriation, and this is always done under the guidance of a point of view, which fixes that with regard to which what is understood is to be interpreted' (Heidegger, 1987 [1927]: 191). Elsewhere Heidegger states that the 'development of the understanding' is what 'we call "interpretation", and that in any act of interpretation 'the understanding appropriates' that which 'is understood by it' (Heidegger, 1987 [1927]: 188). In Heidegger's hermeneutics, then, to interpret a text and to appropriate it are the same thing. For Heidegger all interpretation is necessarily associated with an act of appropriation which involves an attempt to take control of a text by imposing oneself upon it.

The notion of 'appropriation' also has a part to play in the hermeneutic thought of Paul Ricoeur (Ricoeur, 1976, 1995a). I should emphasize, therefore, that the meaning which it has for Ricoeur is quite different from that employed here. Ricoeur rejects the view that the act of appropriation should be associated with placing the meaning of a text 'under the domination of the subject who interprets [sic]'. In his view, to understand is *not* to 'project oneself into the text' (Ricoeur, 1981a: 182). Rather it is to be associated with a certain 'relinquishment of the self' (Ricoeur, 1983b: 183). Thus appropriation, for Ricoeur, has nothing to do with the idea, which can be found in the work of both Heidegger and Gadamer, of a 'projection of the prejudices of the reader into his reading' (Ricoeur, 1983b: 190). Ricoeur insists that 'relinquishment' of the self, or of the ego of the reader, 'is a fundamental moment of appropriation', which therefore must be distinguished from 'any form of "taking possession"' (Ricoeur, 1983a: 191). Given these remarks, as James Risser has noted, 'one has to wonder' why Ricoeur 'chose this word' [i.e. 'appropriation'] 'at all' to characterize his own approach to the reading of texts (Risser, 1997: 234). The irony here is evident. In order to challenge a pre-existing way of thinking about the notion of appropriation, which he associates with the work of Heidegger, Ricoeur appropriates for his own purposes the meaning of the concept of appropriation. Throughout the present work the understanding which I have of the notion of appropriation is closer to that of Heidegger and Gadamer than it is to that of Ricoeur, without being identical to it. I associate my own understanding with Poststructuralism, especially the views of Michel Foucault and Gilles Deleuze, although not those of Jacques Derrida (Burns, 2011b).

The notion of appropriation can be connected to that of a 'struggle for recognition', along the lines famously laid down by Hegel in the so-called 'Master-Slave Section' of his *Phenomenology of Spirit* (Hegel, 1977 [1807]: §§178–96, 111–19). Both G. Douglas Atkins and Danny J. Anderson have suggested that the relationship between a reader of a text and its author can be seen as a conflict between author and reader analogous to the struggle for dominance or superiority which Hegel associates with the relationship between 'master' and 'slave' (Atkins, 1983: 87–8; Anderson, 1989: 151). This is a struggle for ownership and control of the meaning of a text, which is seen as an item of property. The key issue, therefore, is who is to be 'master' so far as the meaning of a text is concerned, the author or the reader, and who is to be 'slave'?. As G. D. Atkins puts it, if we think of the relationship between author and reader along these lines then 'what emerges is a battle of wills between text and critic' [i.e. author and reader] which can be associated with a relationship of reciprocal or 'mutual coercion'. In this struggle author and reader are 'caught in an inevitable and ceaseless oscillation' in which neither 'dominates' or 'acts as master to the slave-other' (Atkins, 1983: 87–8). This is not to say, of course, that either the author or the reader will be entirely successful in the struggle between them to become 'master' in relation to the other. On the contrary, as Atkins suggests, the struggle between them may have no ultimate resolution in that sense. Nor will there necessarily be a compromise solution arrived at in the sense of a third position, some kind of theoretical synthesis along the lines indicated above, which is equally acceptable to both parties. Rather, as again Atkins suggests, what emerges may well be a third position, but one which is in some way or other unstable or which 'oscillates' between the two extremes associated with the positions of author and reader.

One obvious point to note here is that in English the word 'appropriate' can be associated with the idea of 'taking possession', or trying to make something an item of property for oneself. It can also be associated with the notion of 'objectification', and therefore 'enslavement'. So it would not be too difficult to connect a discussion of the relation between author and reader as a 'struggle for recognition' along the lines just indicated to the idea appropriating texts and the ideas contained within them. To attempt to appropriate a text is precisely to involve oneself in such a struggle. To appropriate the text in the strict sense of the term implies that one has been entirely successful in this struggle. To the extent that either author or reader is not then what emerges can be seen as some kind of 'compromise' position, albeit one which would be in some way imposed or enforced rather cooperatively agreed.

The idea of appropriation as here understood can be associated with a certain way of thinking about Poststructuralism, and the Poststructuralist approach to the reading of texts, with its suggestion that 'there are no interpretations, only appropriations'. This phrase echoes Nietzsche's use of the similar phrase, 'there are no facts, only interpretations' in *The Will to Power* (Nietzsche, 1968: 267), although of course the word 'interpretation' is used quite differently there by Nietzsche from the way it is used here. Given this it is not too surprising that M. H. Abrams has associated the approach to meaning which is usually associated with Poststructuralism or 'deconstruction', not with Hegel's idea of a 'struggle for recognition', as I have done, but rather with Nietzsche's notion of the 'will-to-power' (Abrams, 1991b [1989]: 240).

Later, in Chapter 3, I will argue that the concept of appropriation in the sense outlined above is a valuable one for those who are interested in Aristotle's reading of the works of other classical authors. I focus on Aristotle's *Rhetoric* and on the reading of Sophocles's *Antigone* which Aristotle presents there. In this reading Aristotle associates the Antigone with the concept of a 'universal law', which he also refers to as the 'law of nature' (Aristotle, 1995h: 1368b1–10, 2178; 1375a25–35, 2190). In short he considers what might be referred to as a 'natural law reading' of the *Antigone*. It is not entirely clear whether Aristotle endorses this reading himself, although he does appear to do so. What is clear, however, is that he objects to the use to which the concept of natural law is put by Sophocles, at least according to this particular reading of the play. In my view this natural law reading of the *Antigone* is implausible as a proposed interpretation of it. I suggest, therefore, that it is better seen as an attempted appropriation of Sophocles's text, and of the ideas contained within it, in the sense outlined above. One of the aims of Chapter 3, therefore, is to consider Aristotle's *Rhetoric*, especially the reading of the *Antigone* contained within it, as a case study which might be used to assess the value of the theoretical framework deployed above.

Establishing the Meaning of a Text by Negotiation

The third approach to hermeneutic understanding might be said to represent a compromise between or a theoretical synthesis of the first two. It is this approach which is associated especially with the work of Hans Georg Gadamer referred to earlier (Gadamer, 1975a [1960]). From this point of view, the act of hermeneutic understanding is always an historical enterprise. This is so not simply because the author of a text is an historical being, rooted in a particular society, a particular culture and a particular time, but also, and more importantly, because the readers of texts are also historical beings who share the cultural assumptions of their own society and their own time, and who understand the texts produced by thinkers of the past in the light of these. It follows from this, of course, that the meaning which is given to texts written in the past can and will alter. Indeed, this meaning will be different at different times, precisely because the assumptions of those doing the reading inevitably alter over time, as the society in which they live evolves historically. Nevertheless, it might still be said that these background assumptions do set a limit, at any one time, to the range of possible readings that might legitimately be given of a specific text by an individual reader living in a particular society at that time.

From the standpoint of this third approach, therefore, it is not the case that 'anything goes' so far as the process of hermeneutic understanding is concerned, or that all readings are equally valid. Here the meaning of a text is something which, at least in a given society at any given historical time period, is relatively fixed and stable. However, as we have seen, this meaning can and does change over time. Thus the meaning of a text is something which is in a sense being constantly negotiated and renegotiated. Gadamer sees this process as representing in effect some sort of dialogue between the author of the text and its reader, or perhaps more accurately between an individual (the author) who is a member of a society or culture at an earlier stage in its own historical development and an individual (the reader) who is a member of that same society at a later stage in that development. Gadamer refers to this process as a sort of 'fusion of horizons' between author and reader (Gadamer, 1975a [1960]: 340). It is historical continuity or tradition which makes this fusion of horizons (and hence the hermeneutic enterprise itself) possible. Without it the act of understanding a text could not take place at all.

Although it is not quite so extreme as the second approach described above, that of 'appropriation', partly because it is much less individualistic and more communitarian, Gadamer's historicist hermeneutics nevertheless shares with that second approach a sympathy for the view that the meaning of a text is at least in part something which is added to it by the reader, or created in the process of hermeneutic understanding. Although in his case meaning should be thought of as being produced and reproduced through some process of negotiation between the reader of a text and its author. Like the advocates of the second hermeneutic approach, therefore, Gadamer attaches much less importance than Quentin Skinner does to the idea that the aim of hermeneutic understanding is to uncover the intentions of the author when we read texts, or when we are attempting attempt to establish their meaning. Unlike Poststructuralists, however, Gadamer does not go so far as to suggest that we can ignore the intentions of the author altogether.

This way of thinking about Gadamer's hermeneutics, with its idea that the meaning of a text or of the concepts contained within it is established by a process of negotiation between author and reader, sees this process as being a benign or peaceful and cooperative one. Within it both author and reader have an important part to play. They mutually support and complement one another. Together they collaborate in establishing the meaning of a text. Moreover this meaning is not that of either the author or of the reader, as initially understood. For each could be said to have compromised with the other in the process of the negotiation of meaning. The end product of this process of negotiation and compromise may, therefore, be seen as a theoretical synthesis of their two respective initial positions: the 'thesis' and the 'antithesis'. This puts one in mind of a certain reading of Hegel of course. The Poststructuralist critics of this view would argue, against it, that such a process of negotiation of meaning by peaceful and cooperative agreement between author and reader is either impossible or simply not achievable in practice. On that view what appear to be examples of this way of establishing meaning will inevitably turn out, on closer analysis, to be better understood by reference to the notion of appropriation, not that of negotiation – that is to say, a process of attempted appropriation which turns out in the end to be only partially successful. In this way the meaning of text and the ideas which they contain can and do alter over time. However this change in meaning takes place more slowly that it would otherwise have done. It is evolutionary rather than revolutionary – more of a process than an 'event'.

A Fourth Hermeneutic Approach? Establishing the Meaning of a Text by Reconstruction

It might be suggested that there is a fourth type of activity which might be engaged in by those who read texts, namely that of 'reconstruction'. The concept of reconstruction is understood differently by different authors. For example both Anthony Lisska and Daniel M. Nelson employ this term to refer to contemporary readings of texts from the history of political thought, specifically the writings of St. Thomas Aquinas, the purpose of which is to 'bring them up to date' by demonstrating the relevance of the ideas which they contain for contemporary ethical and political problems (Lisska, 1997: 2, 11–12, 41, 82, 140, 159, 165, 168, 186; Nelson, 1992: xi–xii, 2, 5, 8, 10, 28, 128–30, 141). This idea also, perhaps, lies behind Alasdair MacIntyre's attempt to initiate a revival of interest in the thought of Aristotle, understood as a form of 'virtue ethics' (MacIntryre, 2006, 2006a [1999], 2000 [1981], 1990, 1988). In these cases, as Lisska notes, one aspect of the process of reconstruction involves detaching and abandoning certain ideas or beliefs which for some reason are no longer considered to be tenable. In the case of Aristotle, for example, the ideas in question are those related to what MacIntyre refers to as his 'metaphysical biology' (Lisska, 1997: 39, 67–8, 189–90). In the case of Aquinas, Lisska has in mind the beliefs associated with Christian theology (Lisska, 1997: 12–14, 95–6, 109, 113, 115, 119–20, 127).

A second feature sometimes associated with the notion of reconstruction, which may or may not be connected to the first, has to do with the resolution of logical contradictions between the different assertions which are made by an author about the same subject either within or between texts. For example there are times when Aristotle writes like a 'conventionalist' or ethical relativist, but there are also times when he writes like a 'naturalist' or a natural law theorist of some kind. Such contradictions may be merely apparent, as I think this one is. I shall say more about that in Chapter 4. However they could also be real. If they are real, and cannot be resolved, then the reader of the text is left with a dilemma. In such a situation it will be possible for two diametrically opposed readings of the same text to be offered, each of which might possess the same degree of plausibility, in which case all hope of offering a single defensible interpretation of the text will be lost. The readings in question must then be thought of as being little different from appropriations, in the sense indicated earlier. The specific choice of reading made may in these circumstances reflect the interests and concerns of the individual reader, it being assumed that, although they are incompatible with one another, nevertheless each of these readings, neither of which is comprehensive, will be equally well supported by the evidence provided by the text. On the other hand, these contradictions might be apparent and not real. As such they are in principle resolvable, one way or another. However, in such cases there will always be a number (at least two) of different possible ways of resolving them, some of which will be more plausible than others. It is clear from this that on closer examination what is presented as a reconstruction of a text, or of the ideas of its author, may well turn out to be either an interpretation of it, on the one hand, or an appropriation of it on the other.

The notion of reconstruction has an obvious application to the study of ancient political thought, where our sources relating to the views of particular authors are often fragmentary and/or corrupt, and where, in some cases, none of the works of a particular author have survived. It also might be employed to refer to a reading of a text which is offered in a situation where the intentions of the author of the text remain unknown, or cannot in practice be discerned. The writings of the ancient Greek atomist Democritus are a case in point here.

Another example of this is the writings of Aristotle. We have seen that Kelsen makes much of this in his critique of natural law readings of Aristotle.

A good example of a 'reconstruction' in this sense is provided by Alasdair MacIntyre's reading of Aristotle, although MacIntyre does not himself employ the term. MacIntyre considers himself to be an Aristotelian thinker. However, he does not think that describing oneself in this way necessarily implies a commitment to everything which Aristotle says about all subjects, especially not, for example, the reprehensible views which Aristotle advances in defence of slavery in the *Politics*. MacIntyre has the following extremely interesting remarks to say about his own reading of Aristotle, and about the relationship which exists between his own Aristotelian views and those which were held by Aristotle himself:

> [T]he argument that has led us up to this point is one that has drawn systematically on the conceptual and argumentative resources of Thomistic Aristotelianism. But while it is important to notice this, it is also important to notice how much of this account of political community and political justification is at odds with Aristotle himself, and not only because it rejects his exclusion of women and slaves from citizenship. For Aristotle believed falsely that the life of productive labour of a farmer, for example, was incompatible with the political life. And here he needs to be corrected, on the basis of his own principles (MacIntyre, 1997: 250–1).

These remarks indicate clearly that, in MacIntyre's view, there is a contradiction in Aristotle's thinking, for example when he defends the institution of slavery or excludes women from citizenship. At such times Aristotle is 'at odds' with himself and 'needs to be corrected on the basis of his own principles'. MacIntyre evidently believes that his own political thought, which is based on that of Aristotle, and which he considers to be in some sense 'Aristotelian', does just this. The issue, however, is whether MacIntyre's reading of Aristotle could be considered an 'interpretation' in the strict sense of the term. For it is not at all clear that all of the ideas associated with MacIntyre's reconstruction of Aristotle's thought are attributable to Aristotle himself. Indeed, as MacIntyre concedes, some of them were explicitly rejected by Aristotle. Moreover, this also raises the following further question. In what sense can the ideas associated with Macintyre's reading be said to be authentically Aristotelian, or accepted as a legitimate continuation of Aristotelianism as an intellectual tradition?

It might be asked whether reconstruction is in fact a fourth possible approach to the readings of texts? For the tripartite conceptual schema introduced earlier appears to exhaust all of the available possibilities so far as the readings of texts is concerned. We have just seen, however, that at least some reconstructive readings of texts cannot plausibly be considered to be 'interpretations' of them. This leaves only two other possibilities. Either they are best thought of as 'appropriations' or they should be associated with Gadamer's notion of establishing the meaning of a text by a process of negotiation between author and reader. However, with the exception perhaps of Nelson's reading of Aquinas, it does not seem reasonable to consider any of the reconstructive readings alluded to above as being straightforwardly appropriations of the texts with which they deal. It seems far more plausible to suggest, rather, that they have more in common with Gadamer's idea that the meaning of a text is established by a process of negotiation between author and reader, both of whom are working within the same intellectual tradition.

One of the ways in which the meaning of a concept changes or evolves historically over time, within the framework of a particular intellectual tradition, might be connected to the notion of reconstruction as here understood. There is a similarity here between the idea that those who engage in such acts of reconstruction are seeking to address (and perhaps attempt to resolve) a contradiction of some kind (real or apparent), and Mark Bevir's understanding of conceptual change, which focuses on the idea of resolving 'dilemmas' which I discuss below (Bevir, 1999: 176, 230, 235, 246–7, 263; 2000: 299). In my view, however, these remarks relating to the reconstruction of texts within intellectual traditions have more to do with characterizing how conceptual change of this kind occurs than it does with why it occurs – or what some commentators would refer to as the 'causal mechanism' by means of which it occurs. It is to a consideration of issues of this kind that I now turn.

Concepts and Their Meaning

How is the meaning of concepts, like that of natural law, established; and how and why do the meaning of concepts changes over time? Let us begin our examination of these issues by asking what is a concept? Or what do I mean by the word 'concept'? I shall use this word to refer to a general or abstract idea, what philosophers usually call a 'universal'. I shall assume that concepts are intimately associated with, and expressed by, the words of a particular language, or a number of languages. In short, as the later Wittgenstein suggests, and as Quentin Skinner also states, we may say that 'possessing a concept' is, if not always then at least in a large number of cases, 'equivalently a matter of knowing the meaning of a word', and this amounts, in turn, to being able to use the word which is associated with that concept appropriately (Wittgenstein, 1972: 20; Skinner, 1995 [1989]: 7).

However, understanding the nature of the relationship which exists between words and concepts is not a straightforward matter. In natural languages a concept is usually, but not necessarily, associated with just *one* word or shorthand phrase which expresses it and which might be said to name it. It is, however, possible for the members of a particular linguistic community to possess a concept even though they do not (yet) possess a name for it, or a shorthand linguistic expression to designate it. As Terence Ball has rightly said, 'to have a word for X is to be in possession of the concept X. Yet one may possess a concept without having a word to express it' (Ball, 1988: 16; see also Burns, 2000b; Skinner, 1995 [1989]: 7–8). I shall argue later that this idea is of some significance for those interested in the history of the concept of natural law.

Why are concepts meaningful? What gives them their meaning? What, indeed, do we mean when we talk about concepts having a meaning? When considering these questions it is useful to distinguish between a traditional way of thinking about meaning, which can be associated with the thought of both Plato and Aristotle, and a more recent view which can be found in the writings of the later Wittgenstein. From the standpoint of the more traditional view, like all concepts, the concept of 'natural law' and that of a 'natural law theorist' are meaningful because they can be defined. There is a 'closed' list of essential characteristic features, that is to say beliefs, the presence of each of which in the writings of a particular individual is necessary, and the presence of all of which is sufficient, to justify the classification of that individual as a natural law theorist.

The work of Richard Wollheim illustrates very well the traditional or 'essentialist' way of thinking about natural law and natural law theory. Wollheim appreciates that, throughout its long history, the doctrine of natural law has changed considerably, and has engendered a number of different 'variants and modifications'. Accordingly, he suggests, if we are to speak meaningfully about *the* doctrine of law it is necessary for us to isolate those features which all of these different varieties of natural law theory have in common. We must offer 'a minimal characterization of the doctrine of natural law'. Wollheim does not question whether it is possible to do this. He simply assumes that it *is* possible, as the term 'natural law' or its linguistic equivalent, for example the Latin *lex naturalis,* has 'been used over the centuries to designate a remarkably persistent doctrine' (Wollheim, 1967: 405). Wollheim then goes on to present his readers with what he claims is such a 'minimal characterization' of the concept of a natural law, or of *the* doctrine of natural law, and of the features which are necessarily associated with each of its particular forms, no matter how much they might differ in certain 'accidental' respects.

Readers familiar with what Cicero says about natural law in the passage from the *De Republica* cited above will recognize immediately the similarity between what Wollheim considers to be a minimal characterization of the concept of natural law and the natural law theory of the Stoics. According to Wollheim's account, which is also shared by numerous other commentators, there are three defining characteristics associated with the concept of a natural law theory. To be correctly described as a natural law theorist it is necessary, in his view, that a person should subscribe to the following three beliefs, namely: (i) that there are certain principles of morality or justice which are universally valid, applying in all societies, in all places and at all times; (ii) that these principles are apprehensible by the faculty of reason of the individual moral agent; and most important of all (iii) that these principles constitute a 'higher' standard of justice or law which might be used by individuals to critically evaluate the laws (positive laws) of the society in which they live.

From the standpoint of the traditional theory of meaning, then, when we describe someone as a natural law theorist what we must have in mind is that they (necessarily) subscribe to these three principles. Any theorist who does not subscribe to all three of these principles could not, properly speaking, be said to be a genuine natural law theorist at all. The problems associated with applying this way of thinking about the meaning of concepts generally, and that of the concept of natural law in particular, to Aristotle, specifically to what Aristotle says about natural justice or law in his *Nicomachean Ethics*, are readily apparent.

How does this way of thinking about meaning differ from that of the later Wittgenstein? I suggested above that for Wittgenstein too possessing a concept amounts to knowing the meaning of a word. In Wittgenstein's opinion, however, this amounts in turn to being able to use the word which is associated with that concept appropriately (Wittgenstein, 1972: 20; Skinner, 1995 [1989]: 7). On this view, to possess a concept is to understand, and to be able to follow, the linguistic convention or rule which regulates the use of the word which expresses or designates it within a particular linguistic community. This account of what it is to possess a concept is based upon the theory of 'meaning in use' which was developed by Wittgenstein in his *Philosophical Investigations*. Again, this Wittgensteinian way of thinking about the meaning of concepts is relevant for those wishing to understand the historical emergence of the concept of natural law in ancient Greece.

According to the later Wittgenstein for a concept like that of a natural law to be meaningful it is not necessary that it be either definable or defined. All that is required is that there must be at least some linguistic convention which regulates its use. That is to say, there must be an open list of criteria which regulate the legitimate application of the concept, and which enable us to differentiate between correct and incorrect instances of its employment. Concepts of this sort have what Frederick Waismann has referred to as an 'open texture' (Waismann, 1978: 38). In the case of the concept of natural law, if such a rule is to exist it is not necessary that there should be certain essential features which *all* natural law theories possess (and must possess) in common. All that is necessary is that the various different natural law theories should share at least some characteristic features in common with other theories which have in the past themselves been considered to be natural law theories. All that is required is that different types of natural law theory should have what Wittgenstein refers to as a 'family resemblance' to one another (Wittgenstein, 1969: 31–7; 1972: 1, 17–20, 25–7).

The difference between Wittgenstein's view of meaning and the more traditional view, associated with the writings of Plato and Aristotle, is not that Wittgenstein's view associates meaning with the existence of linguistic rules or conventions which regulate the use of concepts or words, whereas the traditional view does not. Rather, it is that Wittgenstein associates the meaning of a concept with the existence of flexible rules which cannot be mechanically applied, whereas the traditional view, to the contrary, associates the meaning of a concept with the existence of strict rules which are applied inflexibly or mechanically, without attention being paid to the different circumstances associated with particular cases. The irony here of course is that, as John McDowell has noted, this critique of Aristotelianism rests on ideas about rules and what is involved in rule following that are recognizably 'Aristotelian' (McDowell, 1998b; 1998c).

I suggested earlier that it is possible for the members of a particular linguistic community to possess a concept even though they do not have a short-hand label to name it or express it. But it may also be of course that, within a particular group of language users, the same word or linguistic expression can designate or express quite different concepts. For example, it is possible for the descriptive label 'natural law theorist' to be legitimately withheld from an individual thinker even if he or she does employ the expression 'natural law (or its equivalent in another language), if it should be decided that the meaning which this expression has for the theorist in question does not resemble closely enough the meaning which the expression is traditionally thought to have. An example of this is the employment of the Greek expression *nomos physeos* by the character Callicles in Plato's *Gorgias*. At one point, when discussing the beliefs of those who reject what today is often referred to as 'the moral point of view' and whose conduct is devoted entirely to the pursuit of their own self-interest as they understand it, Plato has Callicles say that such men 'follow nature – the nature of right – in acting thus; yes, on my soul, and follow the law of nature' (*nomos physeos*) (Plato, 1996 [1925]), 483e, 384–7). It is arguable that this particular linguistic usage is a paradoxical one, given that both the idea of natural law and the linguistic expression used to designate it are usually associated with the rejection rather than the affirmation of the views upheld by Plato's Callicles. The fact that Callicles employs this phrase *nomos physeos* does not, therefore, justify the conclusion that he could legitimately be characterized as a 'natural law theorist'. I shall say more about this issue when discussing 'the nature versus convention debate in classical Athens in Chapter 4.

We may illustrate the relevance of Wittgenstein's theory of 'meaning in use' for our understanding of the history of the concept of natural law by referring to an example. Let us assume, then, that it is in the writings of Cicero that what Saul Kripke refers to as an 'initial baptism' of the concept of natural law takes place (Kripke, 1988 [1972]: 96). To adapt a phrase of Michael Freeden's, Cicero can be thought of as 'the original exemplar whose authority is acknowledged by all' of the 'contestants' in the debate over the meaning of the concept of natural law, and the place and time of its historical emergence (Freeden, 1996a: 55). Cicero may, therefore, be considered unquestionably to be a paradigmatic example of a natural law theorist, or perhaps even *the* paradigmatic example of a natural law theorist – that is to say, somebody who employs the concept of natural law in his own writings without intending to reject the validity of the concept or criticize those who use it. In the case of Cicero the language in which the concept is formulated and expressed is Latin, and the corresponding phrase is *lex naturalis*. Moreover, let us also assume that in his particular case the meaning of this concept can indeed be 'unpacked' by reference to the three component concepts which are referred to by Wollheim, given that Wollheim's understanding of this concept is so similar to that enunciated by Cicero in his *De Republica*.

Now it is clear that, from the Wittgensteinian point of view, the meaning of this concept could in principle alter after Cicero, if the expression *lex naturalis* comes to be employed in a new and different way by other members of the same linguistic community. But what about the period before Cicero, in a situation where we are talking about the members of a different linguistic community who use a different language, that of ancient Greece? Here we need to distinguish between ancient Greece at the time of the Stoics, on the one hand, and in the classical period associated with Plato and Aristotle on the other. So far as the later period is concerned, it might perhaps be argued that there is no great problem. Cicero is widely considered to be an unoriginal thinker who simply translated into the Latin language both the concept of natural law and the equivalent linguistic phrase which was used to express it by the Greek Stoic thinkers before him. Many commentators also think (rightly or wrongly) that the Greek phrase in question was νομος φυσεος (*nomos physeos*). I shall say more about this issue in the Conclusion.

But what about the earlier period, the classical period when Aristotle was writing? The issue here is not that of finding an equivalent Greek expression which could be translated into Latin as *lex naturalis*. For we have seen that the members of a linguistic community can possess a concept even if they do not (yet) also possess a particular short hand label to express it or to designate it. From the Wittgensteinian point of view, classifying somebody as a natural law theorist might be justified even if the individual in question did not in fact employ the expression *lex naturalis* (or an earlier equivalent in the Greek language) provided their beliefs are considered to be sufficiently similar to those of the paradigmatic natural law theorist Cicero. Rather the important question is whether the ancient Greeks before Cicero did in fact possess the concept of natural law, irrespective of whether they had a short-hand phrase or label to name it. Moreover, with respect to this question, the issue is not whether the ancient Greeks possessed exactly the same concept of natural law as that of

Cicero, but whether they possessed a concept which was sufficiently similar to that of Cicero to justify the claim that it could legitimately be regarded as an early formulation of what was later to be considered as *the* concept of natural law. In Chapters 1 and 3 of this book I examine the 'natural law passages' in the writings of Aristotle in connection with this particular issue.

Conceptual History: Intellectual Traditions

So much for concepts and their meaning. Let us now consider the issues of conceptual change and of conceptual history. As John Gunnell has noted, talk about 'changes in concepts' is ambiguous. It might mean one or other of two things. For 'in speaking of conceptual change in any realm of discourse', Gunnell insists, 'it is necessary to distinguish between changes *in* a concept and changes *from* one concept to another. Failure to make this distinction has plagued much of the practice of conceptual history' (Gunnell, 1998: 650). According to Gunnell, conceptual history in the sphere of political thought differs from that of the natural sciences for this very reason. As Gunnell puts it, 'what we would think of as conceptual revolutions in natural science are not, for the most part, points in the history of a concept but changes from one concept to another' (Gunnell, 1998: 650). It is evident that when making this remark, Gunnell had the work of T. S. Kuhn in particular in mind (Kuhn, 1970 [1962]). Following Gunnell's suggestion, I shall clarify what I mean by conceptual change by considering four different senses of the term. Some of these are more relevant to the present discussion than others. I list them all here for the sake of completeness.

In the first place we might imagine a situation in which, not only a word or label, but also a concept itself, does not (yet) exist for the members of a particular linguistic community. In such a situation, conceptual change may take the form of conceptual innovation involving an initial process of concept formation, or the crystallization of existing ideas or beliefs into a new concept which is not initially associated with any word or linguistic expression which names it. This process of initial concept formation might involve the combination of other concepts which up until then were thought of by the members of a linguistic community as being unconnected with one another, and perhaps even in some way logically opposed to one another. It might involve a new association of concepts, one which had not been considered appropriate or even possible before. One obvious example of this which is of obvious relevance for the present work is the bringing together of the concepts of *physis* and *nomos* so as to produce the concept of natural law in ancient Greek political thought. I shall say more about this issue in Chapters 3 and 4. Another example is the combination of the concept of 'dialectics' in philosophy with that of 'materialism', so as to generate the concept of 'dialectical materialism', in Germany in the nineteenth century – a conceptual innovation which has been attributed variously to Frederick Engels, Joseph Dietzgen and Georg Plekhanov (see Burns, 2002b).

There is an issue here of course as to whether it is appropriate to describe a concept which emerges in this way as 'new', given that it has been produced by a process of combination of pre-existing ideas or concepts. For this does suggest that the concept in question was not entirely new. As Siep Stuurman has noted, one should perhaps think of such a process of concept formation as being 'not about totally new ideas', but rather 'new combinations of elements of old discourses'. Nevertheless there is evidently an 'element of creativity' or novelty associated with it, even if the concepts associated with it are not simply thought up 'out of the blue' along the lines suggested by, for example, T. S. Kuhn and Michel Foucault (Stuurman, 2000: 317–18).

Secondly we might, as Melvin Richter has noted, think of conceptual change taking place in a situation where although a linguistic community already possesses a certain concept it has not yet acquired a word or linguistic to designate that concept (Richter, 1995: 9). In these circumstances, it does not seem inappropriate to describe the coining such a word as being part of (perhaps the end point of) a process of conceptual innovation. One example of this might be Aristotle's attempt to formulate a short-hand linguistic expression to designate the concept which today we refer to in the English language as the concept of natural law. Here we have a situation where an individual provides an expression to identify or pick out a concept which has already come into being in the linguistic community, of which they are members, but which has not yet received a name.

Thirdly, we can imagine a situation in which the members of a particular linguistic community already possess a concept, with a word or linguistic expression to designate it. In these circumstances conceptual change might again take the form of conceptual innovation where one concept is simply replaced by another, completely different one, associated with different a word or linguistic expression where the second word or linguistic expression has a completely different meaning from the first. After such a process of conceptual change the members of the linguistic community in question no longer think about the world in terms of the first concept at all. Instead they do so by employing a completely different concept. This is the type of change which T. S. Kuhn and Michel Foucault have in mind when they talk about conceptual change (Kuhn, 1970 [1962]; Foucault, 1994 [1966]). For both Kuhn and Foucault conceptual change is thought of as being instantaneous (like a Gestalt switch). It is associated with the replacement of one 'paradigm' (Kuhn) or 'discourse' (Foucault) by another. Conceptual change of this kind is radically discontinuous rather than continuous. It is 'revolutionary', in Kuhn's sense of the term.[2]

It is obvious that from the point of view of this third way of thinking about conceptual change it is impossible to write the history of a concept, for example the concept of natural law, if the purpose of history is to map out or trace a process of change or development of the meaning of that concept over time. It is for this very reason that Foucault preferred to employ the term 'archaeology' rather than 'history' to describe what he was doing when he examined the problem of conceptual change in a variety of social science disciplines in his writings of the 1960s (Foucault, 1994 [1966]: xxii). From the point of view of this third way of thinking about conceptual change, the meaning of the words or concepts associated with one paradigm or discourse, at an earlier time, are completely different from those associated with a later paradigm or discourse, even within the same academic discipline, say that of astronomy, chemistry, physics, medicine, jurisprudence or ethics. The perspectives associated with these paradigms or discourses are therefore 'incommensurable' in Kuhn's sense of the term. As Kuhn puts it, 'because it is a transition between incommensurables, the transition between competing paradigms cannot be made a step at a time'. Like a 'gestalt switch', it must 'occur all at once' or 'not at all' (Kuhn, 1970 [1962]: 150).

In the Conclusion I shall criticize the views of commentators who maintain that the transition from Aristotle's way of thinking about ethics and politics and that of later Stoic thinkers can be thought of in this way, especially those who suggest that a central feature of this alleged paradigm shift in the ethical and political thought of the ancient world was associated with the introduction by the Stoics of an entirely new concept, and consequently also the introduction into the lexicon of political thought of an entirely new phrase by means of which this new concept could be expressed, namely 'natural law'. Against this view I argue that it is better to think of the relationship between Aristotle and later Stoic thought in terms of the principle of continuity (of a certain kind) rather than that of discontinuity.

Fourthly, when talking about conceptual change we might mean an alteration in the meaning of a particular concept like that of natural law over time. In other words, we might have in mind a situation in which the same linguistic expression comes to have, not a completely different meaning, but a partially different meaning. In the context of our example, this amounts to saying that the linguistic expression which is used to designate the concept of natural law comes to be used in a somewhat different way by the members of our linguistic community. It comes to be applied by the members of that community in certain circumstances or to certain things which it had not in the past been thought of as applying to before. In the terminology of Gottlob Frege, this would involve an alteration of both the sense and the reference of this expression (Frege, 1977a). It is, of course, not difficult to imagine how creative individuals, willing and able to follow existing linguistic conventions or rules in new and imaginative ways for reasons of their own, might play a part in such a process.

This way of thinking about conceptual change is associated with the view that the meaning of a concept can evolve slowly over time. If the use and hence also the meaning of a concept, or the particular word or linguistic expression with which it is associated, is extended so that it is considered to have a legitimate application to new situations or cases and therefore comes to be used by the members of a particular linguistic community living at a later time in a slightly different way from the way in which it was used by the members of that same community at an earlier time, then we may say that for the members of that community the meaning of the concept in question has altered over time and that, therefore, conceptual change of yet another kind has taken place.

This view of conceptual change indicates, as Mark Bevir has suggested, that linguistic contexts can 'overlap'. On this view, when thinking about conceptual change or the history of a concept, we might employ the notion of 'overlapping linguistic contexts' and how we might relate it to the idea of an 'intellectual tradition' (Bevir, 1994: 668). More specifically, this understanding of conceptual change allows us to use the later Wittgenstein's theory of meaning to develop the notion of an intellectual tradition within which conceptual change takes place along these evolutionary rather than revolutionary lines. David Boucher and others have observed that the idea of an intellectual tradition, understood in this sense, is associated with the notion of evolutionary and not revolutionary change, of 'continuity in and through a process of change' (Boucher, 1985: 108–11, 114–18; Bevir, 1994: 668; Greenleaf, 1968; Haddock, 1974; Wolin, 2004a [1964]: 23–26). Similarly, Andrew Lockyer has argued that the range of problems which a particular group of political theorists writing at different times have attempted to answer, together with the answers that they give to these problems, may be said to 'constitute a tradition of discourse'. These problems and answers, and hence the tradition of discourse with which they are associated, 'have a history' precisely because the concepts which the theorists in question use to formulate and solve these problems 'have different meanings in different contexts', meanings which change over time as a consequence of 'changing political and social arrangements' (Lockyer, 1979: 217). The concept which undergoes such a process of change can legitimately be said to be 'continuous' or to retain is 'identity' despite the fact that it lacks a fixed essence. It is not continuous because there are some things about its meaning that never change, or never could change, but basically because the process in and through which its meaning alters over time for the members of a given linguistic community is a slow one. From this point of view, as again David Boucher has pointed out, intellectual traditions in the history of political thought are 'fluid'. They undergo change while at the same time retaining their identity, because all of their features 'do not change at once' (Boucher, 1985: 113–4).

In my view the history of the concept of natural law provides a good illustration of how this evolutionary model of conceptual change helps us to understand how an intellectual tradition and the core concepts associated with it can develop over time. This model suggests that it might be legitimate to talk about such a thing as *the* natural law tradition despite the obvious diversity which exists in the ideas of those theorists who have, historically, employed the concept of natural law, whether or not they also employ the linguistic expression *lex naturalis*. It shows that it is possible for someone to talk meaningfully in this way about the history of the concept of natural law without being an 'essentialist'. It also shows that we may refer to the existence of relatively stable concepts like that of natural law in the history of political thought, even if at the same time we also acknowledge that the meaning of these concepts, at a particular moment in time, depends on the specific linguistic context in which they are used.

From this standpoint it is entirely legitimate for us to speak of such a thing as *the* natural law tradition provided that when we do so we are not assuming that it must be possible to offer a precise definition of the concept of natural law. It makes perfectly good sense to say that two different theorists writing in different societies, or in the same society at different times, might nevertheless be said to belong to the same tradition of political thought, even though when they use the same terminology it is evident that they do not mean the same thing by it, and even on occasion when they mean something completely different by it. As Sheldon Wolin has noted, 'history never exactly repeats itself'. The political experience of one age, although no doubt similar in at least some respects to that of another, 'is never precisely the same'. In such situations, all that is necessary for us to be justified in referring to the existence of a continuous 'natural law tradition' is that there should indeed be a 'family resemblance' (Wittgenstein) or a 'chain of communication' (Kripke) between their respective uses of the concept in question (Kripke, 1988 [1972]: 96; also 91). In other words, all that is necessary is that we should be able to trace some historical line of connection between the beliefs of the two theorists whose views we are comparing. Moreover, there is no reason to think that the concept of natural law is unique in this regard. As Terence Ball has observed, the reason why the vast majority of the concepts which are of interest to the historian of political thought 'elude fixed or final definition' is precisely because they possess 'historically mutable meanings' (Ball et al., 1985: x), that is to say meanings which change in this fourth sense. It is arguable that empirically the historical development of most of the other concepts in the lexicon of the historian of political thought is captured better by this fourth, evolutionary model of conceptual change than it is by the 'revolutionary' assumptions associated with the views of Kuhn and Foucault. If we think of conceptual change along these lines it would in principle become possible for us to trace the evolution of the meaning which a concept like that of natural law has for the members of a particular linguistic community over time. It would also become possible in principle for us to write the history of this particular concept and, thereby, of the ongoing intellectual tradition associated with it.

Why Does Conceptual Change Occur?

I have suggested that one approach to thinking about the issue of how conceptual change occurs involves the idea that individual language users start to employ a familiar concept, or the linguistic phrase which expresses it, in a new and different way. This raises the question of why they do this. In recent methodological debates a number of commentators have emphasized the importance of rhetoric for our understanding of the historical development of key political concepts (Ball, 1988: 14–17; Palonen, 1997, 1999, 2000; Richter, 1995: 120–1, 141, 152–3; Skinner, 1999: 60–73; Stuurman, 2000; also Gunnell, 1998). Melvin Richter, for example, has claimed that at certain times in the history of political thought, especially in periods of rapid economic, social and political change, key concepts have been 'redefined or redescribed by political actors seeking' either to 'reconcile contradictions in their own thought', or alternatively to 'knock out or neutralize concepts used by their adversaries' (Richter, 1995: 141; also 120–21, 152–53).

Something like this idea is also central to what Quentin Skinner has referred to as the notion of 'paradiastole,' or 'rhetorical redescription' (Skinner, 1996: 10–11, 142–53, 156–72, 174–80; also Skinner, 2002b, 2002d; see also Palonen, 2003b). This involves, in the manner of contemporary 'descriptivist' moral philosophers, finding alternative descriptive labels with which to characterize certain actions – it being assumed that the particular label which one chooses to apply to an action will differ depending on whether one's intention is either to praise or to blame the person who performs it. As Skinner notes, from this point of view, 'there is no categorical distinction between descriptive and evaluative terms: some descriptions serve at the same time to evaluate' (Skinner, 1996: 145). To illustrate the idea of paradiastole Skinner cites a 'late-Roman rhetorical treatise' in which 'someone who is insanely reckless is called courageous, or when a prodigal is called a good fellow, or when an infamous person is called illustrious' (Skinner, 2002d: 91). Cases of paradiastole, therefore, always involve the issue of the meaning of the corresponding terms, or descriptive labels, and their application to the circumstances of particular cases. In short they are always matters, as Skinner notes, of 'interpretation' (Skinner, 1996: 151). According to Skinner, the term 'paradiastole' is 'Hellenic', and therefore 'postdates' Aristotle's *Rhetoric* (Skinner, 2002d: 90). Nevertheless Skinner concedes that the *concept* which he associates with the term can be found much earlier. Indeed, he suggests that it is employed in the writings of Thucydides. In my view however, as Skinner also acknowledges (Skinner, 1996: 140, 156, 161), the concept of paradiastole (if not the term) can also be found in the writings of Aristotle. The example of describing an action as being either 'courageous' or 'fool-hardy' is used by Aristotle to illustrate his theory of 'the mean' in the Book II, Chapter 7 of the *Nicomachean Ethics* (Aristotle, 1995f: 1107a33–1107b4).

Mark Bevir has also addressed the issue of conceptual innovation and change. Bevir suggests that we can associate intellectual traditions with 'webs of belief', and that the ideas associated with intellectual traditions, thought of in this way, can be thought of as changing in consequence of the fact that the individuals who propound them attempt to resolve certain 'dilemmas' with which they are confronted once the new ideas, or of new ways of thinking about old ideas, have emerged (Bevir, 1999: 29, 176, 221–43). In his view, then, the driving force behind conceptual innovation is the desire for logical consistency that most philosophers and social theorists have, given that they employ sophisticated theoretical concepts in order to engage in some way with the world around them, and given that this is evidently in some sense therefore a 'rational' enterprise. Against this view however, as some of Bevir's critics have noted, it is arguable that Bevir overlooks the importance of such things as interests, power and conflict as driving forces which lie behind the employment of individual language users in particular socio-historical contexts (Palonen, 2000: 304, 307; Stuurman, 2000: 311–12). Rightly or wrongly, these things are often considered to be irrational or non-rational forces in politics, the existence and importance of which ought not to be overlooked by those who are interested in the issue of conceptual innovation or change.

Of these two different ways of thinking about the dynamics of conceptual change I have more sympathy for that of Skinner than I do for that of Bevir. This brings me to the issue of the theoretical framework that is deployed in the present work and, in particular, my own way of accounting for the process by means of which conceptual innovation, or changes in the meaning of concepts, takes place. So far as this question is concerned I think it is useful to again deploy the theoretical framework introduced earlier when discussing the reading of texts, especially the notions of 'appropriation' and 'negotiation'. In this case, though, we are talking about the appropriation or negotiation by individual language users, not of the meaning of texts, but rather of the meaning of words or concepts, like that of natural law, which are employed, not only by the authors of texts, but also by other language users in the wider linguistic community.

Thinking about the relationship between the author and the reader of a text, along the lines of an Hegelian 'struggle for recognition' puts one in mind of the following oft-cited remarks of Humpty Dumpty in Lewis Carroll's *Through the Looking Glass* which touch on the issue of the meaning of words:

> 'When I use a word', Humpty Dumpty said in a rather scornful tone, 'it means just what I choose it to mean – neither more nor less'. 'The question is', said Alice, 'whether you *can* make words mean different things'. 'The question is', said Humpty Dumpty, 'which is to be master – that's all' (Hirsch Jr., 1976: 51–3; see also Abrams, 1991b [1989]: 240; Scruton, 1983: 38; Weldon, 1953: 28).

The point being made here has initially to do with the meaning of words, but is also has an obvious relevance to a discussion of the meaning of texts. There is of course more to the meaning of a text than the meaning of the words and sentences which compose it. But establishing the meaning of the words and sentences which compose a text is at least part of what is involved in establishing the meaning of the text as a whole. So the issue of whether establishing the meaning of words is indeed a matter of free choice or of the exercise of power (as Hobbes suggested); whether the meaning of words generally, and of the words contained within a text in particular, can or cannot be changed at the whim of an individual, especially an individual reader, is evidently an important one for those interested in questions of hermeneutics.

One of the claims made in the present work, especially in Chapter 3, is that this way of thinking about the dynamics of conceptual change, by reference to the attempted appropriation by individual language users of the meaning of existing concepts currently in use, can be connected to what Aristotle says about the concept of natural law both in his *Rhetoric* and elsewhere. Aristotle can fruitfully be seen as someone who was engaged in a form of conceptual politics of this kind: a struggle for recognition over and around the meaning of the concept of natural law and the legitimate employment of this concept in political argument and debate. In this struggle Aristotle's strategy was not to reject outright the concept of natural law but, rather, to appropriate it for his own particular cause. In effect Aristotle sought to transform the meaning of the concept in such a way that, far from being used to develop a radical critique of existing society, its laws and institutions, on the contrary it could be put to use by those seeking to defend them. I go on in Chapter 4 to consider the implications of this reading of Aristotle for those who wish to locate his ethical and political thought against the background of the 'nature versus convention debate' in ancient Athens.

Structure

The first three chapters of the book are devoted to an examination of three of the works of Aristotle. In Chapter 1, I examine what Aristotle says about natural justice or law (*physikon dikaion*) in Book V, Chapter 7 of his *Nicomachean Ethics*. I focus on the issue of Aristotle's understanding of the tri-partite relationship between natural justice, legal or conventional justice and political justice and explain why, for Aristotle, natural justice or law is not a higher standard of justice which might be used to critically evaluate the civil laws or principles of political justice of any society.

In Chapter 2 I consider Aristotle's *Politics* from the point of view of the concept of natural law. I also say something about the merits and demerits of the 'virtue ethics' reading of Aristotle which is usually associated with the work of Alasdair MacIntyre. Here, not surprisingly, I claim that the notion of 'rule following' has an important part to play in Aristotle's understanding of an ethical or virtuous life. I say something about the strengths and weaknesses of the interpretations of Aristotle which are offered by Fred Miller Jr. and Hans Kelsen respectively and argue that neither captures the way in which the concept of natural law is incorporated into Aristotle's political thought as a whole. I also draw attention, here and elsewhere, to some interesting affinities between the political thought of Aristotle and that of Hegel.

In Chapter 3, I examine the natural law passages in Aristotle's *Rhetoric*, especially the natural law reading of Sophocles's *Antigone* which is presented there. I argue that this is best seen as an attempted appropriation of Sophocles's text rather than an interpretation of it. I also suggest that what Aristotle says about the concept of natural law in the *Rhetoric* can fruitfully be seen as an engagement on his part in the kind of politics which I associate above with the appropriation, not so much of texts, but rather of concepts currently in use in the wider linguistic community, which may or may not be found in texts. In the *Rhetoric* Aristotle alludes to a certain way of thinking about the concept of natural law in classical Athens which is strikingly similar to that later associated with Stoicism, but which he himself rejects. One aspect of Aristotle's involvement in this kind of politics is his attempt to redefine the concept of natural justice or law in such a way that its potential to contribute to a radical critique of existing society is undermined. Again, therefore, Aristotle can be seen as attempting to appropriate the concept of natural law and its meaning for his own particular cause. The consequence of this is the account of the concept of natural justice or law that he presents in the *Nicomachean Ethics* which is discussed in Chapter 1.

In Chapter 4 I say something about 'the nature versus convention' debate; in classical Athens in connection both with the thought of Aristotle and with the issue of the emergence of the concept of natural law. I argue that there was in fact not one but two such debates. One of these has to do with the issue of 'moralism versus immoralism', and is clearly enunciated in the writings of Plato, especially the *Gorgias.* The other is the debate between advocates of 'naturalism' and 'conventionalism' or ethical relativism. The remarks made by Aristotle about natural justice or law in the *Ethics* can be seen as a contribution to the second of these debates. It is sometimes suggested that there is no evidence of the existence of this second debate, and therefore of the position known as 'naturalism', in the writings of fifth-century thinkers before Plato. On this view Plato was the first person to defend naturalism in the history of political thought. Against this I argue that it is not implausible to assume that naturalism, and therefore some form of natural law theory, emerged in Athens in the fifth century amongst the Sophists. One consequence of this is that it must not be assumed that all of the Sophists who lived in the fifth century BCE embraced conventionalism.

In the Conclusion I draw the threads together and make some remarks about the continuities which exist between the remarks which Aristotle makes about natural law and the views of the Stoics. I also draw attention to the irony that Aristotle's criticisms of the use to which the concept of natural law was put by his contemporaries may have inadvertently led to the endorsement by later Stoic thinkers of the conception of natural law to which he so strongly objected and which he had drawn to their attention.

Notes

1 Here and throughout references are given to the *Complete Works of Aristotle* edited by Jonathan Barnes (Aristotle, 1995a [1984]), in two volumes. I include the marginal manuscript number first, followed by the page number. The pagination is consecutive over both volumes.

2 I associate such a view of conceptual change with the early work of Quentin Skinner in Burns, 2011b.

Chapter 1

Natural Law in Aristotle's *Nicomachean Ethics*

Introduction

I shall begin by making two preliminary observations. First, in this chapter I focus on the *Nicomachean Ethics* and ignore what Aristotle has to say about natural law in his *Rhetoric*. As we shall see in Chapter 3, the value of the latter as a source for Aristotle's views on natural law is a matter of dispute.[1] Second, the Greek term employed by Aristotle should strictly speaking be translated into English as 'natural justice'. Leo Strauss prefers to use the expression 'natural right' rather than either 'natural justice' or 'natural law' (Strauss, 1968a: 81). His reason for doing so is that he associates the notion of law with that of the command of some superior, an idea which according to Strauss is to be associated with the later history of political thought, and is absent from Aristotle's writings (Burns, 2010b: 56). As M. Salomon Shellens has pointed out, however, many commentators employ the phrase 'natural law' in this context (Salomon Shellens, 1959: 74). In the following discussion, I shall use this example and use the terms 'natural justice' and 'natural law' interchangeably.

Aristotle's remarks concerning natural justice or law (φυσικον δικαιον, *physikon dikaion*) in Chapter 7 of Book V of the *Nicomachean Ethics* are of the greatest significance, and have been much discussed.[2] The passage from the *Ethics* in question is fundamental for our understanding of the history of political thought in general, and for the history of natural law theory in particular. It is also of the greatest importance for our understanding of Aristotle's system of a political thought as a whole, and especially for the assessment of the role which the notion of natural law has to play within it. It is for these reasons that, as M. B. Crowe has pointed out, it has 'always attracted commentators' (Crowe, 1977: 22). To elucidate its meaning, however, is by no means an easy task. This is so for three reasons. In the first place, it is highly compressed. As Strauss has emphasized, it takes up 'barely one page' of the *Nicomachean Ethics* (Strauss, 1974: 156). In the second place, it is ambiguous and therefore obscure. Pierre Destrée has claimed that this passage is, 'in the opinion of all contemporary commentators, one of the most obscure' in the history of philosophy (Destrée, 2000: 221). And Crowe has rightly pointed out, not only that it leaves 'more than one tantalizing question unanswered', but also that 'where there is ambiguity commentators sometimes find what they wish to find' (Crowe, 1977: 25). In the third place, Aristotle's words appear at times to be downright inconsistent. It is, indeed, difficult to disagree with P. F. Sigmund when he says that they are 'confusing' (Sigmund, 1971: 9), and possibly also self-contradictory and confused. The passage in question, therefore, evidently has its dangers for the would-be interpreter.

What follows is intended to be an attempt to at least partially elucidate the meaning of this passage from the *Ethics*. In the terminology which I presented in the Introduction, I offer as a 'reconstruction', or a reconstructive interpretation, of the views expressed by Aristotle in this passage, and of Aristotle's natural law theory as a whole. It must be conceded, however, that this attempt is an exploratory one. Some readers may consider it to be tendentious – a reading which is much closer to being an 'appropriation' than an interpretation of Aristotle's political thought. All interpretations of this kind (including this one) should be treated with the greatest caution. The justification for making the attempt lies in the fact that the passage in question *is* so important and influential, and yet clearly does require a reconstructive interpretation if it is to be understood at all. I shall begin by presenting the passage in question in full. I will then subject it to a detailed analysis. The purpose of this analysis is to clarify some of the passage's ambiguities, to make explicit some of its concealed presuppositions, and in particular to uncover Aristotle's attitude towards the relationship which exists between natural law and positive law:

> [1134b, 18] Of political justice part is natural, part legal - natural, that which everywhere has the same force and does not exist [20] by people's thinking this or that; legal, that which is originally indifferent, but when it has been laid down is not indifferent, e.g. that a prisoner's ransom shall be a mina, or that a goat and not two sheep be sacrificed, and again all the laws that are passed for particular cases, e.g. that sacrifice shall be made in honour of Brasidas, and the provisions of decrees. Now some think that all justice [25] is of this sort, because that which is by nature is unchangeable and has everywhere the same force (as fire burns both here and in Persia), while they see change in the things recognized as just. This, however, is not true in this unqualified way, but is true in a sense; with the gods it is perhaps not true at all, while with us there is something that is just even by nature, yet all of it is changeable; but still some is by nature, some not by nature. [30] It is evident which sort of thing, among things capable of being otherwise, is by nature, and which is not but is legal and conventional, assuming that both are equally changeable. And in all other things the same distinction will apply; by nature the right hand is stronger, yet it is possible that all men should come to be ambidextrous. The things which are just by virtue of convention [1135a] and expediency are like measures; for wine and corn

> measures are not everywhere equal, but larger in wholesale and smaller in retail markets. Similarly, the things which are just not by nature but by human enactment are not everywhere the same, since constitutions also are not the same, though there is but one which is everywhere and by nature the best [5] (Aristotle, 1995e: 1134b18–1135a5, 1790–91).

It should be readily apparent that this passage does undoubtedly contain a number of ambiguities, and perhaps also a number of downright inconsistencies, but this does not mean that no sense at all can be made of it, or that the attempt to reconstruct its meaning is not worthwhile. What is required here is indeed a reconstruction of Aristotle's views on natural law and its relationship to positive law, and it is in the nature of reconstructions that they can always be carried out in different ways. It must, however, be conceded that it is probable that no one interpretation of this passage will (or could) succeed in resolving all of the inconsistencies which it contains into an account of Aristotle's views on natural law which is both comprehensive and entirely coherent. All interpretations of this passage, including the one offered here, will have their own peculiar difficulties. A reconstruction which, as it should do, renders Aristotle's ideas (or some of them) coherent may not be a comprehensive interpretation of Aristotle's thought as a whole. Indeed, it could not possibly be a comprehensive interpretation if it is true that some of the contradictions with which it deals are not apparent but real.

Terminology: Natural Justice, Legal Justice and Political Justice

One point of central importance to note about this passage is that in it Aristotle appears to refer to *three* different types of justice. These are what he calls 'political justice' (πολιτικον δικαιον, *politikon dikaion*), 'natural justice' (φυσικον δικαιον, *physikon dikaion*), and 'legal' or 'conventional justice' (νομικον δικαιον, *nomikon dikaion*). This is unusual, in that most commentators today who write about these matters adopt the bipartite approach of the Stoic tradition. They make a straightforward distinction between just two types of justice or law, namely natural law on the one hand and positive law on the other.[3] Aristotle's system of classification is more sophisticated than this. It is true that he makes a distinction between natural justice and legal or conventional justice. In addition to this, however, he also suggests that what he calls 'political justice', on the one hand, and legal or conventional justice on the other, are not exactly the same thing. In his view, legal or conventional justice is but a 'part' of political justice. This raises the question of how we should use the term 'positive law' when discussing Aristotle's political thought. Should we use this term to refer to Aristotle's *nomikon dikaion* (νομικον δικαιον). Or, rather, should we use it to refer to Aristotle's *politikon dikaion* (πολιτικον δικαιον). A number of commentators have observed that the term 'positive law' is typically used to refer to the former and not the latter. It tends to be employed as a synonym for what Aristotle himself refers to as 'legal or conventional justice' (Yack, 1990: 219; Salomon, 1937: 120–7; Salmond, 1895: 127; also Suarez, 1995b: II, XIX, 3, 343; II, XIX, 5, 345). I note in passing that this identification appears to have been made for the first time during the medieval period. For it was then that the term 'positive law' (or its Latin equivalent) came into use (van den Eynde, 1949: 41–9; Kuttner, 1936; Ullmann, 1975: 62). Most commentators acknowledge that the features which at that came to be associated with positive law are those which Aristotle had earlier associated with legal or conventional justice. The identification of Aristotle's notion of legal or conventional justice with positive law is, therefore, not too surprising. However, if we think that it is important to preserve Aristotle's conceptual distinction between 'legal or conventional justice' and 'political justice', then that leaves us with the problem of finding an appropriate English expression, which employs the term 'law', for Aristotle's *politikon dikaion*. To talk about 'political law' in this connection seems clumsy. I shall, therefore, employ the English phrase used by students of Roman law during the medieval and early modern periods, and employ the phrase 'civil law' to express Aristotle's notion of *politikon dikaion*.

J. W. Salmond has noted that Aristotle does make a theoretical distinction between 'political justice' and 'legal or conventional justice'. In Salmond's opinion, however, this distinction is 'of no theoretical importance' (Salmond, 1895: 127). Against this, however, I shall argue that this distinction is extremely significant for those who wish to adequately understand Aristotle's thought. In particular, it is impossible for us to comprehend Aristotle's view of the relationship which exists between natural law and positive law unless we have properly grasped the significance of this fundamentally important conceptual distinction – which lies at the very heart of Aristotle's doctrine of natural law, and hence also of his political thought as a whole.

The Unchangeability of Natural Law and the Idea of Moral Necessity

Are the principles of natural justice changeable or unchangeable? Aristotle's remarks about the changeability or unchangeability of the principles of natural justice in the passage under discussion appear to be inconsistent with one another. At the beginning of the passage he clearly implies that natural justice is '*un*changeable' (ακινετον, *akineton*). For he says that it 'has everywhere the same force'. The example which he uses to illustrate what he means by this is the fact that 'fire burns both here and in Persia'. Moreover he contrasts natural justice with legal justice, which (later on) he says is 'changeable' (κινετον, *kineton*). Towards the end of the passage, however, Aristotle confuses his readers by asserting that, like legal justice, natural justice is *also* in a sense changeable. He says that both natural justice and legal justice are 'equally changeable'. One of our problems, therefore, is to make sense of what Aristotle is saying here, so as to resolve this apparent contradiction. What we must consider is how it is possible for Aristotle to maintain that we can clearly distinguish between justice which is natural and justice which is legal or conventional, despite the fact that both types of justice might be said to be equally changeable.

Although the meaning of the terms is ambiguous, Aristotle's remarks about the 'changeability' and 'unchangeability' of natural justice can, initially, be associated with the notion of moral validity. That this is so is evident from the fact that, after contrasting natural justice with legal or conventional justice, Aristotle goes on to assert that legal or conventional justice, which is most definitely changeable, has to do with actions which are 'originally indifferent'. In other words, it has to do with the enjoining, forbidding, or permitting, of actions which are in themselves indifferent when considered from the moral point of view.[4] In these cases there is, as it were, no moral necessity which dictates either that the actions in question ought to be performed, or that they ought not to be performed. The clear implication which lies behind these remarks is that those principles of justice which are unchangeable and which 'everywhere have the same force', namely the principles of natural justice, have to do with the enjoining or forbidding of actions which are not morally 'indifferent'. In so far as actions of this sort are concerned, there is a moral necessity which dictates either their performance or their non-performance.

Aristotle does not appear to give any examples, in the passage quoted, of those actions which are not morally indifferent. However he does provide us with such examples in Book II of the *Nicomachean Ethics*. There he says that:

> not every action . . . admits of a mean; for some have names that already imply badness . . . adultery, theft, murder; for all these and suchlike things imply by their names that they are themselves bad, and not the excess or deficiencies of them. It is not possible, then, ever to be right with them; one must always be wrong . . . simply to do any of them is to go wrong (Aristotle, 1995e: 1107a9–14, 1748).

This is an entirely secular approach to understanding the concept of natural law. There is a striking resemblance here between the thought of Aristotle on this subject and that of Hugo Grotius, despite the gulf in time which exists between the writing of Aristotle's *Ethics* and the publication of Grotius's *De Jure Belli ac Pacis* in 1625 (Grotius, 2005 [1625]).[5] Grotius was to become famous in the seventeenth century, if not notorious, for suggesting that the natural law is unchangeable in the sense that it would retain its binding force even if it were granted (which could not of course be granted without great impiety or wickedness) that there is no God (Grotius, 2005 [1625]: Prolegomena, XI, 89; I, I, X, 5, 155). Indeed, Grotius likened the truths of morality and ethics, as also did a number of thinkers associated with the 'intellectualist' school of ethics in the seventeenth and eighteenth centuries, to those of arithmetic and geometry (Grotius, 2005 [1625]: I, I, X, 5, 155). According to Grotius, like the proposition '2 + 2 = 4', so also the proposition that 'murder is wrong' can be known with certainty, simply because it cannot be denied without contradiction. It is an absolute or necessary truth discoverable by the faculty of reason. Consequently, it is a proposition which ought to be accepted as true by all rational beings, always and everywhere – at all times and in all places. This is part of what is implied when it is (rightly) claimed that it is a precept of *natural* law.

It is commonly acknowledged that Grotius thought in this way about all of the moral principles which he took to be principles of natural law. What is much less often appreciated however is that when enunciating this view in the *De Jure Belli ac Pacis*, like Aquinas and Suarez before him (Suarez, 1995b: II, VI, 11: 197; II, XV, 4, 288), Grotius refers explicitly to the above passage from Aristotle's *Ethics* as his primary source of inspiration. Grotius tells his readers that 'this is Aristotle's meaning' when he says in Book II, Chapter 6 of the *Ethics* that 'some things are no sooner mentioned than we discover depravity in them' (Grotius, 2005: I, I, X, 5, 155). Grotius goes on to explicitly endorse Aristotle's view that the acts of murder and theft are essentially or necessarily unjust, as the 'very words' imply injustice or a 'crime' (Grotius, 2005 [1625]: I, I, X, 6, 156). In his view, to state that an act is an act or murder but that it is nevertheless just and not unjust is 'manifestly' to 'imply a contradiction'. Hence just as even God himself, who is omnipotent, 'cannot effect that twice two should not be four', so also in Grotius's view God cannot effect that 'what is intrinsically evil', such as an act of theft or murder, 'should not be evil' (Grotius, 2005 [1625]: I, I, X, 5, 155). Despite their disagreement in respect of other, fundamentally important issues, then, this is in fact a similarity between the natural law theory of Grotius and that of Aristotle and not a difference, just as it is a similarity between what I have referred to elsewhere as the Stoic conception of natural law and that of Aristotle (Burns, 1996b: 15–24).

Grotius's debt to Suarez here should not go unmentioned. This is obvious to anybody who reads the *De Jure Belli ac Pacis* of Grotius (1612) and the *De Legibus ac Deo Legislatore* (1625) of Suarez together. It is Suarez for example who pointed out, just thirteen years before Grotius published his magnum opus, that according to Gregory of Rimini 'even if God did not exist' the dictates of natural law 'would still have the same legal character which they actually possess, because they would constitute a law pointing out the evil that exists intrinsically in the object' (Suarez, 1995b: II, VI, 3, 190). It was Suarez who argued before Grotius that our knowledge of the natural law is a knowledge of certain 'eternal truths'. The propositions enunciating the precepts of natural law are, he claims, 'eternally true' because 'the principles themselves' are 'necessarily true by their definition' (Suarez, 1995b [1612]: II, XIII, 3, 259; also II, XIV, 19, 280). Suarez insists that ethical 'truths' are no different from the 'necessary propositions' discussed by logicians. For their 'falsity in a single instance is no less inconceivable' than the falsity of such necessary propositions. In the sphere of ethics, he argues, every 'natural precept' is characterized 'by the absolute truth which is necessary from the very nature of the case' (Suarez, 1995b [1612]: II, XIV, 10, 273–4). Indeed, he maintains that truths of this kind are 'necessary propositions' which are derivable 'by an inevitable process of deduction'. Thus 'they cannot fail or be false in any individual case' (Suarez, 1995b [1612]: II, XVI, 3, 312). In short, according to Suarez, the truth of these ethical propositions cannot be denied without contradiction. Just like Grotius then, although again before him, Suarez also follows Aristotle by holding that the truth of the proposition that 'murder is unjust' does not depend on the will of God. Finally it was Suarez who, again before Grotius, agreed with Aquinas that for this very reason 'not even God', who is of course presumed to be omnipotent, 'is able to grant a dispensation' from the duty to obey the natural law. For 'just as a natural precept cannot be abrogated' so also 'it cannot be changed' and consequently 'cannot be subject to dispensation' (Suarez, 1995b [1612]: II, XIV, 10, 274). In Suarez's opinion 'a contradiction is involved in conceiving of one and the same thing', for example the duty to refrain from committing acts of murder or theft, 'as being obligatory and as not being obligatory' at the same time, or as being obligatory in general, but not in this particular case (because a dispensation has been granted by God). Thus Suarez maintains that 'a contradiction is involved' also 'in conceiving that anything of this sort is subject to dispensation' (Suarez, 1995a [1612]: II, XV, 16, 297). As Suarez puts it elsewhere, God 'cannot act contrary to His own justness'; and yet God 'would so act' if He ever 'granted license' to anybody 'to do that which is *per se* intrinsically unjust', as he would be doing if he granted a dispensation to someone to commit an of theft or murder (Suarez, 1995b [1612]: II, XV, 16, 297).

It is clear from the above passage from Book II of the *Ethics*, which is cited by Aquinas, Suarez and Grotius, that Aristotle believed that there are some actions which are by their very nature morally wrong and that it is possible for us to have knowledge of this, and of what might be referred to as 'moral truths' or 'moral facts'. I shall argue later that for Aristotle this is genuinely 'scientific' knowledge in the sphere of ethics. In this respect Aristotle's ethics, as a number of commentators have noted, is similar to the doctrine which today is referred to as 'moral realism' (see Arrington, 1989b; Boyd, 1988; Charles, 1995; Heinaman, 1995; McDowell, 1995; Platts, 1988; and Sayre-McCord, 1988b). It is also similar to the doctrine held by some moral philosophers today which is known as 'descriptivism' (Brennan, 1977: 36, 41, 44–57, 64–5, 119; Hare, 1963; Hudson, 1969b, 1970b; Kovesi, 1967: 26, 32, 109; Jost, 1979: 41–8). In Aristotle's ethical thought the actions in question are considered to be essentially or necessarily wrong, and the type of 'necessity' that we are talking about in this context is strict logical necessity. The 'wrongness' of murder, theft and adultery is logically implied by the meaning of the terms which we use to describe such actions. Aristotle took the view that if we understand the meaning of these terms then, at the same time, we must necessarily also understand that we are under a moral obligation not to perform the actions which they describe. According to this reading, then, Aristotle would have agreed with Grotius and Kant that there can be no moral justification for the performance of such actions. To accept that a particular action is an example of an act of murder, theft or adultery and then go on to maintain that nevertheless its performance is morally permissible, would indeed from Aristotle's point of view be to contradict oneself. As we have seen this is also the view which was held, later, by Aquinas and Suarez, who both cite the above passage from Aristotle's *Ethics* as a source for it Aquinas, 2006 [1975b]: 2a2ae, 67, 7, 83; Suarez, 1995b: II, VI, 11, 197).[6]

An important consequence of this is that Aristotle was of the opinion that actions such as murder, theft and adultery must necessarily be morally wrong always and everywhere, in all societies, at all times and in all places. All societies ought to have (and on one reading *do* have) legal systems which contain principles of political justice which forbid the performance of such actions. The principles of justice associated with these actions possess a moral validity which is universal, and not simply parochial or historically specific. This is part at least of what Aristotle appears to have in mind when he refers to the principles of natural justice as being 'unchangeable'.

The Relationship between Natural Justice, Legal Justice and Political Justice

A further point to note about Aristotle's discussion of natural justice in the *Nicomachean Ethics* is that the meaning of the opening sentence of the long passage presented above is ambiguous. Aristotle says there that 'of political justice part is natural, part legal'. There is some truth, therefore, in Hans Kelsen's claim that for Aristotle 'natural law is simply a constituent part' of 'the positive law of the state' (Kelsen, 1973a: 131), although it would have been better if Kelsen had employed the term 'civil law', or something similar, rather than 'positive law'. The crucial question, however, is what exactly should this be taken to mean. For Aristotle's remarks might be interpreted in two quite different ways, one of which (the second) is preferred here.

According to the first interpretation, what Aristotle has in mind when he makes these remarks is what we may refer to as a 'vertical' division of a system of political justice into those laws which are entirely natural in so far as their substantive content is concerned, on the one hand, and those laws whose content is entirely legal or conventional on the other. This approach, fundamentally, is that of the Stoic conception of natural law (Burns, 1996a: 15–23). From this point of view, a (civil) law with a content which is entirely natural is simply a principle of natural law which has been incorporated into the legal system of a particular society and which has, thereby, been provided with a coercive sanction. In the light of Aristotle's statement that what characterizes natural justice, as distinct from legal justice, is that it 'everywhere has the same force', this implies a division of a body of civil laws into just two categories. In the first category we may place those laws which have a substantive content which is entirely 'unchangeable' from the standpoint of their moral validity. These laws deal with matters of moral necessity, and are valid in all societies everywhere. In the other category we may place those laws which have a substantive content which is entirely 'changeable', concerning which there is no moral necessity and which, therefore, may legitimately vary from society to society, from time to time, and from place to place.

According to the second interpretation, however, when Aristotle makes these remarks he is thinking of something quite different altogether. On this interpretation, he has, rather, in mind what we may refer to as a 'horizontal' division of a system of political justice into two 'parts'. Considered from this second point of view, each and every individual principle of political justice (or civil law) within a system of political justice is thought of as having, at one and the same time, both a part which is natural and a part which is legal or conventional. From this standpoint, there is no principle of political justice which is either entirely natural, or entirely legal or conventional, so far as its substantive content is concerned. Each principle of political justice is thought of as having a part which relates to some matter of moral necessity, while at the same time also having another part which relates to something which is a matter of indifference from the moral point of view.

A great deal of the confusion surrounding what Aristotle has to say in the long passage we are analysing arises because he does not himself distinguish clearly between these two different ways in which we can conceive of a body of law being divided into 'parts'. This confusion is added to by the fact that Aristotle actually adopts both approaches, quite unsystematically, in the ensuing discussion of natural justice. Moreover, it is further compounded by the ambiguity of the original Greek text of the *Ethics*:

> του δε πολιτικον δικαιον το μεν φυσικον εστι το δε νομικον, *tou de politikon dikaion to men physikon esti to de nomikon* (Aristotle, 1900: 1134b18–19).

Some English translations of this sentence do not pick up on this ambiguity. To cite just one example, let us consider the translation offered by H. Jackson. In his commentary on the *Ethics*, Jackson suggests that this Greek sentence should be translated as follows: 'Of the πολιτικον δικαιον there are two *kinds*, natural and conventional' (Aristotle, 1879: 39; see also Aristotle, n.d.: 145; Aristotle, 1965: 147; Yack, 1990: 220). This particular translation clearly suggests that Aristotle has in mind what I have termed a vertical division of a system of political justice into its component parts. It therefore lends itself to just one particular interpretation of the meaning of the Greek text, and hence also to just one particular interpretation of Aristotle's views on natural law and its relation to both positive and civil law, an interpretation which sees Aristotle as a forerunner of Stoic natural law theory. The translation of W. D. Ross above is superior because it leaves open the possibility that what Aristotle may actually be thinking of is a 'horizontal' division. This leads to a quite different interpretation of Aristotle's views on natural law and of his political thought as a whole.[7]

Aristotle appears to be thinking of what I have termed a 'vertical' division of a system of political justice into its component parts when he acknowledges, later on in the passage under discussion, that it is possible for some principles of political justice to be entirely legal or conventional in so far as their substantive content is concerned. These principles are those which are 'passed for particular cases', or which have to do with the 'provisions of decrees'. In both of these cases it would seem that Aristotle is prepared to allow that the specific content of the law does not in any way relate to a matter of moral necessity. If, however, we set aside what Aristotle says about the provisions of decrees and the laws passed for particular cases, it would appear that, in the rest of the passage, when he talks about a system of political justice being divisible into its component parts what he has in mind is what I have termed a 'horizontal' division rather than a 'vertical' one.

One significant implication of these remarks is for Aristotle *none* of the remaining civil laws of the society in question should be thought of as having a substantive content which is entirely natural with respect to its substantive content. He suggests that there is no civil law which has a substantive content which relates entirely to matters of strict moral necessity. There is no civil law which has a moral validity which is, in its entirety, strictly universal in scope. Hence there is *no* civil law which has a substantive content which is entirely 'unchangeable', in the moral sense of that term. According to this interpretation, then, the best way to characterize Aristotle's attitude towards those principles of political justice which are not entirely legal or conventional would be to say that in his view such principles must be thought of as being divisible 'horizontally' into two component principles of justice, one of these principles being a principle of natural justice and the other being a principle of legal or conventional justice.

What Are the Principles of Natural Law?

In the passage under examination Aristotle appears unwilling to provide specific examples of principles which he considers to be principles of natural justice. The only examples to which he refers are those relating to the practice of ransoming of prisoners and to the practice of offering sacrifices. At first sight, however, these appear to be examples of principles of legal or conventional justice, rather than examples of precepts of natural justice. This has led at least one commentator, Leo Strauss, to maintain that one of the reasons why Aristotle's discussion of natural justice is ambiguous, or so 'singularly elusive', is that 'it is not illumined by a single example of what is by nature right' (Strauss, 1974: 156). If my interpretation of Aristotle is correct, however, then Strauss's claim is not justified. This is so because, from this point of view, the principles of justice to which these examples refer are not what Aristotle would consider to be principles of legal or conventional justice. They are, rather, principles of political justice. And it follows from this, given that these principles have a 'part' which is natural as well as a part which legal or conventional, that these two principles must necessarily also provide us with examples of what Aristotle would consider to be principles of natural justice.

We may illustrate this point by considering as an example the principle that 'a prisoner's ransom shall be a mina'. Aristotle suggests that it is a matter of convention that a prisoner's ransom shall be a mina. According to the interpretation advanced here what this means is that it is a matter of indifference, morally speaking, that a prisoner's ransom shall be a mina, as opposed to something else. Here the principle that 'a prisoner's ransom shall be a mina' is considered to be an example, not of a principle of *legal* or conventional justice, but of a principle of *political* justice. As such, this principle may be thought of as having two constituent 'parts'. On the one hand there is the principle of justice which states that 'all prisoners shall be ransomed'. On the other hand there is the principle of justice which states that a prisoner's ransom 'shall be a mina'. The first of these principles is a principle of natural justice. In Aristotle's view, it is not a matter of moral indifference whether prisoners should be ransomed. On the contrary, this is a matter of strict moral necessity. Prisoners ought to be ransomed. All *poleis* ought to include such a principle within their respective systems of political justice. I find it difficult to accept, therefore, Ross J. Corbett's claim that 'Aristotle's own examples' of principles of natural justice 'have nothing to do with morality' (Corbett, 2009: 235). The second principle, however, does not relate to a matter of moral necessity. The question as to what, exactly, a prisoner's ransom ought to be is a matter of indifference from the moral point of view. This question, therefore, in Aristotle's opinion, is a matter of 'convention'. It is to be decided in a morally arbitrary manner by the positive law of a particular *polis* at a particular time. Aristotle, then, would acknowledge that in some *poleis* the ransom demanded for a prisoner will be a mina, whereas in others it will not, and that this variation is one which is entirely legitimate from the moral point of view.

Aristotle does not make an explicit distinction between legal or conventional justice which is customary and legal or conventional justice which is enacted or made, that is to say, statute law. It would, however, be a mistake to assume automatically, as W. A. Robson appears to do, that he must have had customary law in mind here (Robson, 1935: 243–5). As G. R. Morrow has pointed out, the idea of legislation, or the creation of 'new' law, is by no means alien either to Greek political experience or to Greek political thought at this time (Morrow, 1948: 38). This is, indeed, evident from what Aristotle himself has to say about this issue in chapter 9 of Book X of the *Ethics*.

I note in passing that the above interpretation of Aristotle is also the one presented by Aquinas in his commentary on the *Nicomachean Ethics*. According to Aquinas, Aristotle's attitude towards the principle that 'a prisoner's ransom should be a mina' is that:

> It is *natural* justice that a citizen who is oppressed without fault on his part should be aided, and consequently that a prisoner should be ransomed, but the fixing of the price pertains to *legal* justice, which proceeds from natural justice without error (Aquinas, 1964: 443).

Here, as also in other matters, Aquinas seems to me to have been a thorough student of Aristotle's *Ethics*. He presents a thoughtful and careful reading of Aristotle's views, which he himself also endorses. In my view Aquinas's doctrine of natural law is best seen as a continuation of, rather than a significant departure from, the Aristotelian natural law tradition.

From the standpoint of the interpretation of Aristotle presented by Aquinas, which is also that of Francisco Suarez, those principles of justice which forbid the performance of actions which are necessarily wrong, such as murder, theft and adultery, would be considered by Aristotle to be principles of natural justice or natural law (Suarez, 1005a: II, XV, 11, 202). It is true that Aristotle does not state explicitly that this is so. All he says in the long passage under examination is that it is 'evident' which principles of justice are natural and which are legal or conventional. This conclusion is, however, clearly implicit in the remarks which Aristotle makes about the notion of unchangeability, on the one hand, and about actions such as murder, theft and adultery on the other. For Aristotle says that the principles of justice forbidding murder, theft and adultery 'must always be wrong', and this implies that, morally speaking, these principles are unchangeable. He also suggests, however, that those principles of justice which are 'unchangeable' and which have 'everywhere the same force' can, for this very reason, be said to be 'natural'. It is principles of this sort that, in the later scholastic natural law theory developed by Aquinas and others, are referred to as the 'secondary' precepts of natural law (Aquinas, 2006 [1966]: 1a2ae, Q. 94, 4, 89).[8]

It is a further consequence of the interpretation presented here that if Aristotle accepts that the secondary principles of justice which forbid murder, theft and adultery are principles of natural justice, then he is logically committed to accepting that there is yet another, more general principle which is also a principle of natural justice. This principle, indeed, is what might be termed the supreme principle of natural justice, or the 'primary' precept of natural law. It is the principle from which actions like murder, theft and adultery derive their status as actions which are necessarily wrong or unjust. This principle encapsulates Aristotle's belief that the very idea of justice, understood in its 'particular' sense, is necessarily related to that of equality (το ισον, *to ison*) (Aristotle, 1995e: 1129a32–1129b2, 1782). It states that those who are equal in some relevant respect ought to be treated equally in (relevantly) similar circumstances.[9] Aristotle does not himself give this principle a name. I shall, however, follow a tradition which has developed since the time of Aristotle and refer to this principle as the principle of equity. Like Aquinas and Suarez, so also Aristotle appears to have thought these secondary principles of natural law can be derived from the principle of equity by a process of deductive reasoning (Aquinas, 2006 [1966]: la2ae, Q. 94, 4; 87–9; Q. 94, 6, 97; Q. 95, 2, 105–7; Suarez, II, VIII, 2–3, 218–9; II, X, 12, 229–30; II, XIII, 3, 259; II, XV, 2, 286; II, XVI, 3, 312).

That the English term 'equity' is derived ultimately (via the Latin *aequitas*) from the Greek το ισον (*to ison*) has been maintained by a number of commentators (see Riley, 1948a: 10–18; but also Maine, 1965a: 34). However it is important to note, as Francisco Suarez observes, that the English word 'equity' used in this more general sense must be distinguished from the same term when it is used to translate the Greek word επιεικεια (*epieikeia*). According to Suarez, the term 'aequitas' is customarily interpreted as having a 'twofold sense'. For in one sense 'it stands for natural equity, which is identical with natural justice'. And in this sense equity 'is not an emendation of [legal] justice (ius), but rather the source of the rule thereof'. Suarez also observes however, following Aristotle and Aquinas, that the notion of equity may also be understood in another sense, as being a 'prudent moderation of the written law, transcending the exact literal interpretation of the latter' (Suarez, 1995b [1612]: I, II, 9–10, 34–5; also II, XVI, 1–16, 309–25). Aristotle discusses equity in this second sense, επιεικεια, in Book V, Chapter 10 of the *Ethics*. In the account which he offers equity in this more technical sense is a legal principle which is supposed to deal with 'problem cases' which call for 'a correction of the law where it is defective owing to its universality' (Aristotle, 1995e: 1137b26–33, 1796).

In my view the concept of equity, understood in the first of these two senses, lies at the very heart of the doctrine of justice which Aristotle develops in the *Nicomachean Ethics*, and therefore of Aristotle's political thought as a whole. Indeed, it might be said that Aristotle's principal task throughout Book V of that work is to arrive at a definition of the concept of justice understood in its 'particular' sense – which he does by relating it to the notion of equity. As Georgio del Vecchio has put it, Book V of the *Ethics* contains Aristotle's elucidation of the concept of particular justice, as it is 'generically understood' (Del Vecchio, 1952: 23). That is to say, it contains an account of the concept of particular justice understood in the strict sense of the term and 'without qualification' (απλος δικαιον, *haplos dikaion*) (Del Vecchio, 1952: 23; see also Gauthier and Jolif in Aristotle, 1970; Jackson in Aristotle, 1879: xx, 100–4; Newman in Aristotle 1881–1902: Vol. 3, 192; Salomon Shellens, 1959: 89). Such a reading of Aristotle's intentions implies that, although it may not appear so on the surface, Book V does possess, at least implicitly, an underlying, coherent structure.[10]

Moreover in certain situations, namely within what Aristotle refers to as the sphere of 'rectificatory' or 'corrective' justice (διορθοτικον δικαιον, *diorthotikon dikaion*), where it is assumed that all those involved *are* in fact equal in all relevant respects, the principle of equity may be said to reduce itself to, and is indeed an alternative formulation of, the precept of morality known as the Golden Rule: 'Do not to another what you would not have done to yourself'. That this is so is something which has been noted on a number of occasions. Georgio del Vecchio, for example, has provided an excellent account of Aristotle's views on justice, an account which strongly emphasizes the importance which Aristotle attaches to the Golden Rule (del Vecchio, 1952: 84, 187–8; see also Hamburger, 1951: 52; Perelman, 1967b: 25–7; Spooner, 1914: 311; Hertzler, 1934: 423; Marc-Wogau, 1967b).

It has been noted that, quite apart from any (implicit or explicit) reference to it in the writings of Aristotle, there is a close connection between the notions of equity, natural justice and the Golden Rule. We have seen that Suarez made this connection in the early seventeenth century. Much more recently E. H. Snell also has pointed out that in the English language, 'the term equity is used in various senses'. However, in its most popular sense, as in the case of Suarez, 'it is practically equated to natural justice' (Suarez, 1995b: II, VII, 2, 209; II, VII, 5, 211; II, VII, 8–9, 213–14; Snell, 1915: 1). Similarly, R. Newman has argued that 'the central concept of pure equity' is the Golden Rule (Newman, 1973: 28). This view is also shared by R. Snyder, who insists that equity 'denotes the spirit and habit of fairness, justness and right dealing which should regulate the intercourse of men'. The basic principle of equity, therefore, is the rule 'of doing to all others as we would have them do to us' (Snyder, 1973: 38). Indeed, as we have just seen, this belief that equity, the Golden Rule and natural justice are the same thing that has a long history, a history which predates Suarez and which can be traced back to Aristotle himself (Snyder, 1973: 33–43; Perelman, 1980: 34–43; Raphael, 1946; Maitland, 1936; Maine, 1965a; Allen, 1951: 383–425; Vinogradoff, 1923, 1943). To cite just one example, as both Aquinas and Suarez observed, the identification of natural justice with the notion of equity, understood by reference to the Golden Rule can be found in the history of the canon law of the Catholic Church after the publication of the *Decretum Gratiani* in the mid-twelfth century (Aquinas, 2006 [1996]: 1a2ae, Q. 94, 4, 87, 91; Suarez, 1995b: II, VII, 8–9, 213–14). This text is usually considered to be significant because within it, for the first time, the notion of natural law is explicitly and authoritatively associated with the fundamental principles of Christian morality as we find these expounded in both the Old and the New Testaments of The Bible. This way of thinking about questions of jurisprudence is also significant for any attempt to understand the part which the notion of natural law, or the idea of equity, has to play in the history of English law and legal theory throughout the medieval period, into the sixteenth century and beyond. Christopher St. German's *Doctor and Student* (St. German, 1974 [1524]), which was published in the early sixteenth century and relies heavily on the thinking of Aquinas and Gerson, is especially interesting in this regard.

Setting aside these other issues for the time being, however, the important point for present purposes is that Snell's claim that the notion of equity can, in certain situations, be more or less identified with the Golden Rule, because in both cases what we find is a legal and moral principle which seeks to capture the essence of justice, and therefore also of natural justice, by reference to some formulation or other of the idea of 'reciprocity', is one with which Aristotle would have entirely agreed. It is, therefore, extremely difficult to accept Steven B. Smith's extravagant claim that there is 'no Aristotelian equivalent' either of 'the Kantian Categorical Imperative' or of 'the commandments of the Decalogue' (Smith, 1991: 138–9). It is also difficult to agree with Julia Annas's assertion that the notion of impartiality 'does not figure in Aristotle' (Annas, 1993b: 450). Indeed, it seems to me that the idea of impartiality is central to Aristotle's understanding of the concept of justice in the *Ethics*, which in turn is the foundation upon which the political thought developed in the *Politics* is built. To claim that Aristotle was not concerned with the idea of impartiality is to suggest that we can understand Aristotle's ethical and political thought without considering his theory of justice. In my view, however, Aristotle's theory of justice, and also therefore his conception of natural justice or law, is absolutely central to his political thought as a whole.

The Character of Political Justice

For Aristotle, the principles of natural law are what I refer to as formal principles of morality or justice (Burns, 1996a: 36–41). The primary principle of natural law, the principle of equity, is a formal principle because, although it states that equals ought to be treated equally in relevantly similar circumstances, it does not state which persons are to be considered as equals, how they are to be actually treated, or which circumstances are to be considered as relevantly similar. The secondary principles of natural law, such as those forbidding murder and theft, are formal principles because, although they state that we ought not to perform such actions, they do not state which particular actions are to be considered as falling into these 'forbidden' categories. If these principles are to be of any practical value they need to be provided with a definite substantive 'content'. They must be combined with certain principles of legal or conventional justice, the purpose of which is to establish which acts are to count as acts of 'murder', 'theft' and so on. For Aristotle, this is the principal task of legal or conventional justice. In the terminology of the later scholastic natural law theory, the principles of legal or conventional justice provide the formal principles of natural justice with a more detailed specification, or what later Scholastic natural law theory refers to as a 'specific determination' (Aquinas, 2006 [1966]: 1a2ae, Q. 95, 2, 103–7; 1969: 255; Suarez, 1995b: II, XV, 26, 305; II, XIX, 10, 350; II, XX, 2, 351).

Moreover, as this task is carried out by principles of justice which are not natural, but legal or conventional, then it follows that in Aristotle's view it does not actually matter how, in particular, the specific determination of the concepts of 'murder' and 'theft' is carried out. This is something which is arbitrary when considered from the moral point of view. There is no reason, morally speaking, why this ought to be done in one way rather than another. As they are precepts of legal justice, and not natural justice, the principles of justice which carry out the task of determination are changeable in one of the senses in which Aristotle uses this term. Morally speaking, they can and do vary from society to society. At this level it is not the principle of moral universalism, but that of historical or cultural relativism, which reigns.

According to Aristotle, then, practical moral problems cannot be solved by an appeal to the principles of natural justice alone. Nor, in Aristotle's opinion, can they be resolved solely by an appeal to a law which is purely legal or conventional. Such problems can only be solved by the joint application of a principle of natural justice and a principle of legal or conventional justice, in combination with one another. It is Aristotle's view that, apart from one or two exceptions already noted, principles of these two types never actually exist apart from one another. They always exist in combination with one another, and they are always associated with a specific principle of political justice, of which they constitute the integral, component 'parts'. From this point of view, most of the principles of political justice of a *polis* are principles of natural justice which have been given a more specific interpretation or 'determination' by certain principles of legal or conventional justice. These principles of political justice may, therefore, be considered to be particular concrete manifestations of the formal principles of natural justice. The principles of political justice just *are* the principles of natural justice, when considered from the standpoint of the specific, historically given character of their many, and various, possible modes of existence. It is only after they have been so interpreted that it is possible for individuals to follow the principles of natural justice in practice.

For Aristotle, it is only by so far as they have been specifically interpreted by positive law that the principles of natural justice or law might be said to exist empirically at all. They exist immanently within the principles of political justice of a particular polis. Employing the terminology of Hegelian metaphysics, we might say that the 'individual' or 'concrete' existence of the principles of natural justice depends on their being given a specific determination in civil law. From the standpoint of Hegel's philosophy, which was greatly influenced by that of Aristotle, a precept of natural justice is an 'essence' (Hegel, 1975: §112, 162–6). This principle manifests itself, or 'appears', in a given society at a certain time, as a 'particular' principle of 'political justice' or civil law (Hegel, 1975: §14, 19–22; §§ 21–4, 33–7; §38, 62; §45A, 73; §48A,78; §61, 95; §80, 13–15; §82, 120; §112, 163; §115, 166; §119, 174; §128, 184–90; §145, 204–7; §160, 223–8; §181, 244–5). To think of a principle of civil law in this way, as a combination or 'synthesis' of an underlying 'essence' with an empirically accessible 'appearance,' is to think of it in its 'actuality' (Hegel, 1975: §142, 200–2; §163, 226); see also Burns, 1996a: 66–74, 1995, 1998a).

It is for this reason that Salmond's claim, noted earlier, that the distinction between 'political justice' and 'legal justice' is of no theoretical importance for our understanding of Aristotle's political thought is not well founded. To fail to appreciate the significance of this distinction is, in my opinion, to misunderstand completely Aristotle's view of the relationship which exists between natural law, positive law and civil law. It is to misunderstand completely what Aristotle means when he says that natural justice is a 'part' of political justice. One important implication of this interpretation of Aristotle's claim that of political justice 'part is natural, part legal' is that when a principle of natural justice, like that forbidding murder or theft, is incorporated into the system of political justice of a particular society it is not merely ratified, or provided with a coercive sanction. The principles of political justice of a particular society are not simply principles of natural justice to which nothing, apart from a coercive sanction, has been 'added'. Hence, also, these principles of political justice are not exact copies or reproductions of the principles of natural justice, down to the smallest details, so far as their substantive content is concerned. On the contrary, when the precepts of natural justice are incorporated into the legal system of a given society they are not only given a coercive sanction, but they are also at the same time modified in some way. They are modified by being combined or amalgamated with principle of legal or conventional justice. A principle of political justice is the synthetic or compound principle which results from such a process of combination. It is this 'concrete' principle of political justice which is enforced by coercive sanctions (Burns, 1996a: 18–19; Finnis, 1980: 28, 281; Kelsen, 1972a: 416).

It does not seem inappropriate at this point to draw the attention of the reader to the views of Richard Hooker on this subject in his *Of the Laws of Ecclesiastical Polity* (Hooker, 1836 [1593]). Hooker's starting point is the Aristotelian suggestion that 'some kind of regiment the Law of Nature doth require; yet the kinds thereof being many, Nature doth not tie to any one, but leaveth the choice as a thing arbitrary' (Hooker, 1836 [1593]: I, X, 5, 304). Hooker then goes on to argue that there are two types of human law, one of which possesses a character which is 'mixed'. As Hooker puts it, 'all laws human, which are made for the ordering of politic societies, be either such as establish some duty whereunto all men by the law of reason did before stand bound; or else such as make that a duty now which before was none. The one sort we may for distinction's sake call "mixedly", and the other "merely" human.' (Hooker, 1836 [1593]: I, X, 10, 310; also I, X, 10, 311). In Hooker's schema duties which are 'merely human' relate to principles of conventional justice, as Aristotle understands the term. It should however be noted that the contrast which Hooker draws when discussing this issue is not between those duties which are merely conventional and those which are natural. It is, rather, between those duties which are merely conventional and those duties which are 'mixed', that is to say which are both natural and conventional at the same time.

Nevertheless it must be conceded that Hooker's understanding of what this involves is somewhat different from that presented above. For in the case of those duties which are 'mixed' duties, Hooker maintains that the human element relates to the issue of enforcement and punishment only. Thus, for example, having stated that 'in laws that which is natural bindeth universally, that which is positive not so', Hooker goes on to consider the act of theft. This is, he says, an act which is 'naturally punishable' because theft is intrinsically wrong or unjust. Hooker goes on to claim that 'the kind of punishment' for the act of theft' is a matter for 'positive' law. Consequently 'the particular determination of the reward or punishment', he maintains, 'belongeth unto them by whom laws are made' (Hooker, 1836 [1593]: I, X, 6–7, 306). I note in passing that similar views relating to punishment and penalties can also be found occasionally in the writings of Aquinas and Suarez (Aquinas, 2006 [1966]: 1a2ae, Q. 95, 2, 107; Suarez, 1995b [1612]: II, XII, 1, 253), although Hooker's account differs from theirs because, as both Aquinas and Suarez make plain elsewhere, the core issue for them is not what the punishment for theft is going to be, but rather which acts are to be considered acts of 'theft' properly so called and which are not.

The Changeability of Natural Law

As I noted earlier, at the beginning of the passage under discussion, Aristotle says that what characterizes natural justice is the fact that it is unchangeable. I have already considered one interpretation of what he might possibly have meant by this. Later on in the passage, however, he goes on to acknowledge that all principles of justice, those of natural justice included, are changeable. These two statements appear to flatly contradict one another. Our present problem, therefore, is to consider whether these apparently contradictory statements might be reconciled, and if so how. Aristotle provides us with a hint as to how this problem might be solved when he says that natural justice is indeed changeable, but only 'in a sense', and not in an 'unqualified way'.

This suggests that he takes the view that natural justice might also be said to be *un*changeable, although again only in a sense, and not in any unqualified way. In short, these remarks indicate that Aristotle is of the opinion that the principles of natural justice are in one sense changeable and in another sense not so, depending on the point of view from which we consider them.

Earlier I related the notion of changeability to that of moral necessity. With respect to the question of the moral validity of the precepts of natural justice, it appears to be a clear implication of Aristotle's later admission that these principles are changeable after all that they are not associated with matters of strict moral necessity and do not possess a universal moral validity. This is Leo Strauss's understanding of Aristotle. If we take as an example the principle of natural justice or law forbidding theft, if this interpretation were correct it would imply that for Aristotle the act of theft might, in certain circumstances, be morally permissible. Hence it is acceptable, morally speaking, that the legal systems of some societies might on occasion permit acts of theft. Interpreted in this way, Aristotle's remarks support the view that he is sympathetic either towards moral relativism or towards ethical consequentialism.

However, in my view it is unlikely that this is what Aristotle was thinking of when he acknowledged that natural justice is, after all, at least in one sense changeable. There are three reasons for doubting the validity of this particular interpretation of Aristotle's meaning. The first is that, as we have seen, Aristotle is perfectly clear, elsewhere in the *Ethics*, that the precepts of natural law forbidding acts like murder, theft and adultery, just *are* strictly universal when considered from the standpoint of their moral validity. In Aristotle's view questions of moral validity are matters of logical necessity. Hence they are associated with principles which possess a strict universality. The second is the fact that, towards the end of the passage, Aristotle suggests that, where political constitutions are concerned, there is but one 'which is everywhere and by nature the best'. This clearly implies that, with respect to questions of moral validity, Aristotle associates something being natural with its being strictly universal. The third is that if this is what Aristotle means when he says that the principles of natural justice are at least in one sense changeable, then it becomes extremely difficult, if not impossible, to explain the particular sense in which he considers that these principles remain '*un*changeable'.

It follows from this that either my earlier account of what Aristotle means by the 'unchangeability' of natural justice is incorrect (which in my view it is not), or that Aristotle does in fact contradict himself when he says that natural justice is both 'unchangeable' and 'changeable' (which in my view he does not), or, finally, that Aristotle means something else when he says that the principles of natural justice are, at least in a sense, changeable. The problem, here, is that of establishing what else he might possibly mean. Now there is in fact an alternative account of Aristotle's claim that the principles of natural justice are either unchangeable or changeable, which has nothing to do with the notion of moral necessity. According to this alternative account, when Aristotle speaks of a principle of justice being unchangeable what he has in mind is the notion that the principles in question are not morally but empirically universal. That is to say, they can be found within the positive legal systems of all societies, at all times and in all places. This is a matter of fact which is confirmable (if only in part) by empirical observation. This analysis of Aristotle's remarks fits in very well with what he has to say elsewhere, both in the *Ethics* and in his other writings, about what is involved when we say of something that it is 'natural'. For there is a general tendency for Aristotle to associate something's being natural with its being universal, that is to say, with its being 'necessary' in the specific sense that it applies in all possible cases – in the same way that fire burns both here and in Persia (Aristotle, 1995b: 73b25–29, 119; 88b30–89a3, 146; 1995e: 1134b25–26; 1180b11–22). From the standpoint of this interpretation, as J. R. Kroger has noted, for Aristotle 'what is natural is also necessary'. At the same time, however, 'only universal practices can be natural, for if a practice is necessary, it must be followed universally' (Kroger, 2004: 918). Thus when Aristotle admits later on in the passage under discussion that the principles of natural justice are in fact changeable after all, at least in one sense of the term, what he is doing is acknowledging that, although these principles are certainly morally universal, nevertheless they are not empirically universal. There is a sense in which they are not found in the systems of political justice of all *poleis* in all times and in all places.

Even when considered from this alternative point of view, however, that which relates to the notion of empirical universality rather than to the notion of moral necessity, Aristotle's remarks concerning the changeability of the principles of natural justice remain ambiguous. For they can still be interpreted in two quite different ways, only the second of which, in my view, is to be preferred. According to the first of these interpretations, the principles of natural justice would be unchangeable if they were to be found universally, incorporated within the systems of political justice of all societies at all times (Begin, 1959: 88; Maritain, 1958: 84–94; Strauss, 1974 [1953]: 9, 97–8). Similarly, they would be changeable if their occurrence was *not* strictly universal in that sense. Thus, when Aristotle says that the principles of natural justice are in a sense changeable it follows, according to advocates of this interpretation, that what he is suggesting is that there are some societies in which the principles of natural justice, or particular concrete manifestations of them, are not to be found at all. Despite the fact that these principles possess a moral validity which is universal, there are nevertheless some societies which 'fail' to incorporate these principles into their own systems of political justice. There are, for example, some societies which enjoin or permit the performance of certain actions, such as murder, theft and adultery, which are forbidden by natural justice.

We may illustrate this by considering an example. Let us take the principle of natural justice which states that theft is wrong. And let us assume that, for Aristotle, from the standpoint of its moral validity this principle *is* strictly universal. In other words, the act of theft, according to Aristotle, is necessarily wrong, always and everywhere. No individual could ever be justified, morally speaking, in committing an act of theft; and no society could ever be justified in permitting the performance of the act of theft in and through its system of civil law. In this sense, at least, the precept of natural justice forbidding theft certainly is unchangeable. However, in certain societies this might not be recognized. The principle may 'fail' for some reason. For, as Aristotle puts it, 'things are objects of knowledge in two senses'. Some things are known 'without qualification', and some things are known only 'to us' (Aristotle, 1995e: 1095b1–3, 1731). Though morally universal, the principle of justice forbidding theft might not be empirically universal, precisely because the systems of political justice of at least some societies wrongfully permit it. There are occasions when both Aquinas and Suarez argue in a similar way; although there are also occasions when they take a different view.

On the other hand, however, Aristotle's claim that the principles of natural justice are at least in one sense changeable might be interpreted differently, although still in a way which relates to the question of their empirical universality, as opposed to that of their moral validity. According to this second interpretation (which is the one favoured here) it is Aristotle's view that the principles of natural justice are strictly and entirely unchangeable when considered from the standpoint of the moral validity. Furthermore, it is Aristotle's view that these principles are also strictly unchangeable when considered from the standpoint of their empirical application, at least in one sense. In other words, these principles can indeed be found incorporated within the systems of political justice of all societies, in all times and in all places. From this point of view, then, the problem that we have when interpreting Aristotle's remarks regarding the changeability of natural justice is that of explaining how it is possible for Aristotle to consistently maintain that the principles of natural justice are empirically universal in this sense and yet in another, different sense, are not so. The solution to this problem, in my view, lies in the fact that the principles of natural justice may be considered from two quite different standpoints. They may be considered either as purely formal principles of justice, on the one hand, or they may be considered as substantive or concrete principles of justice on the other.

If we consider the principles of natural justice as formal principles then these principles are, empirically speaking, entirely unchangeable. According to my preferred interpretation, it is Aristotle's view that, in addition to possessing a moral validity which is universal, these principles of natural justice are also empirically universal. They are to be found in the systems of political justice of all societies at all times, without exception. On the other hand, however, it must not be forgotten that these formal principles of natural justice can only exist at all in so far as they are combined with certain principles of legal or conventional justice, as integral component elements of corresponding principles of political justice, which are to be found in the legal systems of particular societies at particular times. It is Aristotle's view that these principles of political justice are particular concrete manifestations of the formal principles of natural justice. They *are* the principles of natural justice in so far as the latter are considered from the point of view of their particular empirical existence. It seems clear enough, however, that these principles of political justice do in fact differ from one another in certain respects. For the formal principles of natural justice do not and need not morally speaking manifest themselves always in precisely the same way. Thus, considered, as concrete principles of justice the principles of natural justice are not 'unchangeable', but 'changeable'. Both morally and empirically, the particular manner in which they manifest themselves can and does vary from society to society, from time to time, and from place to place. It is in this way, then, by emphasizing that the normative precepts of natural justice may be thought of either as formal principles, on the one hand, or as concrete principles on the other, that it is possible for us to explain how Aristotle can maintain without contradiction that natural justice can be and is both changeable and unchangeable at the same time.

As I have already alluded on more than one occasion to the similarities which exist between the thought of Aristotle and that of Hegel, I shall take the opportunity to note here in passing that the principles of 'natural justice' in Aristotle's political philosophy can be thought of as playing the same role as the principles of 'abstract right' do in that of Hegel (Hegel, 1979; Burns, 1995, 1996: 42–5). Ernest J. Weinrib has made the interesting claim that 'in Hegel's legal philosophy what Aristotle calls *corrective* justice appears as abstract right' (Weinrib, 1991–92: 423). It seems to me, however, that it would be more accurate to say that it is in fact what Aristotle refers to as '*natural* justice' which appears in Hegel's philosophy of law as the notion of 'abstract right'. It must be conceded, however, that there is a close relationship in Aristotle's ethical thought between the idea of natural justice and that of corrective justice. For in Aristotle's view the basic principles of natural justice, such as those forbidding the acts of murder, theft and adultery, are also principles of corrective justice and vice versa.

Is Aristotle a Natural Law Theorist or a Legal Positivist?

This question has been answered in different ways by commentators on Aristotle's political thought. Some, perhaps most, claim that Aristotle is a natural law theorist, indeed the first natural law theorist in the history of political thought. He is the founder of the natural law tradition. As Max Salomon

Shellens has pointed out, 'philosophers and historians almost invariably claim that Aristotle is the father of natural law' (Salomon Shellens, 1959: 72; see also Crowe, 1977: 19; Destrée, 2000: 220; Friedmann, 1967: 10; Friedrich, 1963: 22–23). Others, however, have emphatically denied this. Indeed some, like Hans Kelsen, have maintained (or at least strongly implied) that Aristotle rejects the notion of natural law altogether (Kelsen, 1957a,b, 1973a; Yack, 1990: 216). We may begin by asking whether or not Aristotle would allow that the principles of natural justice could possibly serve as a yardstick for measuring the justice or injustice of political justice, or civil law, for as we have seen this is usually considered to be a defining characteristic both of natural law and natural law theory. In so far as the principle of equity is concerned, it seems evident that in Aristotle's opinion no positive law could possibly come into conflict with the demands which are placed upon us by this fundamental principle of natural justice. For this principle is a purely formal principle. It states that equals ought to be treated equally in similar circumstances, and Aristotle gives to positive law the task of deciding who are equals and precisely how these equals are to be treated. From Aristotle's point of view, therefore, any civil law at all, in so far as its specific content is concerned, is consistent with the principle of equity. A civil law could only be unjust or unfair, from this point of view, if it were actually administered unfairly. From the standpoint of concrete or substantive justice, the principle of equity is clearly incapable of providing a means of differentiating between those civil laws which are just and those which are unjust. This is a point which has been well made by Alf Ross, who has noted that 'it is indeed impossible' to derive 'from the formal idea of equality' any sort of demand 'with regard to the content of' a legal order (Ross, 2007a [1959]: 274, 280). It is also a point which has been acknowledged by Hans Kelsen, specifically in connection with the thinking of Aristotle. According to Kelsen, it is Aristotle's view that, as 'a rationalistic moral philosophy is not capable of determining the content of a just order', that is to say, is not capable of answering the questions 'which differences between individuals are relevant and which irrelevant', then it follows that such matters must be left 'to the state', that is, 'to the positive legislator' (Kelsen, 1957a: 133; see also Kelsen, 1961: 439–40). It follows from this, as again Ross has noted, that justice in the formal sense 'cannot be a legal-political yardstick or an ultimate criterion by which a law can be judged' (Ross, 2007a [1959]: 274, 280).

Similar remarks might be made about the more specific principles of natural justice forbidding actions such as murder, theft and adultery. These principles also possess a formal character. They need to be given a specific interpretation or a definite substantive content if they are to be applied in practice. And it is Aristotle's view that this task be carried out by positive law. Under these circumstances it is evidently a logical impossibility for positive law to conflict with the requirements of natural law. Thus, here also, it is quite impossible for natural law to serve as a standard of measurement by means of which the justice or injustice of positive law might be evaluated. Jeremy Bentham once claimed that it is logically impossible for a positive law to permit the act of murder, because although by definition 'murder' is an act of 'wrongful killing', nevertheless in the final analysis the notion of what is 'wrongful' is defined by positive law (Bentham, 1977a: 42–3; see also Burns, 1996a: 34–41). This view has a parallel in the political philosophy of Hobbes of course (Hobbes, 1998 [1642]: VI, 16, 86–7; also XIV, 10, 158–9; XVI, 10, 192; XVII, 10, 213–4). In my opinion, however, the ultimate origins of it are to be found in the philosophy of Aristotle.

The peculiarity of Aristotle's doctrine of natural law, and of his understanding of the relationship which holds between natural law, positive law and civil law appears not to have been noticed by most of the commentators who associate Aristotle's political thought with the natural law tradition. It *has*, however, been noted by Kelsen, who maintains that Aristotle should not be considered to be a 'genuine' natural law theorist at all, precisely because Aristotle does not consider natural law to be a yardstick for the evaluation of positive law, and because, in Kelsen's view, such a belief is a necessary precondition for any genuine natural law theory. Kelsen maintains, not entirely accurately, that for Aristotle 'natural law is simply a constituent part of the positive law of the state'. He also suggests that in Aristotle's view that the principles of natural justice 'consist of those norms which are much the same in all legal orders'. However, Kelsen also goes on to point out that, under these circumstances, 'this so-called natural law cannot exercise the function essential to all natural law proper, of operating as a standard of evaluation for positive law'. Within Aristotle's system, Kelsen rightly argues, one cannot 'distinguish, by appeal to natural law, between a just and an unjust system of law'. Thus, Kelsen finally concludes, despite his employment of the term 'natural justice' Aristotle cannot be regarded as a 'genuine' natural law theorist in the strict sense of the term. For he gives to the notion of natural law 'a meaning which is entirely otiose from the standpoint of a genuine natural law theory'. Aristotle employs the concept of natural law, or natural justice, 'only to vindicate positive law' (Kelsen, 1973a: 132).

What is interesting about Kelsen's interpretation of Aristotle's views on natural law is that, throughout, Kelsen simply assumes, unquestioningly, that a system of political thought cannot be a genuine natural law theory if it denies that natural law is a standard for evaluating what Kelsen refers to as 'positive law'. This assumption, which is certainly to be found in the Stoic and some other natural law traditions, but is entirely absent in others, is for Kelsen definitive of the very notions of 'natural law' and 'natural law theory' per se. It is precisely because he makes this unfounded assumption that Kelsen comes very close to making the contrary claim that, far from being a natural law theorist, Aristotle is in fact an early forerunner of the modern doctrine known as 'legal positivism', a doctrine to which Kelsen himself subscribes. Thus, according to

Kelsen, it is Aristotle's view that 'positive law' and 'positive law alone' is 'just'. Hence 'positive law and justice coincide'. And this amounts, in Kelsen's view, as it might be said to do in the case of all legal positivists, 'to an unconditional glorification of positive law' (Kelsen, 1957a: 126; 1973a: 131).

According to Kelsen, then, Aristotle denies (if only implicitly) that there *is* such a thing as natural justice or natural law. It should be clear from the analysis presented earlier, however, that in my view Aristotle does not do this at all. What he actually denies is that there is such a thing as natural justice or natural law in the specific sense in which Kelsen understands that term. What Aristotle denies is the existence of a natural law, understood as a higher standard of justice which might in certain circumstances be used to critically evaluate civil laws and the political constitutions with which they are associated. Aristotle does *not* deny that there is such a thing as natural law in a different sense from this. Nor, therefore, does he reject the notion of natural law outright and embrace the doctrine of conventionalism.

Donald N. Schroeder has maintained that 'Aristotle's legal ideas fit into neither the natural law nor the positivist tradition, but have certain features in common with both' (Schroeder, 1981: 30; see also Shiner, 1994: 1248, 1261–63). If by '*the* natural law tradition' Schroeder has in mind what I have referred to elsewhere as the Stoic conception of natural law, then there is some truth in this claim. On the other hand, however, it might be suggested that this assessment is erroneous to the extent that it assumes that there is just *one* natural law tradition. Against Schroeder, I would argue that Aristotle is most definitely a natural law theorist in *some* sense of the term, although the natural law theory to which he subscribes is one which most commentators today would consider to be of an unconventional type. Aristotle does not subscribe to the Stoic conception of natural law, which dominates the understanding current thinking about natural law and natural law theory. As Kelsen rightly points out, Aristotle does not regard the principles of natural law as constituting some ideal standard of justice which individuals might use to critically evaluate positive law.

I am, therefore, in complete agreement with F. D. Wormuth when he says that Aristotle 'had no conception of a natural law which annuls positive law' (Wormuth, 1948: 59; see also Yack, 1990: 220, 234). This does not mean, however, as Kelsen wrongly suggests, that Aristotle is not a natural law theorist at all. All that it means is that there are important differences between Aristotelian natural law theory and the Stoic conception of natural law. For Aristotle adheres to what may be termed a 'formal' conception of natural law. To employ the terminology associated with the different political ideologies, whereas Cicero and the Stoic conception of natural law are the forerunners of the liberal natural law theory of modern times, Aristotle is the founding father of a conservative conception of natural law which is to be found in the writings of figures such as Montesquieu, Burke and Hegel. So far as the relationship between the thought of Aristotle and that of Hegel, in particular, is concerned it seems to me that Pierre Aubenque is correct when he says that Aristotle's conception of natural law 'is far from allowing us to define precise criteria for judging the legitimacy of this institution or of that law'. Aubenque is also correct when he says that Aristotle and Hegel are in agreement that 'nature' or natural law serves to justify the 'conventions' associated with the 'concrete morality' (*Sittlichkeit*) of particular societies (Aubenque, 1980: 157).

Given the central role which Aristotle's discussion of the principle of equity has to play in the argument of Book V of the *Nicomachean Ethics*, and given that Aristotle's discussion of justice in the *Ethics* is a preliminary to his treatment of the same subject in the *Politics* (Aristotle, 1995h: 1280a16–19, 2031; 1282b16–20, 2035), the claim made earlier that, for Aristotle, the principle of equity is the fundamental principle of natural justice is of considerable importance. For it implies that Aristotle's brief discussion of natural justice in Chapter 7 of Book V of the *Ethics* is of much greater significance for our understanding of his political thought as a whole than is usually supposed. I find it difficult to agree, therefore, with R. G. Mulgan when he argues that 'the idea of natural law as such does not play an important role' in Aristotle's system of political thought (Mulgan, 1977: 141). Neither can I agree with Dennis Lloyd when he asserts that 'the doctrine of natural justice' played 'little part in Aristotle's *Ethics*' (Lloyd, 1959: 65). Nor, finally, can I agree with P. E. Sigmund when he insists that although 'a conception of fundamental natural law or natural justice was present' in Aristotle's writings 'it was not developed or integrated with the rest of his thought' (Sigmund, 1971: 12). All of these commentators have, in my opinion, misunderstood Aristotle's views on natural law, especially his understanding of the relationship which exists between natural law and positive law. Had they properly understood what Aristotle has to say about natural justice, legal justice and political justice in the *Ethics* they would not have been so quick to relegate the notion of natural law to the status of a footnote to Aristotle's system of political thought as a whole – and an embarrassing footnote at that. If Aristotle's position is properly understood, then the notion of natural justice or law is placed where it truly belongs, and where later scholastic natural law theory of Aquinas quite rightly places it, at the very heart of Aristotle's political thought.

The Possibility of Scientific Knowledge in Ethics and Politics

Usually, when Aristotle talks about true knowledge, or genuinely 'scientific' knowledge, he associates the term with those things which occur as a matter of necessity. As he puts it, 'the object of scientific knowledge is of necessity' (Aristotle, 1995e: 1139b19–36, 1799; 1140a31–1140b4, 1800). However,

Aristotle associates the notion of 'necessity', in turn, with empirical 'universality', that is to say with universality of occurrence. He observes that 'some occurrences are universal', for they are what they are 'always and in every case', and 'to hold in every instance and always is of the nature of the universal' (Aristotle, 1995b: 96a8–10, 158–9). In his view, this is the difference between 'knowledge', in the strict sense of the term and mere 'opinion'. For example at one point he states that 'scientific knowledge and its object differ from opinion' precisely because the former is 'commensurately universal' (Aristotle, 1995e: 1180b14–22, 1865–66; 1995a: 88b30–35, 146). This means that it is knowledge of something which applies in every case, or which 'belongs to every instance of its subject' (Aristotle, 1995b: 73b25–29, 119). A clear implication of these remarks is that for Aristotle anything which does not occur always and in every case could not, strictly speaking, be said to be 'universal'. Neither could it be said to be 'necessary'. Nor therefore, in his view, could it be said to be a possible object of genuine or scientific knowledge.

When Aristotle says that those things which are 'natural' are '*un*changeable', in the passage under discussion, his remarks are entirely consistent with what he has to say about scientific knowledge, and its relationship to the notions of necessity and universality, elsewhere in his writings. It follows from this that for Aristotle it *is* possible for us to have genuinely scientific knowledge in the spheres of morality and politics. Such knowledge relates precisely to the principles of natural justice, in so far as these principles may be said to be necessary and universal principles which are unchangeable because they have 'everywhere the same force'.

On the other hand, however, there are obvious difficulties associated with this interpretation of Aristotle. For example, as is well known, elsewhere in the *Ethics* Aristotle explicitly rejects the view that in the sphere of politics genuinely scientific knowledge is possible at all. Aristotle's reason for adopting this position can be associated with his belief that even the principles of natural justice can be said to be changeable, in one sense of the term. There are, he occasionally concedes, *no* principles of justice which possesses the quality of strict universality of occurrence which he associates with genuinely scientific knowledge (Aristotle, 1995e: 1094b13–27, 1730; 1103b26–1104a9, 1743–44). The problem with *this* reading, though, is that if these remarks are taken literally a logical implication of them is the denial by Aristotle of the very existence of natural justice. This is a problem because it is clear from what Aristotle says in the passage from Book V of the *Ethics* that I am analyzing that he does not wish to commit himself to such a view. This raises the issue of whether it is possible for us to reconcile the apparently conflicting remarks which Aristotle makes in relation to this question and if so how.

In my opinion, *this* alleged contradiction in Aristotle's thinking is again apparent and not real. It can, therefore, be resolved. The way forward here is to recognize that for Aristotle it is possible for us to discuss questions of morals and politics at two different levels, namely the level at which normative principles are formal or abstract, on the one hand, and the level at which they are substantive or concrete, on the other. If we are content to be satisfied with general principles relating to natural justice, then Aristotle holds that it certainly is possible for us to make statements in this sphere which have a universal applicability, and which, therefore, do possess the status of genuinely 'scientific' knowledge. If, however, we wish to focus, not on these general principles, but on specific details regarding moral or political questions; or to the application of these general principles to the circumstances of particular cases; then at this lower level 'scientific' knowledge is not possible. For here we have entered the sphere of legal or conventional justice, and in that sphere, the sphere of the determinate and the particular, Aristotle insists that there are no principles of justice at all which possess a universal validity. It follows from this, however, that there cannot be any substantive or concrete principles of justice which possess a universal validity either. That is why Aristotle insists in the *Ethics*, as Hegel was to do after him, that 'precision is not to be sought for alike in all discussions', and that in matters of morality and politics we 'must be content' to 'indicate the truth' only 'roughly and in outline' (Aristotle,1995d: 1094b12–14, 1730; 1104a1–5, 1743–44). To continue with my earlier comparison of the political thought of Aristotle with that of Hegel, the reader is reminded at this point that the 'double title' title of Hegel's most well known work of political philosophy is *Natural Law and Political Science in Outline: Elements of the Philosophy of Right* (Hegel, 1979; Burns, 1996a). When he first published his magnum opus in 1817 Hegel chose to give it a recognizably Aristotelian title.

It is for this reason that Aristotle maintains in the *Ethics* that laws are a product of the 'art' of politics (Aristotle, 1995e: 1181a24–1181b1); and it is for this reason, also, that he argues that, in matters of legislation, guidance is to be found by the application of 'phronesis', 'prudence' or 'practical wisdom' (φρονεσις), rather than by scientific knowledge in the strict sense of the term (Aristotle, 1995e: 1140a24–1140b30, 1800–01). Aristotle points out that prudence is concerned, not with 'universals', but rather with 'particulars', and as a result is in some situations actually more useful than genuine or scientific knowledge, which is concerned with universals. The example which Aristotle gives to illustrate this point is an interesting one. He refers to the routine principle of every day conduct which stipulates that 'light meats are good for you'. For Aristotle, this is a universal principle and hence a matter of genuine scientific knowledge. This principle is, however (to employ the terminology adopted earlier) a formal principle. For, as Aristotle himself points out, it is possible for a man to know 'that light meats are digestible and wholesome', and yet for him *not* to know 'what sorts of meats are light'. In these circumstances, Aristotle suggests, a person who relied on scientific knowledge alone would not succeed in producing 'health'. The man of prudence, on the other hand, may well be unfamiliar with the general principle that light meats are good for you. He may lack genuinely scientific knowledge in this particular area. And yet at the same time he could be familiar with the particular principle that, for example, 'chicken is wholesome'. According to Aristotle, such a person is in practice more likely to produce health than someone who relies entirely on general principles. Aristotle goes on to say that an adequate understanding of politics (and practical affairs generally) actually requires an appreciation of *both* types of principle, the general and the particular, and the relationship which exists between the two. It requires both scientific knowledge of general principles *and* prudence or 'practical wisdom' regarding the way in which these general principles can be and are applied to the circumstances of particular cases (Aristotle, 1995e: 1141b8–20, 1802). The analogy between what Aristotle says here about this principle that 'light meats are digestible and wholesome' and what he says in the passage from Book V of the *Ethics* under discussion about the principle that 'a prisoner's ransom shall be a mina' is readily apparent. Indeed, it is quite striking. This particular example clearly supports the interpretation that I presented above of Aristotle's understanding of the relationship which exists between natural law and positive law.

Aristotle on Natural Law and 'The Politics of Interpretation'

It is clear that the 'specific determination' of the abstract principles of natural law has to do with establishing or fixing the precise meaning of certain core moral or legal concepts, for example the concepts of murder, theft and adultery. Not surprisingly, therefore, the act of determination has been connected by a number of writers with the 'interpretation' of the meaning of legal terms. As we shall see in Chapter 3, Aristotle says some interesting things about this issue in the *Rhetoric*, especially in relation to the meaning of the concepts of murder and theft. Pierre Destrée has rightly suggested that Aristotle recognizes the possibility of a 'plurality of interpretations' of the precepts of natural law, citing the natural law which forbids murder as an example. According to Destrée, Aristotle holds that 'all human beings acknowledge the law forbidding murder'. At the same time, however, Destrée maintains that Aristotle also argues that 'it is possible to interpret this law differently'. So far, so good. In my view, however, Destrée is mistaken when he goes on to say, as he does, that this 'does not mean' that for Aristotle 'there are no interpretations which are better than others' (Destrée, 2000: 234). On the contrary, that is exactly what it does mean. Given that, in Aristotle's view, the principles of justice which determine more particularly what in a given society at a given time is going to count as an act of murder are not principles of natural justice, but rather principles of legal or conventional justice, it follows that for Aristotle all such interpretations are equally legitimate when considered from the moral point of view.

It should however be noted that the notion of interpretation, understood in this sense, is somewhat different from that referred to in the Introduction to the present work. It will be remembered that there the distinction between the activity of interpretation and that of appropriation is that in the former case we are talking about the *discovery* of meaning by the reader of a text, whereas in the latter we are talking about the *creation* of meaning by the reader of a text. These considerations apply generally to all texts. Consequently they apply also to legal texts and the issue of how the meaning of the concepts contained within them is to be established. With respect to this issue it is evident that the process of establishing or fixing the precise meaning of terms such as 'murder' and 'theft', as envisaged by Aristotle, does not fall neatly into either one or the other of these two categories. This is so because it is in part a creative act, involving the production of new meaning by a reader, but not entirely so. From this point of view, by applying the concepts of murder and theft, or the laws which forbid these acts, to the particular circumstances associated with novel situations one thereby changes the meaning of these concepts by extending their denotation, or the range of their application. At the same time, however, the kind of analogical reasoning which is involved here undoubtedly does involve 'rule following', and hence the principle of continuation of the past. The person who undertakes this task is familiar with the linguistic rule or convention which gives these notions the meaning which they currently have, and might be said to be following this rule, albeit in a novel and creative way. We are not, therefore, talking here about a situation in which the meaning of these core concepts is being entirely created *de novo*. It is assumed that the meaning of these concepts after this process of interpretation is not completely different from what it had been before, but only partially so.

It is not difficult to connect this way of thinking about the interpretation of meaning to what Aristotle says elsewhere about the virtue of prudence or practical wisdom, or indeed what he says about equity in the sense of *epieikeia*, in the *Nicomachean Ethics*. For in both cases we are talking about the issue of applying general rules to the circumstances of particular situations. In the case of *epieikeia* the situations in question are new ones which were not envisaged by the legislator and which are conceived to be 'hard' or 'problem cases' (Dworkin, 1978b). Consequently, according to Aristotle, the equitable interpretation of the law requires an effort to establish what the original intentions of the author of the law in question were. In these situations the alteration of the meaning of the concepts involved ought to be 'in the spirit' of the law in question, even if it involves going beyond 'the letter' of the law as it is has been up to now and is currently understood.

Nor is it difficult to connect Aristotle's views on this subject to those of the later Wittgenstein so far as the latter is interested in developing a theory of meaning which is built around the notion of 'meaning in use', that is to say, the idea that what gives concepts (or the words which are used to express them in a particular natural language) their meaning is the fact that there is some linguistic convention which regulates their use (see Burns, 2011a). The affinity between the views of the later Wittgenstein on this subject and those expressed by Aristotle in the *Nicomachean Ethics* is obvious, though it has been little discussed.[11] Finally, it is also possible to connect Aristotle's views on this issue to the hermeneutic philosophy of Hans Georg Gadamer referred to in the Introduction, especially to Gadamer's notion of the hermeneutic circle. For the activity of 'interpretation', understood in this Aristotelian sense, arguably does involve a process of negotiation of meaning along something like the lines indicated by Gadamer. As we saw earlier, however, there are different ways of thinking about what such a process of negotiation involves, according to one of which it can be associated with the attempted, but not entirely successful, appropriation of the meaning of a particular word or concept.

So far as the interpretation of the concept of natural law, and of associated concepts such as 'murder', 'theft' and 'adultery' is concerned, Aristotle says some interesting things in the *Rhetoric*, which can be connected to the discussion of his views on natural law presented above. For example at one point he observes that 'it often happens that a man will admit an act, but will not admit the prosecutor's label for the act nor the facts which the label implies' (Aristotle, 1995i: 1373b38–1374a17, 2188). So, Aristotle goes on, 'he will admit that he took a thing, but not that he stole it; that he struck someone first, but not that he committed outrage; that he had intercourse with a woman, but not that he committed adultery; that he is guilty of theft, but not that he is guilty of sacrilege, the object stolen not being consecrated', and so on (Aristotle, 1995i: 1374a1–5, 2188; see also Aristotle, 1995g: 1221b19–25, 1934). Here, as Aristotle rightly notes, 'whether our aim is to establish a man's guilt or to establish his innocence', in order to make 'the justice of our case clear', it is necessary that we be 'able to distinguish what is theft, outrage or adultery from what is not' (Aristotle, 1995g: 1374a1-5, 2188). Alternatively, one might say that it is necessary to possess the rhetorical techniques required for successfully persuading a jury, in a court of law, that the action committed falls under our own preferred description, rather than that of our opponent. Everything here depends on the success or failure of our efforts to appropriate the concepts of, in this case, murder, theft and adultery, for our own particular cause.

The relevance of these remarks for our understanding of Aristotle's views on natural law, and the relationship which exists between natural law, positive law and civil law, is readily apparent. For as we have seen Aristotle's view is that, in the end, it is for the law of the *polis*, and therefore also for its courts of law, to decide whether an action is or is not an act of murder, theft, adultery and the like, and therefore contrary to the requirements of natural justice or law. This is a matter of what Hobbes was later to refer to as the 'authentic interpretation' of the precepts of natural law (Hobbes, 1991: II, XXVI, 8, 190–1; see also Hobbes, 1998: VI, 16, 86–7; XIV, 9–10, 158–9; XVI, 10, 192; XVII, 10, 213–4). As such it has to do with establishing the precise meaning and application of the core concepts associates with the fundamental principles of natural law, such as those forbidding murder, theft and adultery. The similarity between the views of Hobbes and those of Aristotle in respect of this issue is readily apparent. Moreover, it should not be forgotten that Hobbes translated Aristotle's *Rhetoric* into English. So on this occasion the connection between his own views on the relationship which exists between natural law and 'civil law' is direct and immediate. As Hobbes puts it, Aristotle held that 'because the defendant does many times confess the fact, but deny the injustice; as that he took, but did not steal; and did, but not adultery; it is necessary to know the definitions of theft, adultery, and all other crimes' (Hobbes, 1839–45c: 445). For Hobbes, as for Aristotle before him, establishing this was the task of the civil law. More to the point however, for present purposes, Aristotle's treatment of the concept of natural justice or law (*physikon dikaion*) in the *Nicomachean Ethics*, and of the 'law of nature' (*nomos koinos*) in the *Rhetoric*, might be seen as a classic illustration of a rhetorical manoeuvre of this kind. Here, too, what is involved is a struggle with others over the meaning of a particular concept, in this case the concept of natural justice or law. And once again everything depends, in the end, on the extent to which one is successful in the effort to appropriate the concept for one's own particular cause. I shall say more about this in Chapter 3.

Notes

1 See Barker, 1969 [1948]: xxxiv; Bryce, 1901: 566–68; Friedrich, 1963: 23; Hamburger, 1951: 39, 65; Kelsen, 1973: 135; Ritchie, 1894: 191, 1895: 30; Sigmund, 1971: 9–10; Salmond, 1895: 127; Strauss, 1974: 156; von Leyden, 1985: 84; Watson, 1966: 66; Wormuth, 1948.

2 See Aubenque, 1980; Bodéüs, 1999; Burns, 1998a, 2002a, 2003; Corbett, 2009; Crowe, 1977: 17, 117–18; Destree, 2000; Dherbey, 2002; Kelsen, 1957a, 1957b, 1973a, 1973b; Miller Jr., 1989, 1991, 1997; Morrall, 1977: 82–3; Ritter, 1969; Renault, 1991; Salomon, 1937; Salomon Shellens, 1959; Remow, 2008; Sigmund, 1971: 2–9; Wormuth, 1948; Yack, 1990, 1993: 128–74.

3 The account presented here is an elaboration on an earlier discussion of Aristotle's views in Burns, 1996: 3, 14, 67–8; see also d'Entrèves, 1974: 174–5; Rommen, 1979: 247.

4 As Ernest Barker points out, Aristotle employs the terms 'justice' and injustice' in a sense which is as much 'moral' or 'ethical' as it is 'legal'. See Barker, 1969: 362.

[5] See also Besselink, 1988; Brett, 2002; Chroust, 1943; Edwards, 1970; Haakonssen, 1985; Hearnshaw, 1926; Schneewind, 1998a; St. Leger, 1962; Tierney, 1997a; Tuck, 1979.

[6] For a different reading of Aristotle see Finnis, 1991:31–37.

[7] A similar translation to that of Ross is provided by Grant, in his edition of the *Ethics*. See Grant in Aristotle, 1865: 126; also Stewart, 1892: 492. Although both Grant and Stewart employ the word 'element' rather than the word 'part.'

[8] See also Aquinas 2006 [1996] la2ae, Q. 94, 5, 93; la2ae, Q. 94, 6, 97; la2ae, Q. 95, 2, 2, 103; Aquinas, 2006 [1969]: la2ae, Q. 99, 2, 35–7; la2ae, Q. 100, 1, 59–61; la2ae, Q. 100, 3, 65–7; see also Suarez, 1995b 1612]: II, VII, 5–7, 211–12; II, VII, 9, 213-14; II, IX, 12, 230; II, XIII, 5, 261; II, XV, 2, 286; and Armstrong, 1966.

[9] Modern discussion of the concept of justice has been greatly influenced by what Aristotle has to say about the subject. See, for example, Berlin, 1955–56; Blackstone, 1967; Ginsberg, 1971a: 50–73; Kelsen, 1957, 1961; Lloyd, 1972; Marc-Wogau, 1967b; Perelman, 1963, 1967b, 1980; Raphael, 1970; Ross, 1959; Williams, 1967; von Leyden, 1985; Winthrop, 1978.

[10] For this issue see Burnet in Aristotle, 1900: 213, 217–24; del Vecchio, 1952: 53, 68; Dherbey, 2002: 125–8; Grant in Aristotle 1865: 108–12; Jackson in Aristotle, 1879: xx, 76, 82–3 and 100–4; Gauthier and Jolif, 1970: 369–73, 385; Marc-Wogau, 1967b: 26–40; Ritchie, 1916 [1894]: 185; Ross, 1964: 212; Stewart, 1892: 431–2.

[11] For a discussion of the notion of a rule, and of rule-following, in the spheres of law and jurisprudence generally see inter alia Dworkin, 1978b; Hart, 1961a, 1961b: 200–02; McCormick, 1994; Twining and Miers, 1986b [1976]. For this issue in relation to the philosophy of Wittgenstein see Patterson, 1992, 2004. For the affinity between the views of Wittgenstein and those of Aristotle see McDowell, 1998a, 1998b: 57–67; Putnam, 1993.

Chapter 2

Natural Law in Aristotle's *Politics*

Aristotle and Human Nature

The starting point for understanding Aristotle's views on ethics and politics is his theory of human nature and his well-known assertion in the *Politics* that man is 'by nature' a social or a 'political animal' (Aristotle, 1995g: 1253a2–3). In the first instance this suggests nothing more than that individual human beings are sociable or gregarious because they are always to be found living together with others in society or in a *polis*. Additionally, however, Aristotle considers it to be a 'characteristic of man that he alone has any sense of good and evil, of just and unjust' (Aristotle, 1995h: 1253a15–17, 1988). According to Aristotle, then, man is by nature a moral or an ethical being, destined to live a life of justice. In his view, as also for Hegel after him, a natural life for human beings is an 'ethical life', or a life devoted to justice. It is this characteristic above all which differentiates the human species from other species of animals. If it is true, as Aristotle says at the very beginning of the *Nicomachean Ethics*, that 'the good has been aptly described as that at which everything aims' (Aristotle, 1995f: 1094a1–3, 1729), then a life of justice represents the 'good' for humanity. This is the ultimate end towards which all human beings ought to strive and to which, in his opinion, they do strive (Aristotle, 1995h: 14–16, 2035). This is the very essence of what it is to be human. Only if we live a life devoted to justice do we satisfy the requirements of our own nature and thereby become 'human' in the strict sense of the term. For Aristotle such an ethical life is not a 'means to an end' but, rather, an 'end in itself', something which is of value for its own sake. The ultimate aim of politics is to enable such a process of personal development to take place. It is political society which makes it possible for us to live a 'good life' in this sense of the term, and thereby actualize our potential as human beings. For to live an ethical life is to live together in harmonious fellowship with others within a political community under a system of civil law (Aristotle, 1995h: 1278b1–5, 2028–29; 1280a31–34, 2031–32; 1281a3–4, 2033; 1325a7–11, 2103).

To fulfil one's potential by living an ethical life in this way is to achieve a condition which at the beginning of the *Nicomachean Ethics* Aristotle refers to by the Greek word *eudaimonia* (Aristotle, 1995f: 1095a15–19, 1730). This term is extremely difficult to translate. It is has in the past been rendered into English by the word 'happiness'. It is clear, however, that for Aristotle somebody whose life is devoted to justice, and who has achieved *eudaimonia*, may not be 'happy' in the sense in which this term is commonly employed by speakers of the English language today. Indeed, such a person might well be unhappy in the everyday sense of that term. Or at least one might say that the achievement of happiness in that particular sense is not really the point of living such a life. This is something which Aristotle's thought has in common with that of both Plato and, later, Immanuel Kant. Recently, dissatisfaction with this traditional translation of the Greek *eudaimonia* by the word 'happiness' has led to alternative formulations being used. Thus *eudaimonia* might also be translated as 'flourishing', 'fulfilment', 'well-being' or 'perfection'. In my view, each of these alternatives has its problems. For example, the use of 'flourishing', 'fulfilment' and 'well-being' all imply that a person who has achieved the state of *eudaimonia* has also arrived at a condition, if not of happiness, then at least of 'contentment' in the everyday sense. But this, too, is not necessarily the case for those who live an ethical life as Aristotle understands it. Similarly, to translate 'eudaimonia' as 'perfection' also has its drawbacks. For if this word is used then it appears that what Aristotle is suggesting is that a person who lives a life devoted to justice, and who has achieved *eudaimonia*, may be thought of as being not merely a 'human being' but rather, going further, as a perfect human being. This translation, therefore, wrongly suggests that for Aristotle those individuals who have achieved *eudaimonia* are different from, and in some sense superior to, other human beings, precisely because they are living an ethical life whereas those other human beings are not. In my view therefore, for all of these reasons, the term *eudaimonia* is best left untranslated.

Justice and Virtue Ethics

By focusing on Aristotle's theory of justice I shall be ignoring a great deal of what Aristotle has to say about other things in the *Ethics*. In particular, I will not be discussing what Aristotle has to say about moral virtue in general or moral virtues such as honesty and courage in particular. Nor will I be discussing Aristotle's famous theory of 'the mean' (Aristotle, 1995f: 1106a14–1107a7, 1747–48). I will, for the most part, consider justice not so much as one of the virtues, but as something which Aristotle associates with a definite framework of moral rules or laws. This brings me into conflict with a number of recent commentators, who consider Aristotle to be an exponent of what is usually referred to as 'virtue ethics', understood as an outlook which detaches the notion of ethics from any association with that of rule following (Annas, 1996;

Burns, 2005a; Collins, 1999; Crisp and Slote, 1997; Darwall, 2002; Gardiner, 2005; Hittinger, 1989; Hursthouse, 1999; Lisska, 1997: 4–5, 51–2; MacIntyre, 2000; Simpson, 1997; Statman, 1997a; Strauss, 1974; Trianosky, 1990). As I have argued elsewhere, Leo Strauss interprets Aristotle in this way in his *Natural Right and History* (Burns, 2010b). However to illustrate this point here I shall refer to the writings of Alasdair MacIntyre.

There are occasions when MacIntyre suggests that the difference between Aristotelian virtue ethics and modern ethical doctrines is that virtue ethics attaches no importance at all to moral rules, as opposed to psychological motivation or moral character, as a determinant of what is just and unjust. For example, at one point MacIntyre claims that for Aristotle 'there is no set of rules' that ought to be followed in any particular ethical situation (MacIntyre, 2006a: 28). MacIntyre also states that 'the most obvious and astonishing absence from Aristotle's thought for any modern reader' is the fact that 'there is relatively little mention of rules anywhere in the *Ethics*' (MacIntyre, 2000 [1981]: 150). The (allegedly) modern 'preoccupation with rules', MacIntyre insists, is an indication of the fact that moral philosophers today tend to adopt a decidedly '*un*-Aristotelian' approach to ethics (MacIntyre, 2000: 153). In MacIntyre's opinion, the 'primary question' for 'modern moralities' is 'what rules ought we to follow?' MacIntyre suggests that whereas 'on the modern view the justification of the virtues depends upon some prior justification of rules and principles', in the ethical thought of Aristotle it does not (MacIntyre, 2000 [1981]: 118–19). Indeed, this is what differentiates 'modern' approaches to ethics from pre-modern ones such as that of Aristotle. The implication of these remarks is clear. Unlike the moralists of the modern era Aristotle is presented as having no interest in the question of how moral 'rules and principles' might be justified. According to MacIntyre, Aristotle holds that 'we need to attend to the virtues in the first place', prior to and independently of any moral rules. For Aristotle justice is 'definable', MacIntyre claims 'independently of and antecedently to the establishment of enforceable rules' (MacIntyre, 1988: 39, 116).[1]

MacIntyre indicates that the 'modern' attitude is perhaps best exemplified by the moral philosophy of Kant. He claims that within the ethical and political thought of Aristotle, unlike that of Kant, it is not moral rules but the moral virtues which 'have the central place' (MacIntyre, 2000: 257). It is because of the absence in 'virtue ethics' of the idea that ethics has to do with moral rules, or 'rule following', that its exponents believe that it represents a radical departure from the other approaches to ethics that have been so influential in the modern era, including Kantian ethics and utilitarianism. For adherents of this approach, ethics has to do with having a virtuous character, or creating a society in which people will have such a character, rather than about individuals concerning themselves with questions of right and wrong, or with laws, duties and obligations. For an exponent of virtue ethics in this sense, then, what makes actions just or unjust is, it would seem, solely the motivation which lies behind them (Statman, 1997b, 21–2, 26–8; Louden, 1997: 189–90). This approach to ethics is sometimes associated with the notion of 'moral particularism' (Hooker and Little, 2000; Irwin, 2000; Sherman, 1997b).

In the preface to his *Whose Justice? Which Rationality?*, which appeared in 1988, MacIntyre states that 'more than one critic' who responded to his defence of Aristotle's virtue ethics in *After Virtue* (1981) 'misrepresented that book' because they saw it as a 'defence of "a morality of the virtues" as an alternative to a "morality of rules"' (MacIntyre, 1998: ix). Against this charge of misrepresentation it might be argued that MacIntyre does on numerous occasions in *After Virtue* give his readers the impression that, as he understands it, Aristotelian virtue ethics is an ethics without rules. The passages cited above are cases in point. It must, however, be conceded that MacIntyre also occasionally makes statements which contradict this assessment of his views (see MacIntyre, 1998, ix, 116, 2000 [1981]: 118–19, 150–2, 200, 257). In other words, either his thinking about this subject is not entirely consistent, or alternatively he expresses himself carelessly at times when discussing it.

Whether MacIntyre's beliefs on this issue have been correctly understood or not, 'virtue ethics' in this sense is now commonly associated with his name. Moreover, largely because of MacIntyre's influence, the view that Aristotle subscribed, not to an ethics of moral rules or laws, but to a 'virtue ethics' understood as an ethics without rules, has become increasingly prominent in the last two or three decades. However, against this reading, it might be argued that although Aristotle certainly can be associated with the notion of a virtue ethics of some kind, nevertheless he is not an exponent of a virtue ethics of this particular type. For in Aristotle's opinion an essential component of what is involved in living an ethical life is obedience to moral rules or laws.

According to Aristotle, an ethical life is necessarily a life devoted to the cultivation of virtue, in particular the virtue of justice. But what exactly does such a life involve? In the *Nicomachean Ethics* Aristotle insists that 'some people who do just actions' are nevertheless 'not yet just', and hence also not yet virtuous, if they do these actions 'involuntarily or through ignorance or for some other reason, and not for the sake of the actions themselves', even though, he continues, they do 'what they should and all the things that the good man ought' to do (Aristotle, 1995f: 1144a14–17, 1807; also 1097a30–1097b7, 1734). When he makes this remark Aristotle is using the word 'just' in two different, though related ways. First he presupposes that one could meaningfully describe an action as just simply because it is a *right* action, even though one could also say that the person who performs it is not acting justly if they do so for the wrong reason. According to Aristotle, then, we can logically separate the question of the justice or injustice of actions, that is to say their rightness or wrongness, from that of the presence or absence of moral virtue, specifically the virtue of justice, in the motivation of the persons who perform them. It follows from this, however, that for Aristotle whether or not an action is indeed just or unjust in at least one sense of the term, in other words whether it is right or wrong, has nothing to do with the motive which lies behind it or the character of the person who performs it. On this reading, Aristotle is of the opinion that even a virtuous motive, for example the desire to act justly, could not transform an action which is intrinsically unjust into one which is just and therefore morally permissible (Aristotle, 1995f, 1107a9–14, 1748). It also follows that in Aristotle's view for an action to be a just action, in the fullest possible sense of the term 'just', it has not only to be appropriately motivated, by the desire to act rightly, it must also *be* objectively right. It must satisfy the requirements of an independent standard of right and wrong which is external to the individual moral agent. In short, it must conform to some rule or law.

Here Aristotle's belief that there are certain actions, such as murder, theft, adultery and lying, which are necessarily unjust seems to me to be extremely important. In this connection, it should be noted that it is a core belief for more than one natural law tradition that there are some actions which are intrinsically wrong, always and everywhere. We do find this idea in the writings of Aristotle, which is of course one of the reasons for thinking that Aristotle is a natural law theorist. But this belief is necessarily associated with the further belief that there are certain moral rules, or principles of natural law, which forbid the performance of the actions in question. If 'virtue ethics' is an ethics without rules, and is based on a certain reading of Aristotle, then its adherents must either deny that Aristotle thinks that certain actions are intrinsically wrong, or they must maintain that although he did hold this view nevertheless it is not central or even particularly important for our understanding of Aristotle's ethical and political thought as a whole. We saw in the Introduction that John McDowell is of this opinion.

It should be noted that the belief that there are certain actions which are intrinsically wrong or essentially unjust implies that Aristotle's ethics should not be thought as a 'consequentialist' doctrine within which the notion of 'the good' is accorded logical priority over that of 'the right' (Burns, 2005a). The belief in the intrinsic rightness and wrongness of certain actions is usually associated with the notion of ethical deontologism, and with the moral philosophy of Kant. It is arguable, therefore, that the fact that Aristotle endorses it implies that Aristotelian ethics is very similar to Kantianism in at least some respects. However, this is not so because both Aristotle and Kant subscribe to a 'virtue ethics' in MacIntyre's sense of the term. Rather it is because both Aristotle and Kant are ethical deontologists with respect to what they consider to be the fundamental questions of right and wrong. In my view, then, the claim made by the advocates of the 'virtue ethics' interpretation that Aristotle thinks of ethical life as a life of 'virtue', understood exclusively by reference to the notions of character and motivation, is mistaken. For although Aristotle's ethical thought certainly does attach importance to character and motivation it *also* attaches importance to the idea that some actions are right or wrong, just or unjust, considered independently, not only of their consequences, but also of the character and motivation of the person who performs them. Like Hegel, Aristotle rejects the view that acting from a certain allegedly 'honourable' motive, such as for example what Kant would refer to as 'the sense of duty', is what actually determines the rightness and wrongness of any one's actions; as if acting 'virtuously' in this way would automatically make an agent's actions right, no matter what it was that they actually did. Indeed, in the *Nicomachean Ethics* Aristotle says explicitly that 'it makes no difference whether a good man has defrauded a bad man or a bad man a good one, nor whether it is a good or a bad man who has committed adultery', for 'the law looks only to the distinctive character of the injury' or injustice, and rightly so (Aristotle, 1995f: 1132a2–5, 1786). This implies, of course, that contrary to the 'virtue ethics' interpretation of his views, Aristotle did attach importance to the idea that ethical life has to do with conformity to certain moral rules, namely those which forbid the performance of those actions which are intrinsically unjust. These rules are inscribed within the principles of political justice, that is to say the laws, of all *poleis* everywhere.

Despite MacIntyre's claim that virtue ethics is quite different from the moral philosophy of Kant, it is arguable, as R. B. Louden has noted, that there is in fact a striking similarity between his virtue ethics reading of Aristotle and Hegel's interpretation Kant's ethics (Louden, 1997a: 189–90; Hegel, 1991: 48–9, 58, 149–50, 162–5, 170–84). To employ the terminology of modern moral philosophy, Kant's ethics as Hegel understood it is both 'subjectivist' and 'non-cognitivist'. It is subjectivist because with its alleged exclusive focus on the idea that the only thing of moral value is the 'good will' of the individual moral agent (Kant, 1993: 7–8), Kant's doctrine, Hegel claims, concedes that there are no objectively valid substantive moral rules which all moral agents are obliged to follow in the same way no matter what the circumstances. It is arguably 'non-cognitivist' because in consequence, Hegel insists, Kant does not allow for the possibility that individual agents might possess any substantive moral 'knowledge', in addition to the knowledge which they have of the Categorical Imperative itself, which is to be understood as a purely formal moral principle.

It is clear from the above that, as interpreted by Hegel, Kant's moral philosophy is strikingly similar to what (rightly or wrongly) is often thought to be MacIntyre's 'virtue ethics'. Given this similarity between MacIntyre's reading of Aristotle and Hegel's reading of Kant, it is not too surprising that a number of commentators have claimed recently that there is an hitherto unrecognized affinity between the ethical thought of Aristotle and that of Kant, two thinkers whose views on ethics have often, as in the case of MacIntyre, been thought to be diametrically opposed to one another (Crisp, 1997: xv; Louden, 1997b). According to this recent re-reading of the relationship between Aristotle and

Kant, each of these thinkers attaches exclusive importance to the role of moral character and motivation in ethics, or to the notion of virtue understood in terms of the concept of a morally goodwill. Neither thinker, therefore, is committed to the idea that ethical life has to do with the conformity of an agent's actions to any objective ethical duties associated with certain moral rules or laws forbidding the performance of actions which are assumed to be intrinsically wrong or unjust. This recent re-assessment of the relationship between the thought of Aristotle and that of Kant, focusing on the similarities rather than the differences between them, is an interesting intellectual project, and one worth pursuing. However, in my opinion it should not be carried out in this particular way. For both Aristotle and Kant are committed to the view that there are certain actions which are intrinsically wrong or unjust, and that it is for this reason that these actions are forbidden by civil law.

In the *Ethics* Aristotle is interested in those actions the performance or non-performance of which is associated with the achievement of *eudaimonia*. It would, however, be a mistake to assume, as John Rawls does, that Aristotle thinks that it is the consequence of either promoting or not promoting *eudaimonia* which constitutes the rightness or wrongness, or the justice and injustice, of those actions which are right or wrong, just or unjust. Nor does Aristotle think, as Rawls erroneously suggests, that the concept of 'rightness' depends logically on that of 'goodness' (Rawls, 1999 [1971]: 21–8). As Michael Slote has noted, Aristotle has a different criterion for assessing the rightness and wrongness, the justice and injustice, of both individual actions and social institutions (Slote, 1992: 89). Aristotle's claim, rather, is simply that human beings only achieve *eudaimonia* when they live an ethical life, a life devoted to justice for its own sake. J. L. Mackie has rightly claimed that according to Aristotle for human beings *eudaimonia* is something which 'intrinsically desirable' (Mackie, 1988: 106). It is not a 'means to an end', specifically happiness, but rather an 'end in itself'. The affinity between the thought of Aristotle and that of Kant with respect to this particular issue is obvious (see Engstrom and Whiting, 1998; Sherman, 1997a).

Brian Tierney maintains that the meaning of the term 'justice' (δίκαιον, *dikaion*) in Aristotle's ethical thought, like that of the term 'virtue' (αρετε, *arete*), is ambiguous. In the case of 'justice', Tierney notes that Aristotle employs this term 'in two senses'. He distinguishes between 'justice as a moral virtue and justice as an objectively right state of affairs' (Tierney, 1997: 21). Moreover, Aristotle also holds that the terms 'just' and 'virtuous' can be applied variously to actions, to the persons who perform those actions, or to the motives of those persons. On this view, for Aristotle an ethical life in the fullest sense of the term is a life of justice in two senses. It is a life in which individual moral agents act justly in the sense of acting rightly. In particular, they refrain from committing actions which are objectively unjust or wrong. At the same time, however, they are also motivated in a certain way. They act justly in the further sense that they do what is right for a particular reason. They act rightly, not because this will make them happy, but simply because it is the right thing to do (see also MacIntyre, 2000 [1981]: 149; 1988: 39, 111, 113; Crisp, 2000: xv). According to this reading of Aristotle it is only if our character is such that we habitually act in this way that we could strictly speaking be said to be just or virtuous persons, and hence also 'human beings' in the strict sense of the term.

It may be conjectured that for Aristotle, just as for Kant after him, each of these two elements is necessary and neither is on its own sufficient for truly just or virtuous conduct. It is only when our actions are objectively right *and* when they are appropriately motivated that these actions and the persons who perform them may properly be said to be just or virtuous in the fullest sense of these two terms (Aristotle, 1995f: 1129a7–12, 1781). So when Aristotle says in the *Ethics* that 'some people who do just acts' are 'not necessarily just' (and hence also not necessarily virtuous) if they do the act ordained by the laws either 'unwillingly or owing to ignorance or for some other reason and not for the sake of the acts themselves' (Aristotle, 1995f: 1144a14–20, 1807), he presupposes that one can meaningfully describe an action as being just in one sense (that is to say, right) even though the person who performs it is *not* acting justly in the fullest sense because they perform the action in question for the wrong reason or with an inappropriate motive. From Aristotle's point of view, such actions are certainly right, but they are not virtuous. Hence, also, they are not completely just.

This aspect of Aristotle's thought has been noted by a number of commentators. Basil Willey, for example, has said that for Aristotle 'a man is not truly and securely virtuous' unless he habitually performs 'right actions' for the right reason (Willey, 1965: 59). William Frankena has observed that, for the ancient Greeks generally, and therefore also for Aristotle, 'being virtuous entails not just having good motives or intentions but *also* doing the right thing' (Frankena, 1980: 52–3). And on one occasion even Leo Strauss suggests, despite his advocacy of a 'virtue ethics' reading of Aristotle elsewhere, that the Greek notion of 'virtue' is to be associated, not with the possession of a certain character or motivation, but rather with the idea of 'the primacy of "law" in classical political thought'. Indeed, here at least, Strauss maintains that the two things, virtue and obedience to law, are 'fundamentally the same' (Strauss, 1973 [1936]: vii).

In my opinion, then, it is a mistake to think that Aristotle subscribed to a form of virtue ethics as MacIntyre appears at times to understand it, that is to say, to think that his sole concern was with the character and motivation of the citizens of a *polis* rather than with the duties and obligations which are associated with the moral rules (or the standards of right and wrong) which, in his view, are inscribed in the laws of that *polis*. Moreover, given Aristotle's claim that truly virtuous persons do what is right, or what they ought to do, for its own sake, simply because it is the right thing to do, it seems to me that it is not inappropriate to suggest that, as in the case of Kant, Aristotle also possessed the notion of 'acting from the sense of duty'.

Some commentators, including MacIntyre, would argue that there is an historical anachronism involved in attributing to Aristotle, or indeed to the ancients generally, the idea of acting from 'the sense of duty'. According to advocates of this line of reasoning, there is a fundamentally important difference between the notion of 'virtue', as Aristotle or any ancient Greek understood it, and that of 'the sense of duty'. For the latter idea is necessarily associated with the notion of the 'individual moral conscience'. However, in their view, the latter idea is a peculiarly modern phenomenon, and is again exemplified especially in the writings of Kant. It is, therefore, a notion which is alien to the thought and experience of classical antiquity. It seems to me, however, that the passages from the writings of Aristotle cited above count against this view. Moreover, speaking more generally, more than one commentator has suggested that the notion of 'a sense of duty' can be found in the moral and political thought of the ancient Greeks. Thomas Reid, for example, in an essay entitled 'Of the Sense of Duty', which is contained in his *Essays on the Active Powers of Man* (1788), insists that this idea is 'not unfrequent among the ancients' (Reid, 1991 [1788]: 274). And Joel Feinberg has argued, much more recently, that for the ancient Greeks generally the 'good man' was someone who attached 'supreme importance' to 'the sense of duty'. Indeed, according to Feinberg, both the Greek and later Roman conception of 'virtue' is 'inseparable from the idea of duty' (Feinberg, 1969: 2–3).

Those who interpret Aristotle as an exponent of 'virtue ethics' in the extreme sense referred to above offer a one-sided account of his views on ethics in general and especially of his views on justice. They focus exclusively on what Aristotle says about the role of psychological motivation and moral character in the *Nicomachean Ethics* and ignore completely what he says about the role of moral rules or laws in the determination of what is just and unjust. They misunderstand Aristotle's view of what it is that makes actions right or wrong and, as a result, offer a partial and incomplete account of his view of what it is that makes actions just or unjust. The fact that Aristotle says relatively little about moral rules or laws in the *Ethics* should not be taken as implying that he considers them to be unimportant for our understanding of ethical life and virtuous conduct, especially where questions of justice and injustice are concerned.

As is so often the case, it seems to me that Aquinas correctly understands Aristotle's views on this subject when he says in the *Summa Theologiae* that for Aristotle 'the lawmaker's wish is to lead men into virtue' and that 'making the citizens good is the wish of every legislator' (Aquinas 2006 [1966]: 1a2ae, Q. 90, 3, 2, 13; 1a2ae, Q. 92, 1, 4, 41; also Aquinas 2006 [1969]: 1a2ae, Q. 100, 9). This was also the reading of Aristotle which was offered, much later, by Francisco Suarez. According to Suarez, natural law 'imposes an obligation as to the mode of practising virtue'. Suarez explains that by this phrase he includes 'everything required in order that an act may be righteous and good in an absolute and moral sense'. One condition for this, he insists, is that the act in question 'shall be inspired by a righteous motive'. This, Suarez maintains, 'was the meaning of Aristotle (*Nicomachean Ethics*, Book II, Chapter IV), when he said that in order that a virtuous work may be performed with [all due] care, it is not sufficient that the acts themselves be just'. For 'it is furthermore required "that the agent shall perform them whilst he is in the following state of mind: first, he shall act knowingly"' and '"secondly, he shall act by deliberate choice and for the sake of those acts themselves"' (Suarez, 1995b: II, X, 11, 240; see also II, VII, 11, 215; II, IX, 6, 226; II, X, 2, 232; II, X, 4, 234; II, X, 10, 240; II, X, 12, 241). On this view, with which I am in agreement, if 'rule following' or obedience to law is not a sufficient condition, it is at least a necessary condition for the achievement of *eudaimonia* as Aristotle understands the term. In my opinion, therefore, the 'virtue ethics' reading of Aristotle has been rightly criticized by some commentators (Buckle, 2002; Statman, 1997a: 10, 19–21, 26–8, 30; Simpson, 1997; Santas, 1997).

Surprisingly, this is something which MacIntyre acknowledges on one occasion, despite the fact that this acknowledgement is inconsistent with his general thesis that Aristotle is an exponent of a 'virtue ethics' in the sense indicated earlier. In *After Virtue* he concedes at one point that 'although there is relatively little mention of rules anywhere in the *Ethics*', nevertheless for Aristotle moral rules do undoubtedly exist. MacIntyre also accepts that it is a 'crucial part of Aristotle's doctrine that certain types of action are absolutely prohibited or enjoined irrespective of circumstances or consequences'. He concedes, therefore, that Aristotle's approach to ethics is '*not* consequentialist' (MacIntyre, 2000 [1981]: 150; see also 152, 169, 186–7, 190, 200, 278; and MacIntyre, 1988: 113–14). In the same passage MacIntyre also accepts that Aristotle endorses the idea of natural law as this is traditionally understood (MacIntyre, 2000 [1981]: 150; see also MacIntyre, 1988: 120–1; Crisp, 2000: xxiii). In my opinion these remarks significantly weaken the force of MacIntyre's occasional suggestion that Aristotelian ethics is a type of virtue ethics which is entirely devoted to a discussion of questions of character and motivation and that it attaches no importance to justice understood as a framework of moral rules or laws.

Given this let us return to MacIntyre's statement, cited earlier, that 'the most obvious and astonishing absence from Aristotle's thought for any modern reader' is the fact that 'there is relatively little mention of rules anywhere in the *Ethics*' (MacIntyre, 2000 [1981]: 150). Furthermore let us accept that this statement is basically correct. Once we have done this, however, the further issue remains of assessing its significance. One way of doing this is to suggest, as at times MacIntyre appears to do, that Aristotle's ethics attaches no importance to moral rules or to rule following as a vital ingredient of ethical life. However this is not the only way in which the significance of this statement might be understood. A second possibility, which is the one favoured here, is that the importance of the idea of 'rule following' for Aristotle's ethical thought far and away exceeds the amount time and attention which he devotes to an explicit discussion of it in the *Ethics*. The passages where he does this are indeed 'marginal' in Derrida's sense of the term. According to this reading, the idea of rule following is one of Aristotle's basic starting assumptions or theoretical presuppositions. It is important because for Aristotle it is the 'taken for granted' starting point of his argument. Indeed, it is arguable that Aristotle took this assumption so much for granted that he did not feel the need to defend it explicitly or discuss it any great length. Paradoxically, therefore, the apparent 'absence' to which MacIntyre refers betokens the very real *presence* of this idea on every single page of Aristotle's text. As MacIntyre acknowledges here at least (if not elsewhere), the fact that Aristotle says relatively little about moral rules or laws should not, therefore, be taken as implying that he considers them to be unimportant either for ethical conduct or for our understanding of what it is to be virtuous and just.

In Aristotle's view, then, the achievement of *eudaimonia* necessarily requires that there be moral rules or laws which serve as a standard of right and wrong for individual moral agents, all of whom are assumed to be the citizens of a particular *polis*. For Aristotle, in the final analysis (although only then), these moral rules are the principles of 'political justice' or the civil laws of the *polis* in which these individuals happen to live. Moreover, given that for Aristotle a human life is an ethical life, and given also that an ethical life is only possible in political society, it follows that Aristotle's views on ethics and politics are closely related to one another. It is for this reason that in the *Nicomachean Ethics* Aristotle maintains that the study of politics (in the broadest possible sense of the term) is the 'highest master science', because it incorporates within itself the study of ethics. As such it is necessarily concerned with 'what is noble and what is just' and 'lays down laws' about what we ought to do and what we ought not to do (Aristotle, 1995f: 1094b5–7, 1730; also 1102a7–10, 1741; 1180b24–26, 1866). Fred D. Miller Jr. has rightly argued that the views expressed in Aristotle's *Ethics*, especially the 'treatise on justice' in Book V, are presupposed throughout the argument of his *Politics* (Miller, 1997: 67; Aristotle, 1995h: 1261a30–31, 2001; 1280a16–18, 2031; 1282b16–20, 2035; 1295a36–38, 2056; 1332a8–10, 2113). In other words, we cannot understand Aristotle's political thought without first coming to terms with the theory of justice developed in the *Ethics*. In my opinion, however, the reverse is also the case. For we cannot understand Aristotle's ethical thought, especially so far as it touches on questions of justice, without relating it to the ideas advanced in Aristotle's *Politics*. In the remainder of this chapter I shall say more about Aristotle's theory of justice in these two works. I shall begin by considering Aristotle's theory of justice as it is outlined in Book V of the *Ethics*, before turning to consider how this theory is applied in the *Politics*.

Aristotle's Theory of Justice

The core argument of Aristotle's *Politics* is built around the theory of justice which is first developed in Book V of the *Nicomachean Ethics*. In order to answer the question of whether the notion of natural justice or natural law has an important part to play (or indeed any part at all to play) in Aristotle's *Politics*, therefore, it is necessary to begin by discussing Aristotle's views on justice in the *Ethics*.[2] Aristotle begins by pointing out that justice is not simply a state of mind, or a moral virtue in MacIntyre's sense of the term, but also has to do with the rightness and wrongness of our actions (Aristotle, 1995f: 1129a19–24, 1782). If we focus on this aspect of justice, Aristotle argues, it is clear that we commonly think about justice in two ways (Aristotle, 1995f: 1130a14–1130b8, 1783–84). Speaking generally, we associate justice with righteousness, or with doing the right thing, that is to say with lawfulness and with obedience to law. From this point of view, to act unjustly is simply to do that which 'is contrary to law' (Aristotle, 1995f, 1129b1–25, 1782), or that which conflicts with the requirements of what Aristotle refers to as the principles of 'political justice' (Aristotle, 1995f: 1134b18, 1790) of one's own *polis*. By law here Aristotle means moral law. However, consistent with his view that the spheres of the ethical and the political are identical, he does not distinguish between this moral law and what later would be referred to as the civil law of a particular society or *polis*. In Aristotle's view, therefore, the principles of political justice of a *polis* might correctly be said to constitute the standard of justice or of right and wrong for its citizens (Kelsen, 1973a: 127–9). This conclusion is a logical implication of Aristotle's understanding of the relationship between ethics and politics, although this is sometimes not recognized. Because the civil laws of a *polis* are also its moral rules, Aristotle cannot (or should not if he is consistent) allow that there is any independent standard of justice by means of which that law might be critically evaluated. As Aristotle himself puts it, the aim of the true politician is to produce good citizens who are 'obedient to the laws' (Aristotle, 1995f: 1102a9–10, 1741) no matter what the specific character of these laws happens to be. For 'whatever is lawful is in some way just' (Aristotle, 1995f: 1129b12–13, 1782).

It follows from this, of course, that for Aristotle there is no independent standard of justice or morality which stands above the system of political justice of a *polis*. There are no 'higher' principles of justice which might be used as a measure or yardstick for evaluating the laws of a *polis* from the standpoint of their justice or injustice. The laws of a *polis* just are the substantive standard or right and wrong, justice and injustice, for all of its citizens. It is for this reason that it has often wrongly been assumed that the notion of 'natural law' could not possibly have any part to play in the moral and political thought of Aristotle. As we saw in Chapter 1, one of the main aims of the present work is to challenge that view.

Aristotle goes on to point out that, more particularly, we associate the concept of justice with that of fairness – a concept which, in turn, is connected to that of equality (Aristotle, 1995f: 1131a10–23, 1785; Aristotle, 1995h: 1282b16–20, 2035; 1301b30–38, 2067). Justice in this second or 'particular' sense has to do with those actions which affect other people, many of which are also regulated by law. The actions which are just or unjust in this second sense therefore constitute only a 'part' of the class of just and unjust actions as a whole (Aristotle, 1995f: 1130b10–15, 1784). They represent a sub-class of those actions which are regulated by law and therefore just or unjust more generally. Most of Book V of the *Ethics* concentrates on developing a theory of justice in this second, particular sense, and with a consideration of its application to various areas of social and political life.

Aristotle's understanding of 'particular' justice is expressed most clearly in the *Politics*, although he makes it plain that the understanding which he has of justice there is the same as the one outlined in the *Ethics*. Aristotle points out that although the concept of justice has to do with that of equality, nevertheless the concept of equality itself requires further clarification. We must, he says, distinguish between two types of equality. He refers to these as 'proportional' equality, on the one hand, and 'arithmetical' equality on the other (Aristotle, 1995h: 1301b30–35, 2067). Like Plato and the Pythagorean School, Aristotle strongly emphasizes the importance of the notion of proportional equality. Indeed, at one point he identifies the notion of justice with that of proportionality. 'This, then', he says, 'is what the just is – the proportional' (Aristotle, 1995f: 131b17–18, 1786). Injustice in the particular sense, therefore, always involves a violation of the principle of proportionality. Aristotle does not deny that the notion of arithmetical equality has an important part to play in ethics and politics; but he insists that its role is a limited one and that we should not apply this concept in circumstances or situations where it is inappropriate to do so. Aristotle thinks that those situations within which the notion of arithmetical equality apply are limiting cases of the more general type of situation covered by the notion of proportional equality. In his view, therefore, the first of these ways of thinking about equality is more important than the second, which he considers to be a special application of the application of the first.

The principle of proportional equality, or of justice as fairness, requires that those who are equal ought to be treated equally if their circumstances are similar in some relevant respect. It also requires that those who are not equal in a relevant respect ought *not* to be treated equally. Unequals ought to be treated differently provided the difference in treatment is proportional to the inequality which exists between them. If this condition is satisfied then according to

Aristotle we may legitimately claim that they have been treated justly even though they have been treated differently. The principle of arithmetical equality has an application in those situations where we may safely assume that the persons involved are as a matter of fact equals and that their circumstances are as a matter of fact relevantly similar. In such situations justice requires not proportional but strictly equal treatment. Here the principle of equity reduces itself in effect to that of pure or simple reciprocity. As we saw in Chapter 1, it is then an alternative formulation of the 'golden rule' of 'doing as one would be done by'. For Aristotle, the principle of equity constitutes the supreme principle of justice, insofar as justice has to do with moral rules or law. Given that a life of justice is something which he thinks is natural to human beings, it follows that for Aristotle this principle is also the most important principle of natural justice. In the *Ethics* he states that there are two areas of human activity, in particular, where this principle of justice has a practical application. These are the spheres of corrective or rectificatory justice, on the one hand, and of distributive justice on the other.

Corrective or Rectificatory Justice

The sphere of corrective or rectificatory justice (διορθοτικον δικαιον, *diorthotikon dikaion*) (Aristotle, 1995f: 1131b25–1132b21, 1786–87) has to do with regulating the social or ethical relationships between the citizens of a particular *polis*.[3] Here, Aristotle concedes, we may assume that the persons involved are as matter of fact equals in all relevant respects. Consequently, in this area, all of these persons should be treated in accordance with the principle of strict arithmetical equality. Citizens should treat one another as equals and they should all be treated as equals by the laws of the *polis*. When this does not happen it is the function of law to correct any imbalance which arises as a result.

In the *Ethics* Aristotle occasionally gives the impression that he thinks that it is the principle of arithmetical equality which applies in the sphere of corrective justice (and only there) whereas the principle of proportional or geometrical equality applies in the sphere of distributive justice (and only there). But, as Konrad Marc-Wogau has noted, this is not entirely accurate (Marc-Wogau, 1967b: 28). In particular it should be noted that in Aristotle's thinking the principle of proportional equality is not confined to the sphere of distributive justice and has an application in that of corrective or rectificatory justice also. For example, at one point Aristotle notes that the principle of simple or strict 'reciprocity', which is evidently associated with the notion of arithmetical equality, 'fits neither distributive *nor* rectificatory justice' (Aristotle, 1995f, 1132b22–30, 1787). In the latter case, the reason for this is because the system of rectificatory justice of a *polis* has to deal with situations, not just of initial harmony or equilibrium between, for example, two citizens who should be assumed to be equals so far as the law is concerned, but also with situations in which that initial equilibrium has been disturbed. To illustrate the weaknesses of offering an account even of rectificatory justice, let alone that of distributive justice, by reference to the notion of pure arithmetical equality, Aristotle notes that 'if an official has inflicted a wound', it would evidently not be just but unjust should he 'be wounded in return'. In other words, according to Aristotle the official who is responsible for seeing that justice is done in the sphere of rectificatory justice and the person who is wounded by him while he is carrying out his duties, and who is a wrongdoer, a lawbreaker, or a criminal, are not to be considered as equals by the law. It is only before the equilibrium which formerly existed between all citizens has been disturbed by some act of wrongdoing that those citizens are to be considered as equals before the law. Thereafter, any adequate account of why the enforcement of the law might be said to be just will necessary require an appeal, not to the notion of arithmetical equality, but to that of proportional equality. Indeed, once such an injustice has occurred, the relationship between the two individuals concerned ceases to be one of equality, between citizens, and becomes rather one of inequality, between an 'officer' who is superior, on the one hand, and a 'wrong doer' who is subordinate or inferior on the other.

It would be a mistake therefore to assume, as Marc-Wogau appears to do, that for Aristotle all of the problems to which the principle of proportional equality applies *must* be problems of distributive justice, and that none of them are problems of corrective justice. It would also be a mistake to assume, as again Marc-Wogau appears to do, that the problems of corrective or rectificatory justice, because they are limiting cases of the application of the principle of proportional equality, must be thought of as being a sub-set of the class of problems of distributive justice (Marc-Wogau, 1967b: 24). According to Marc-Wogau, 'the principle of corrective justice is a special case of that of distributive justice', rather than being a specific application of the principle of proportional equality (Marc-Wogau, 1967b: 24). But to assert this is to make the error of identifying the notion of proportional equality with that of distributive justice, whereas in fact for Aristotle these two notions are not synonymous in meaning. Rather, in his view, the notion of distributive justice and that of corrective justice both fall under a higher conception of justice which is captured by the principle of proportional equality. As Peter Benson has noted, for Aristotle the notion of corrective justice is not 'reducible' in this way to that of distributive justice (Benson, 1991–92: 529–32). Nor, therefore, is the principle of distributive justice the 'master' principle for those wishing to understand either the doctrine of justice, in its particular sense, which is developed by Aristotle, or the structure of the argument which is advanced by him throughout Book V of the *Ethics*.[4]

This is not to say, however, that Benson is right when he claims that for Aristotle corrective and distributive justice 'constitute two qualitatively distinct and mutually irreducible forms of justice' (Benson, 1991–92: 527). It may well be true that in Aristotle's thinking corrective and distributive justice are indeed 'mutually irreducible,' one to the other, but this does not necessarily imply that the two are 'qualitatively distinct'. Benson overlooks, here, the possibility that for Aristotle these two forms of justice might be related to one another because they are linked, as are two species of the same genus, to a third principle of justice which overarches both of them. That principle, which according to Aristotle captures the essence of justice understood in its 'particular' senses, is of course the principle of equity or proportional equality.

Although it is not directly relevant to the task in hand, it is worth observing at this point that there is a striking analogy between the debate which has taken place between students of Aristotle over the issue of what, for him, is the 'master' principle of justice in the *Nicomachean Ethics*, to which all other principles of justice might be reduced, and the much more recent debate over 'politics of distribution versus the politics of recognition' which has taken place between Axel Honneth and Nancy Fraser (Fraser and Honneth, 2001). In the first of these two debates, which relates to the thought of Aristotle, the notion of distributive justice is contrasted with that of corrective justice, and one of the issues addressed is whether for Aristotle either of these two notions of justice can be reduced to the other. In the second debate, between Fraser and Honneth, the participants to which are also seeking a 'master' principle of justice, the notion of distributive justice is contrasted with that of 'justice as recognition', or what I propose to refer to as 'recognitive justice', the origins of which in modern times, as Honneth notes, are to be found in the philosophy of Hegel. Moreover here also, as in the case of the earlier debate over the correct interpretation of the thought of Aristotle, this raises the interesting question of how these two ways of thinking about justice are related to one another. Can the idea of distributive justice be reduced to that of recognitive justice, as Honneth claims? (Honneth, 2001: 234; Fraser and Honneth, 2001: 2–4). Or alternatively, as Fraser sometimes suggests, should we not think of these two notions of justice as being logically separable and mutually irreducible, and, in consequence, embrace what Fraser refers to as 'perspectival dualism' (Fraser, 2001a: 63–4; Fraser, 2001b: 199–200, 208–9, 213, 216–17, 233)?

Engagement with the contributions to this second debate also raises the further question of how the notion of corrective justice, as we find it in the writings of Aristotle, can be related to that of recognitive justice as this is understood by commentators such as Honneth and Fraser, and indeed by Hegel before them? This is not the place to discuss this issue at length. In my view, though, a case can be made out for the view that the basic principle of corrective justice, as Aristotle understands it, and that of recognitive justice as understood by Hegel, and more recently Fraser and Honneth, are in fact one and the same. The difference between Aristotle and these later thinkers is arguably that, unlike Aristotle, but like the Stoic philosophers of classical antiquity, the notion of 'recognitive justice' which can be discerned in their writings can be seen as an extension of the application of the principle of corrective justice beyond the territorial boundaries of not only the ancient Greek *polis* but also of the modern nation state. The outlook of Hegel [sic], Fraser and Honneth is evidently a 'cosmopolitan' one, in one sense of that term.[5] At the same time however, paradoxically, it might be suggested that one of the ultimate sources of inspiration for developing the idea of recognitive justice in this way is a certain reading of the political thought of Aristotle.

With the exception of one interesting passage in the *Ethics*, one thing that Aristotle does *not* do himself is extend the principle of corrective or rectificatory justice to all human beings. Although he does endorse the concept of natural law in some sense, Aristotle does not on the whole, as the Stoics were later to do, believe that all human beings are by nature equals. Nor, therefore, does he endorse the Stoic belief in the existence of a 'cosmopolis' of which all human beings are the member citizens. At least, Aristotle did not in the *Politics* put forward the view that all human beings are by nature equal, and that they have a natural right to be treated as such. Rather, as is well known, he defends the institution of slavery there. He criticizes the view that slavery is necessarily unjust, because it involves treating equals as if they were unequals, and he refused to accept that slavery is, for this reason, 'contrary to nature' (Aristotle, 1995h: 1253b15–1255b15, 1989–1992). Aristotle did not, therefore, on the whole subscribe to a doctrine of natural law in anything like the sense of the later Stoic philosophy. Although, as we shall see in Chapter 3, it is clear from what Aristotle says about slavery in the *Politics* and in the *Rhetoric* that he was familiar with natural law arguments of this kind, nevertheless he emphatically rejected them. This should not, however, be taken as implying that he rejected *all* natural law arguments.

In the *Ethics* Aristotle states that the principles of justice which forbid those actions such as murder, theft and adultery which are intrinsically wrong fall within this sphere of rectificatory justice (Aristotle, 1995f: 1107a9–14, 1748; 1131a1–10, 1784–85). In my view, then, Peter Simpson's claim that Aristotle 'never bothers to give us any reason why adultery or murder is wrong' (Statman, 1997a: 249) is plainly incorrect. For it is clear from what Aristotle says about corrective or rectificatory justice in the *Ethics* that the reason why, in his view, such actions are wrong or unjust is because those who have committed them have done something which they would not have wished to have been done to themselves and consequently have not respected their fellow citizens as their own equals. They have not acted in accordance with the requirements of the principle of equity, interpreted in this particular context as simple reciprocity. Aristotle seems to think that the injustice of actions such as murder, theft and adultery, and therefore the justice of the moral rules which forbid their performance, can be logically inferred from the more general principle of equity or reciprocity combined with what he takes to be certain obvious facts about human nature.

Distributive Justice

Let us now turn to consider Aristotle's views on distributive justice (διανεμετικον δικαιον, *dianemetikon dikaion*) (Aristotle, 1995f: 1131a10–1131b24, 1785–86), which lie at the very core of the argument of the *Politics*, especially Aristotle's well-known classification of the different types of political constitution. This has to do not with 'private' relations between citizens but with matters of common or 'public' concern. According to Aristotle, problems of distributive justice always possess three elements (Aristotle, 1995f: 1131a15–20, 1785). There is some good to be distributed. There is a body of persons amongst whom this good is to be distributed. And there is some standard of distribution which indicates an attribute the degree of possession or non-possession of which is considered to be relevant for determining the extent to which some persons are entitled to receive more and others less of the good in question (Aristotle, 1995h: 1282b14–22, 2035). Aristotle usually, but not always, assumes that these persons are the citizens of a particular *polis*. Sometimes, however, he discusses the situation in which citizenship itself is the good to be distributed. In this case it is the male adult inhabitants of a *polis* who constitute the relevant population. Problems of distributive justice, for Aristotle, have to do with the relationship which exists between individual citizens and the *polis* as a whole.

For Aristotle the principle of equity is a purely *formal* principle. It states simply that both justice and logic require that equals ought to be treated equally in relevantly similar circumstances or that 'like cases be treated alike'. It does not, however, stipulate who are to be considered equal, how they are to be treated, or when there circumstances are to be considered as relevantly similar. It amounts in effect, therefore, to no more than a commitment to the principle of impartiality, 'constitutionalism', or the 'rule of law' in both ethics and politics. This formal principle must be given a particular concrete realization within the principles of political justice of a particular *polis*. An important issue for Aristotle is how this substantive content is to be derived. Here, as Hans Kelsen has rightly observed, in the final analysis this content is provided by the positive law of a *polis* (Kelsen, 1973a: 127; see also Perelman, 1967c: 23–4).

It follows from this that for Aristotle concrete or substantive justice is and must always be mediated by the customs and traditions or the ethical conventions of a particular *polis*. As Gabriella Remow has noted, for Aristotle although 'it is natural for humans to have some form of civilization or state', nevertheless, as in the case of language, 'the particular form of government or state varies depending on the people involved', and in Aristotle's view rightly so (Remow, 2008: 590). It is for this reason that, as we shall see in Chapter 4, within Aristotle's system of political thought broadly understood 'nature' and 'convention' must be thought of as supplementing one another. It is also for this reason that, in Aristotle's opinion, it is necessary for us to make the transition from the study of 'ethics', which deals with abstract or formal principles of justice, and hence also with the principles of 'natural law' which are to be found in the systems of political justice of all *poleis* everywhere, to the study of 'politics' (in the narrow sense of the term), which deals with the concrete actualization of these abstract principles in the historical circumstances of particular *poleis,* and therefore with the *differences* which exist between *poleis* so far as their respective systems of political justice, or their political constitutions, are concerned.

The fact that for Aristotle the principle of equity is a purely formal principle, in the sense just indicated, has led some commentators to characterize Aristotle as an advocate of 'legal formalism' (Weinrib, 1987, 1994; also Raz, 1994). In my view, although this characterization of Aristotle as a legal formalist is certainly in a sense correct, it is nevertheless also potentially misleading. This is so because Aristotle takes care to explain why and how the principles associated with this formal element in his own theory of justice, as it is developed in Book V of the *Nicomachean Ethics,* need to be supplemented by other principles if they are to be made practically effective. In short, if the intention is to provide an account of Aristotle's moral and political thought as a whole, so far as it touches on the notion of justice, then the characterization of Aristotle as a legal formalist tells only one half of the story.

Aristotle's Classification of Constitutions

As is well known, central to Aristotle's political thought is his classification of the various different types of political constitution in the *Politics.* Here Aristotle applies the theory of justice which he develops in the *Ethics.* He considers how the formal theory of justice outlined in Book V of the *Ethics* might be applied to the circumstances of particular cases. In his view a political constitution is a system of substantive justice, or a particular determination of the formal principle of justice which states that equals ought to be treated equally, and likes ought to be treated alike. Aristotle's starting point here is Plato's question 'who should rule?' or who *would* rule in an ideal society? In his view, this is a problem of distributive justice. Aristotle's treatment of this subject is based on two separate arguments. The first focuses on who does the ruling and on the issue of whose interests are promoted by a particular system of government. In all societies, he says, government is 'in the hands of one, or of a few, or of the many' (Aristotle, 1995f: 1279a26–8, 2030). Moreover, government can be either in the 'common interest' or in the 'private interest' of those who rule (Aristotle, 1995h: 1279a28–31, 2030). If we place these two principles together then it is clear, Aristotle argues, that there are just six *pure* types of constitution possible – although in practice these might be combined in different ways thereby generating various types of 'mixed constitution'. The first three pure types are constitutions in which the one, the few, or the many rule in the interests of all (or the common interest) and hence justly. Aristotle labels these types as 'kingship', 'aristocracy' and 'polity' respectively. The other three pure types, which Aristotle calls 'tyranny', 'oligarchy' and 'democracy', are constitutions in which the one, the few, or the many rule in their own private interests and hence unjustly (Aristotle, 1995h: 1279b4–10, 2030). Aristotle describes these as 'corrupt' or 'perverted' constitutions (Aristotle, 1995f: 1160a32–1160b10, 1834, 1995h: 1275b1–2, 2024; 1279a17–30, 2030; 1282b6–12, 2035).

Aristotle also presents a second argument, which takes a slightly different tack. It focuses on the issue of what standard should be used when distributing political power amongst either the citizens or the inhabitants of a *polis*. There are, he suggests, three possible standards of distribution which might be used here, namely wealth, citizenship and moral virtue or goodness (Aristotle, 1995h: 1282b20–1283b25, 2035–35). In all six types of constitution some people have more political power and others less, but in each case the justification offered for this is different. For example, in an oligarchy the standard of distribution is wealth. The wealthy have more power than the less wealthy. Moreover this is considered to be just because the unequal distribution of power is exactly proportional to the unequal distribution of wealth. In a democracy the standard of distribution is citizenship. Here Aristotle assumes that power is distributed between the adult male inhabitants of a *polis* and not just its citizens, and that those inhabitants who are citizens will receive more of this good than those who are not. In this case, however, because all citizens possess the attribute of citizenship to the same degree, justice demands that political power be distributed between them in accordance with the principle of strict arithmetical equality (Aristotle, 1995h: 1317b1–5, 2091; 1318a3–5, 2092). Once again, Aristotle notes that in a democracy this pattern of distribution is considered to be just because it accords with the requirements of the principle of equity (Aristotle, 1995h: 1280a8–22, 2031; 1301a25–30, 2066).

Given that he concedes that in both an oligarchy and a democracy the principle of equity *is* in fact respected, it might well be asked why Aristotle nevertheless occasionally insists that these two types of government are unjust? Why does he think that oligarchy and democracy are corrupt or perverted constitutions? The reason for this is that he does not consider the standards of wealth or citizenship to be relevant standards for the purposes of this particular problem of distributive justice. Hence, he argues, although these constitutions may be said to be associated with 'a kind of justice' nevertheless when evaluated by an absolute standard of justice they are faulty (Aristotle, 1995h: 1301a36–7, 2066). The advocates of oligarchy and democracy are speaking of 'a part of justice only' (Aristotle, 1995h, 1281a9–10, 2033). According to Aristotle, to distribute political power in the way that they do is just as arbitrary as giving more power to some people on the grounds that they are taller than others (Aristotle, 1995h: 1282b27–28, 2035). Aristotle agrees with Plato that ruling is a job like any other and that those who are best fitted to the job should be the ones to do it (Aristotle, 1995h, 1283a23–25, 2036). For Aristotle, the appropriate standard here is nobility, merit or excellence, that is to say moral goodness or virtue, an attribute which is distributed unequally and is possessed to the necessary degree by only a few people, who are therefore 'the best' (*aristoi*) at ruling (Aristotle, 1995h: 1279a35–37, 2030; 1281a4–10, 2033; 1293b1–6, 2053; 1294a9–11, 2054). In Aristotle's opinion, the good life for anyone is only possible if they are brought up in a *polis* which is ruled by such people. On this view, the reason why there is a wide variety of different constitutions is because although in *every* society there has 'always been an acknowledgement of justice and proportionate equality', nevertheless mankind has 'failed' to create a truly just *polis* in practice because it has invariably employed the wrong standard when distributing political power (Aristotle, 1995h: 1301a25–28, 2066; also 1280a9–12, 2031).

For Aristotle as for Plato the people who should rule (and who would rule in an ideal society) are those who know about politics. They are the minority who are educated, virtuous and wise. Aristotle concedes that, as a matter of fact, such people will come from the wealthy, propertied stratum of a *polis*. They possess what he considers to be moderate wealth. He has in mind those who have enough property to be released from the need to work daily for a living (perhaps because they own slaves) and who as a result have sufficient leisure to engage in the pursuits of the mind and to cultivate their higher faculties (Aristotle, 1995h: 1283a14–19, 2036; 1323a36–1324a2, 2100–01; 1328a35–37, 2108; 1328b34–1329a2, 2108–9). Aristotle calls these people the 'middle class' of a *polis* (Aristotle, 1995h: 1295b2–1296a21, 2056–57).

From this standpoint Aristotle's ideal constitution is really a form of aristocracy. However, if this should turn out not to be possible in practice, he allows that a suitable alternative is *polity*. In its pure form polity is an ideal type of democracy in which all citizens are assumed to be virtuous and good. It is therefore, Aristotle concedes, as much an ideal as a pure aristocracy is. Aristotle argues, however, that polity may also be thought of as a type of 'mixed' constitution (Aristotle, 1995h: 1265b28–30, 2008; 1293b33–35, 2053; 1294a19–24, 2054). In his opinion, polity in this second sense is a realistic and hence practically attainable form of democracy in which rule by 'the people' (demos), who are assumed by Aristotle *not* to be virtuous and good, is balanced in some way by the influence of the minority who are wealthy and educated.

Fred D. Miller Jr.'s Natural Law Interpretation of Aristotle

When arguing along the lines indicated above, Aristotle is of the opinion that the best or ideal constitution is one in which political power is distributed, not simply in accordance with the principle of equity or proportional equality but *also* in accordance with the correct standard of virtue or goodness. Only in such circumstances could the distribution of political power be said to be absolutely just. It is clear that this vision of an ideally just constitution might be used as a critical standard for assessing the justice or injustice of existing constitutions. This is, presumably, what Aristotle has in mind when he says in the *Ethics* that there is only one constitution which is 'naturally the best everywhere' (Aristotle, 1995f: 1135a1–5, 1791) and in the *Politics* 'that the unequal should be given to equals, and the unlike to those who are like, is contrary to nature' (Aristotle, 1995h: 1325b7–10, 2103–4).

These remarks lend support to the view that Aristotle is best understood as being a natural law theorist of some kind, and there is also some other evidence in Aristotle's writings which supports such a reading. First, as we have seen, Aristotle states explicitly in the *Nicomachean Ethics* that there is such a thing as 'natural justice'. Second, he states in the *Politics* that man is by nature a *zoon politikon,* destined by nature to live a life of justice together with others in political society under the rule of law. It follows from this that for Aristotle since a life of justice is something which is natural for human beings then *all* justice might be said to be natural justice. Third, in the *Nicomachean Ethics* Aristotle endorses the view that there are some actions which are intrinsically wrong or unjust and implies that the principles forbidding the performance of such actions are principles of 'natural justice' which are valid for all societies everywhere (Aristotle, 1995f: 1107a8–20, 1748). Fourth, like Cicero after him, who said that 'true law is right reason consonant with nature' (*est quidem vera lex recta ratio naturae congruens*) (Cicero, 1966 [1928]: III, XXII, 210–11), Aristotle states in the *Nicomachean Ethics* that generally speaking 'right actions' are those which conform to 'right principles' and that to do that which is right is to follow the dictates of 'right reason' (ορθos λογos, *orthos logos*) (Aristotle, 1995f: 1103b33–5). Finally, in his *Rhetoric* Aristotle appears to acknowledge the existence of a 'law of nature', the characteristic features of which are those traditionally associated with natural law theory, namely that there are certain principles of justice which are universal, eternal and which can be used to criticize existing societies, theory laws and their institutions (Aristotle, 1995i: 1368b5–10, 2178; 1373b1–10, 2187; 1375a25–35, 2190) (see Chapter 3).

In an important work Fred D. Miller Jr. has appealed to statements like those from the *Politics* cited above to support his claim that Aristotle is best interpreted as a natural law theorist (Miller, 1997: vii, 67, 74–5, 191). Miller argues that in these passages Aristotle is committed to the idea that there is a universally valid critical 'standard of justice by which inferior constitutions can be evaluated' and found wanting (Miller, 1997: vii, 187–8). On these grounds he maintains that Aristotle's argument 'supports a theory of natural justice' (Miller, 1997: 16). Miller Jr. attributes to Aristotle, not only the view that there is such a thing as natural law, but also the view that the principles of natural law constitute a higher, critical standard of justice which individuals might use to evaluate positive law, or the customs and conventions of the society in which they live. According to Miller Jr., then, Aristotle's belief that there are objective, universally valid principles of justice or right indicates that, despite the emphasis on the importance of character, motivation and the moral virtues in the *Ethics*, Aristotle's ethical thought might nevertheless be interpreted as a rule governed natural law theory. This last point is something concerning which Miller and I are in agreement with one another.

In the great 'nature versus convention' debate which dominated Athenian politics in the fourth and fifth centuries BCE, which took place between at least some of the Sophists and their critics over the issue of whether justice exists by nature or by convention, which I shall discuss in Chapter 4, Miller claims that Aristotle takes the latter side against the former. In his view Aristotle 'appeals to an objective normative principle' of natural justice and 'not merely to convention or opinion' (Miller, 1997: 14–15). According to Miller, then, Aristotle was an advocate of the doctrine of 'naturalism', and he rejected outright that of 'conventionalism'. Miller therefore aligns himself with those commentators mentioned earlier who have also taken the view that Aristotle is a natural law theorist; perhaps indeed the very *first* natural law theorist in the history of Western political thought, and hence also the founder of *the* natural law tradition.

It is clear from what Miller says about the concept of natural law, in particular his implicit assumption that *all* natural law theorists consider natural law to be a higher standard of justice which might be used to critically evaluate positive law, that like many other commentators he identifies the idea of natural law generally with what is in fact just one particular manifestation of it, which I have referred to as the Stoic conception of natural law. By implication, then, Miller suggests that Aristotle may legitimately be regarded as a precursor to Stoicism because he endorses a conception of natural law which is similar to that of the Stoics, as their views are reported by commentators such as Cicero. For this reason, although I am broadly sympathetic to Miller's suggestion that a natural law reading of Aristotle is not only plausible but actually necessary if we are to properly understand Aristotle's ethical thought, nevertheless I find myself unable to accept the particular natural law reading of Aristotle which is offered by Miller himself.

Hans Kelsen's Conventionalist Interpretation of Aristotle's *Politics*

It cannot be denied that there is evidence to support Miller Jr.'s interpretation of Aristotle. On the other hand, however, there is also at least some significant evidence which counts against it. Indeed, some commentators have rejected outright the view that Aristotle is an advocate of naturalism and have insisted, on the contrary, that he embraces the opposite theoretical position of conventionalism or ethical relativism. Thus, in their view, Aristotle endorses the same conventionalist approach to ethics as that which is usually associated with Sophism (Guthrie, 1971a: 53; Kelsen, 1973c: 122–36, 1957b: 125–36; Kroger, 2004: 917; Morrall, 1977: 98–9; Yack, 1990: 216). W. K. C. Guthrie, for example, has argued that 'on the subjects in which the Sophists were primarily interested, Aristotle's standpoint was in many ways closer to theirs' than to Plato's' (Guthrie, 1971: 53). In recent times, this view that Aristotle was a conventionalist is perhaps most strongly associated with the works of Hans Kelsen (Kelsen, 1973b, 1973c, 1957b, 1957c). Although Kelsen himself does not refer to them all, there are five reasons why one might take this view.

The first of these was the focus of our attention in the preceding chapter. It has to do with what Aristotle says about the relationship which exists between natural justice (*phusikon dikaion*), legal or conventional justice (*nomikon dikaion*) and political justice (*politikon dikaion*) in the important passage in Chapter 7 of Book V of the *Ethics* (Aristotle, 1995f: 1134b–1135a). By 'natural' in this context Aristotle means that which is ethically necessary and which applies universally in every case. By 'conventional' he means that which relates to a matter of moral indifference and is, therefore, merely accidental, a product of the customs and traditions of a *polis*, varying legitimately from *polis* to *polis*. Aristotle states here that natural justice and conventional justice are both a 'part' of political justice. As I suggested earlier, what he means by this is that every principle of political justice is composed of a principle of natural justice combined with a principle of legal or conventional justice. From this point of view, natural justice is something which is immanent within the system of civil law of a *polis*. To serve as a guide to action natural justice must be applied to the specific circumstances of a *polis* and given a determinate existence within its principles of political justice.

According to Aristotle the essence of justice is the principle of equity, which demands that equals be treated equally in relevantly similar circumstances. We saw earlier that this is a formal principle which cannot be applied in practice unless it is given a content that determines which persons are equal, how they should be treated, and so on. For Aristotle the principle of equity is the most fundamental principle of natural justice, and the principles which provide it with a definite substantive content are the principles of legal or conventional justice of a particular *polis*. It follows from this, however, that in Aristotle's view the latter principles must relate to matters which are indifferent from the moral point of view. In other words, if Aristotle's beliefs are logically consistent it ought to be of no importance to him how these things are actually determined in the case of any particular constitution. Indeed, as Kelsen points out, generally speaking Aristotle leaves the task of determination to positive law and he acknowledges that the constitutions of different *poleis*, for example oligarchic and democratic ones, will therefore inevitably differ from one another in these morally irrelevant respects (Kelsen, 1973a: 126–7). This clearly implies, however, that for Aristotle whether a constitution is an oligarchy or a democracy ought to be a matter of indifference so far as our assessment of its justice or injustice is concerned. In so far as oligarchy and democracy are indeed types of constitutional government which respect the rule of law because they do 'treat like cases alike', Aristotle's theory of justice requires that they each be regarded as both natural and just.

The second reason is that Aristotle says things in the *Politics* which directly contradict a natural law reading of his thought. For example, he says that in every *polis* 'the citizen should be moulded to suit the form of government under which he lives' (Aristotle, 1995h, 1337a12–15, 2121). Elsewhere he states that in every *polis* the young must be 'trained by habit and education in the spirit of the constitution, if the laws are democratic, democratically, or oligarchically, if the laws are oligarchical' (Aristotle, 1995h: 1310a14–18, 2080; also 1276b30–33, 2026; 1294a12–15, 2054; 1308b20–25, 2078; 1309b14–15, 2079). Here Aristotle makes no judgment about the ethical merits or demerits of the different types of constitution under discussion. Given these remarks, it is not too surprising that Kelsen has argued that Aristotle is an ethical relativist who agreed with those Sophists who argued that all justice is a matter of convention. In Kelsen's opinion, it is Aristotle's view that 'every positive law must be just' because 'positive law and justice coincide' (Kelsen, 1973a: 127). In the *Politics* Aristotle excludes 'in advance any justice distinct from positive law, which might possibly conflict therewith' (Kelsen, 1973a: 124).

When arguing in this vein, Aristotle has the greatest respect for the ideal of constitutional government generally (Aristotle, 1995h: 1289a12–15, 2046). Here the hallmark of constitutional government is simply that the rule of law is indeed respected and that like cases (as defined by the ethical values of the constitution in question) are indeed treated alike. The phrase 'the rule of law' in this context refers to existing law or to the principles of political justice associated with the customs and traditions of a particular constitution as it currently stands. A constitution is simply a coherent framework of laws, or of principles of political justice, which is impartially applied. For, as Aristotle says, 'where the laws have no authority' or where the laws do not rule 'there is no constitution' (Aristotle, 1995h: 1292a30–32, 2051). There is considerable truth in the claim that constitutionalism in this sense is Aristotle's enduring legacy to the later history of political thought. From this point of view, as Aristotle points out in his *Eudemian Ethics*, constitutions 'are all of them particular forms of justice; for a constitution is a partnership, and every partnership rests on justice' (Aristotle, 1995g: 1241b, 1967). It follows from this though that for Aristotle a constitution is by definition a system of justice and that strictly speaking no constitution could possibly be unjust. On this reading, then, for Aristotle the idea of an 'unjust constitution' is a contradiction in terms. If, therefore, Aristotle wishes to argue that democracy and oligarchy, for example, are indeed 'corrupt' or 'perverted' constitutions then he could not possibly maintain, without contradiction, that the reason for this is that they are 'unjust'. He must have some other understanding of the notion of corruption or perversion which does not assume that constitutions which fall into this category do so because they are unjust.

The third reason for thinking that Aristotle is a conventionalist or ethical relativist is that such an interpretation of Aristotle's politics is consistent with, and arguably required by, the basic principles of Aristotelian metaphysics. According to Aristotle the world generally is composed of a multiplicity of individual things or substances. Each of these is a composite entity associated with a certain matter, on the one hand, and a certain form on the other (Aristotle, 1995c: 1028b33–1029a7, 1624–35; 1033a1–5, 1631; 1033b1–10, 1631–32; 1034b33–1035a2, 1634; 1038b1–10, 1639; 104314–19, 1646). The form of an individual substance is encapsulated within the definition of its concept (Aristotle, 1995c: 1026b1–37, 1620–21; 1028a31–1028b4, 1623–24; 1042a11–19, 1645; 1043a14–19, 1646). This lists the characteristic features which are necessarily associated with this concept, features which are to be found universally in all examples of this type of substance everywhere (Aristotle, 1995c: 1015a34–1015b9, 1603). According to Aristotle, these necessary features constitute the essence of an individual substance (Aristotle, 1995c: 1029b31–1030a6, 1626; 1031a10–14, 1628). They may be contrasted with other features which Aristotle considers to be accidental, which are not to be found in all examples of the type of substance in question (Aristotle, 1995c: 1007a21–24, 1590; 1025a25–29, 1619; 1026b3–5, 1620–21; 1026b35–36, 1621).

Now considered from the standpoint of Aristotelian metaphysics a particular political constitution, for example that of Athens in the fourth century BCE, is an individual substance in the sense just indicated. As such it contains both essential features and accidental ones. For Aristotle, the form or essence with which it is associated is an idea or concept. Given that all constitutions are by definition systems of justice, not surprisingly Aristotle maintains that the concept in question is the concept of justice. In his opinion, therefore, justice is the very essence of any constitution. It is the essential nature of *all* constitutions to be just. Aristotle considers all particular constitutions to be concrete instantiations of the essence of justice. It follows from this, however, that if his ethical and political thought is to be consistent with his metaphysical beliefs

Aristotle cannot or *should* not acknowledge the existence of any independent standard of justice by means of which the constitution of a particular *polis* might be evaluated and declared to be *un*just. According to this interpretation of Aristotle, if the views on justice expressed in the *Politics* are to cohere with Aristotle's metaphysical beliefs then Aristotle ought consistently to adopt the conventionalist position attributed to him by Kelsen.

Considered from this point of view, the only way in which, for example, democracy and oligarchy might be criticized for being unjust is by saying, not that they are 'perverted' types of constitution, but rather that they are not constitutions at all, properly so called, because the rule of law is not respected within them. There are occasions when Aristotle *does* suggest this. For example he suggests at one point that at least one of the forms of democracy is 'fairly open to the objection that it is not a constitution at all' (Aristotle, 1995h: 1292a30–32, 2051). It is clear, however, that if this idea is taken to its logical limit, then it is inconsistent with, and indeed undermines, the six-fold classification of constitutions for which the *Politics* is famous.

More usually, however, Aristotle is willing to allow that democracy and oligarchy are indeed 'constitutions', in the strict sense of the term, albeit corrupt or perverted ones (Aristotle, 1995h: 1279a23–38, 2032; 1301a25–30, 2066). Hence they can also be seen as systems of political justice. For example, at one point he says that in all constitutions, whether these are aristocracies, democracies or oligarchies, we find the same 'notion of justice'. For these constitutions 'all recognize the claims of superiority', though not of course 'the *same* superiority' (Aristotle, 1995h: 1288a). And elsewhere he concedes that we must 'assume as our starting point that in the many forms of government which have sprung up there has *always* been an acknowledgement of justice and proportionate equality' (Aristotle, 1995h: 1301a25–30, 2066). On these occasions, then, Aristotle concedes that democracy and oligarchy are correctly said to be types of constitution and that within them there is therefore respect for equity and the rule of law. Even in a democracy and an oligarchy those who are considered to be equals *are* treated equally and like cases are treated alike. It follows from this, however, that such constitutions could not possibly be 'unjust' in the primary sense in which Aristotle defines this concept in his *Nicomachean Ethics*, the validity of which he presupposes in his *Politics*. It also follows that, whatever else Aristotle might have meant when he declared democracy and oligarchy to be 'perverted' or 'corrupted' constitutions, he could not possibly have meant that he considered them to be unjust.

The fourth reason for thinking that Aristotle is a conventionalist is his attitude towards the issue of the role which 'reason' has to play in ethics and politics. Like later thinkers such as Edmund Burke, who follow him in this regard, Aristotle objected strongly to abstract ethical and political rationalism. With his emphasis on the importance of 'phronesis' or 'practical wisdom' and his appreciation of the limited value which inflexible rules, mechanically applied, have for ethical and political deliberation, Aristotle demonstrates a marked hostility to what today would be referred to as utopian political speculation and the production of blueprints for alleged ideal societies similar to that which can be found in Plato's *Republic.* These are all features of Aristotle's political thought which identify him as a conservative critic of the abstract rationalism of the Athenian 'enlightenment' of the fourth and fifth centuries BCE.

The fifth and final reason for thinking that Aristotle is a conventionalist or ethical relativist is his claim that man is by nature a political animal, which is also logically inconsistent with his remarks about corrupt and perverted constitutions. As again Kelsen has noted, this claim implies that all positive law must 'be regarded as natural law' and hence that '*every* state' is a 'product of nature' (Kelsen, 1973a: 132). Kelsen rightly observes that if this is the case then even those constitutions which Aristotle considers to be perverted, precisely because they might properly be described as being constitutions or states in the strict sense of the term, must *also* be products of nature. Hence, for Aristotle, nature can provide no criterion for the negative evaluation of these constitutions. Any argument criticizing these constitutions could not possibly rest on the claim that their existence is contrary to nature (Kelsen, 1973a: 133). Kelsen maintains that when Aristotle makes this claim what he says stands in 'open contradiction' to one of the main theses of his political theory, namely 'the natural givenneness of *all* states'. Kelsen asserts that this claim is clearly 'at variance with the intellectual scheme of the whole Aristotelian theory' (Kelsen, 1973a: 147) and that it contradicts 'everything that Aristotle otherwise says about the nature of the state'. As we have seen, he also claims on these grounds, that it is 'more than doubtful' that Aristotle's remarks about perverted constitutions being both contrary to nature and unjust are authentic and that it is difficult to avoid supposing that the text of the *Politics* at these points, which is 'so crucial' to the 'alleged natural law theory of Aristotle', is 'not corrupt' (Kelsen, 1973a: 134–5).

Kelsen's explanation for the logical inconsistency in Aristotle's remarks about the justice or injustice of democracy and oligarchy is possibly correct, of course. However, it is also possible that Aristotle's views on this subject are logically inconsistent, or alternatively that they simply altered over time. Nevertheless, adherents of the conventionalist interpretation of Aristotle would agree with the main thrust of Kelsen's argument here. From their point of view, Kelsen is right to suggest that, in the passages upon which Fred Miller Jr. rests his case, the views expressed by Aristotle are inconsistent with his central claim that man is by nature a social and political animal. On this view, then, it makes no sense to say that one type of constitution is better than another, or that there is one constitution which is the best, or that some constitutions must be unjust because they are contrary to nature. Rather, constitutions are simply different from one another, although of course only with respect to their accidental and not their essential features. The reason why a variety of different constitutions exists is not because in some societies the *wrong* standard of distribution is used, but simply because *different* standards of distribution are used.

According to the conventionalist interpretation of his views, then, Aristotle's claim in the *Politics* that there are 'corrupt' or 'perverted' constitutions which are unjust because they are contrary to nature, or alternatively which are contrary to nature because they are unjust, is contradicted by what he says elsewhere in the same text. It is inconsistent with his own metaphysical beliefs. It runs counter to his doctrine that man is by nature a social and political animal. It conflicts with what he says about the relationship between natural, legal and political justice in the *Ethics*. And it ignores the fact that Aristotle emphatically rejected the type of rationalist approach to the problems of ethics and politics which is usually associated with natural law theory, or the doctrine of naturalism. From this point of view, although it seems implausible to deny that Aristotle actually made this claim, nevertheless it would be unwise to base one's interpretation of his political thought as a whole entirely upon the fact that he did so. There are, therefore, again good reasons for questioning the validity of Fred Miller Jr.'s natural law interpretation of Aristotle, precisely because of its undue reliance on this evidence.

As we have seen, the particular 'natural law interpretation' of Aristotle's *Politics*, and of Aristotle's political thought more generally, which is offered by Fred Miller Jr. is open to a number of objections. This does not mean, however, that we should 'throw the baby out with the bath water' and entirely abandon the idea of presenting a natural law reading of Aristotle, for there are alternative ways of thinking about natural law and natural law theory. Nor does it mean that we are compelled to go to the opposite extreme, as Hans Kelsen does, and interpret Aristotle 'as a conventionalist who rejects the notion of natural law altogether' (Kelsen, 1957a, 1973c; Yack, 1990: 216). Rather, we need to consider the possibility that Aristotle adopts a third approach to the 'nature versus convention debate'. I shall say more about this issue in Chapter 4. For the time being I shall merely observe that neither Miller Jr.'s natural law interpretation of Aristotle nor the ethical and constitutional relativist interpretation of Kelsen and others is entirely correct, although each of them has something to be said for it, and that there is a third possible interpretation which removes at least some of the inconsistencies in Aristotle's thinking, though not all of them. Despite the conventionalist critique of it, there is definitely something in Miller Jr.'s interpretation. Aristotle certainly does attach importance to the concept of natural justice or natural law, and no assessment of his ethical and political thought is acceptable which does not appreciate this fact. However, what is alien to the spirit of Aristotle's thinking is the Stoic idea that there is an independent or transcendent standard of substantive justice which individuals might employ to critically evaluate the positive law or the constitution of the *polis* in which they live and declare it to be unjust. With respect to this issue I agree with the conventionalist interpretation of Aristotle, for all five of the reasons suggested above. In my view the remarks in which Aristotle suggests that perverted or corrupt constitutions are both contrary to nature and unjust are indeed, as Kelsen maintains, inconsistent with the central thrust of his general approach to ethics and politics. Kelsen has argued on these grounds that we should set these remarks aside and that if we do the only appropriate conclusion is that Aristotle is not a natural law theorist at all but a conventionalist or ethical relativist whose views are very close to what today is referred to as legal positivism (Kelsen, 1973a: 129–32, 147). But this is going much too far. Kelsen is right to argue that we should set these remarks aside, however, if we do, we are not then compelled to abandon the view that Aristotle is a natural law theorist, albeit in a different sense from that suggested by Fred Miller Jr.

The Relationship between Aristotle's *Ethics* and his *Politics*

We saw in Chapter 1 that for Aristotle the principles of political justice of a *polis* possess a complex structure with component parts. Each principle of political justice has a part which is natural and a part which is merely legal or conventional. But the same can also be said about the constitution, or the entire system of political justice, of a particular *polis*. In Aristotle's view, because a political constitution is the system of political justice of a particular *polis*, it must possess the same basic structure as any individual principle of political justice. A political constitution is, therefore, also a composite entity with component parts, one of which is natural and the other legal or conventional. The first of these is associated with the precepts of natural justice or law and is not, therefore, something which is unique to any particular *polis*. On the contrary, all *poleis* possess these principles. They hold them in common. The second is associated with the principles of legal or conventional justice of a particular *polis*, its peculiar history, customs and traditions. These supplement or complement the principles of natural justice or law in the manner indicated above.

Similar remarks might also be made about Aristotle's theoretical understanding of politics, and of the relationship which exists, not just between the spheres of ethics and politics in any particular society, but also between the disciplines known as 'ethics' and 'politics'. At first sight this suggestion appears to imply that for Aristotle it is the task of the student of ethics to focus exclusively on those features which are natural and which all *poleis* have in common, whereas it is that of the students of politics to focus exclusively on those features of a particular *polis*, or of a number of *poleis*, which are legal or conventional. But this would be a somewhat narrow picture of the discipline of politics as Aristotle understands it. For in the *Nicomachean Ethics* Aristotle argues that the study of politics (understood in the broadest possible sense of the term) is the 'highest master science' precisely because it incorporates within itself, as just one of its component parts, the discipline of 'ethics'. And it is the discipline of politics in this broad sense of the term that is concerned with 'what is noble and what is just' and 'lays down laws' about what we ought to do and what we ought not to do (Aristotle, 1995f: 1094b5–6, 1729–30; 1180b19–26, 1866).

It is arguable, then, that in addition to associating the discipline of politics somewhat narrowly with the study of the empirical and the historically contingent elements of civil law to be found in the political constitutions of particular societies, which he undoubtedly does, Aristotle *also* possesses a much broader understanding of the discipline which incorporates within itself as its two component parts, the disciplines of 'ethics' and that of 'politics' in the narrow sense of the term. In Aristotle's opinion, the student of 'politics' in its widest sense must take an interest in both the 'natural' and the 'legal' or 'conventional' components of the political constitutions which are their objects of study, together with the relationship which exists between the two.

One can, then, think of Aristotle's theory of justice as a whole along the same lines as Aristotle himself thinks both of the principles of political justice or the laws of a *polis* and of the political constitution with which those principles are associated. This also has two component parts, one of which deals with things which Aristotle considers to be 'natural' and the other with things that are 'legal' or 'conventional'. The first of these is to be found in Book V of the *Ethics*. The principles of justice which Aristotle considers to be natural and hence universally valid are presented there in an outline sketch. In his *Politics* Aristotle goes on to discuss the circumstances within which these principles are concretely realized in some of the constitutions of the many different *poleis* in fourth century Greece. This second part of Aristotle's theory is, therefore, concerned not with the similarities which exist between the constitutions of these *poleis*, but with the differences in their history, customs, traditions and conventions.

It is tempting to suggest at this point that for Aristotle it is in the sphere of politics, narrowly conceived, that justice becomes law, or that the principles of natural justice are transformed into 'laws' properly so called, which Aristotle identifies with the principles of political justice of a *polis*. Thus, on this view, in Aristotle's thought the concept of justice is logically prior to that of law. On the other hand, though, it is not clear that it would be correct to do this. Indeed it might be argued that there are two good reasons for not doing it. The first is that such a reading of Aristotle is inconsistent with the view, adopted throughout, that Aristotle's notion of *physikon dikaion* can be translated into English as 'natural law' rather than 'natural justice'. This is not in itself decisive of course. For it might be argued that what this shows is that such a translation is not justified. The second reason is that in Book V of the *Ethics* Aristotle associates the idea of justice in its 'general' rather than its 'particular' sense with that of obedience to law. He indicates very clearly, therefore, that it is the notion of law which has logical priority over that of justice, and not vice versa. However, if it is made plain that what we have in mind is Aristotle's understanding of the concept of justice understood in its 'particular' sense, then it is possible to argue that the concept of justice does have logical priority over that of law, provided that by 'law' one has in mind civil law or the laws which Aristotle associates with the principles of political justice of a particular *polis*.

Each of the two elements referred to above, the 'ethical' and the 'political' or the 'natural' and the 'legal' or 'conventional', is vital for understanding Aristotle's political thought as a whole, so far as it constitutes a comprehensive theory of justice, and neither on its own is sufficient. If we focus exclusively on the former then like Fred Miller Jr. we present Aristotle as a natural law theorist in an excessively rationalistic sense and we lose sight of the historical and relativistic dimension of his views on ethics and politics. If we focus exclusively on the latter then like Hans Kelsen we transform Aristotle into a conventionalist or an ethical relativist and lose sight of the fact that he wishes to defend the existing social order in any society (especially in Athens) by means of reasoned argument and philosophy rather than an appeal to religion, on the one hand, or mere custom and tradition on the other. We need therefore a 'third way'. What this third doctrine amounts to in the end is a sophisticated philosophical justification of the customs and traditions associated with the constitution of any *polis*, no matter what they might be. Aristotle argued that there is a reason or justice which lies beneath and supports these different customs and conventions and that, consequently, in any given case the existing social and political order is not entirely arbitrary and conventional.

In this regard there is, again, a striking similarity between the political thought of Aristotle and that of Hegel. I pointed out in Chapter 1 that the 'double title' title of Hegel's most well-known work of political philosophy is *Natural Law and Political Science in Outline: Elements of the Philosophy of Right* and that when he first published this work in 1817 Hegel chose to give it a recognizably Aristotelian title (Hegel, 1979; Burns, 1996a). Pursuing this comparison between the thought of Aristotle and that of Hegel further, in my view the best way to characterize Aristotle's views is to think of them, as in the case of Hegel, as constituting a form of 'philosophical conservatism'. For Aristotle, just as later for Hegel, it might be said that reason is 'the rose in the cross of the present' (Hegel, 1979: preface, 12). To be more specific, the relationship which exists between the theory of justice advanced in Book V of the *Ethics* and the classification of political constitutions put forward in the *Politics* is strikingly similar to that which exists between Parts One and Three of Hegel's *Philosophy of Right*, which deal with the spheres of 'abstract right', on the one hand, and of 'ethical life' respectively. Hegel's treatment of the notion of 'abstract right' in Part One of his great work is the analogue within his political philosophy of the account of the formal principles of natural justice which is given by Aristotle in Book V of the *Ethics*, just as the notion of 'ethical life' which Hegel develops in Part Three, especially his remarks about political constitutions there, corresponds to Aristotle's account in his *Politics* of the empirical details associated with the constitutions of a variety of historically given individual *poleis* in Greece in the fourth century BCE.

I note in passing that Hegel, too, occasionally employs the notion of 'corrupt' or 'perverted' constitutions in his writings, when talking about what he refers to as 'bad states' (Hegel, 1975: §213, 276; §24A, 41; §135A, 191; 1979: §258A, 279; §270A, 283). It is arguable however that, as in the case of Aristotle, so too in that of Hegel it is difficult to square the suggestion that there are such things as 'bad states' with the broad thrust of his views on philosophy, ethics and politics, at least if by a 'bad state' Hegel had in mind one the laws of which are unjust. I have suggested that for Aristotle the idea of an 'unjust constitution' is logically self-contradictory. The same however could be said of Hegel's notion of a 'bad state'. It might be argued that for Hegel as for Aristotle if 'bad states' exist then this cannot possibly be because they are *unjust* states. Like Aristotle, Hegel thought that no state could possibly be unjust. In his view even a 'bad state' is a 'state' in the strict sense of the term. Moreover all states, properly so called, possess a 'constitution'. They are all associated with a definite framework of laws, and hence also a particular system of political justice or 'ethical life'. This is a reason for concluding that, as in the case of Aristotle, so also the political philosophy of Hegel is fundamentally conservative in terms of its political implications. This reading of Hegel as a 'conservative' has often been offered in the past. However it can fairly be said that it is by no means the most popular reading of Hegel today. Indeed Jon Stewart has referred to it as one of a number of 'Hegel myths and legends' (Stewart, 1996). One of my reasons for drawing attention to the striking affinities which exist between the political thought of Hegel and that of Aristotle is to challenge this view (Burns, 1996a, 1998b, 2002c, 2005b).

Notes

1 For criticism of MacIntyre's 'virtue ethics' reading of Aristotle see Burns (2005a). This raises the issue of the complex, triangular framework of relationships between the thought of Aristotle, Kant and Marx, together with the further issue of the relationship which exists between this framework and the work of Alasdair MacIntyre. For some more recent reflections on these issues see Burns (2011 c).

2 For discussion of Aristotle's views on justice see Berlin, 1955–56; Blackstone, 1967; Ginsberg, 1971a; Kelsen, 1957a, 1961, 1973; Lloyd, 1972; Marc-Wogau, 1967a; Perelman, 1963; Perelman, 1967b: 6–9; Perelman, 1967c: 21-8; Perelman, 1980; Raphael, 1970; Ross, 1959; Williams, 1967; Winthrop, 1978; and von Leyden, 1985.

3 For Aristotle's notion of rectificatory or corrective justice see the contributions to the symposium entitled 'Corrective Justice and Formalism: The Care One Owes One's Neighbor', in *Iowa Law Review*, 77 (1991–92), 403–864, especially Weinrib,

1991–92, 403–26; Benson, 1991–92, 515–624; and Heyman, 1991–92, 851–63; also Marc-Wogau, 1967a.

4 For this issue see also Burnet in Aristotle, 1900: 213, 217–24; del Vecchio, 1952: 53, 68; Dherbey, 2002: 125–8; Grant in Aristotle, 1885: 108–12; Jackson in Aristotle 1879: xx, 76, 82–3 and 100–4; Gauthier and Jolif in Aristotle, 1970: 369–73, 385; Ritchie, 1895: 185; Ross, 1964: 212; Stewart, 1892: 431–2.

5 I discuss the relationship which exists between Aristotle's theory of justice (including his views on corrective or rectificatory justice), Hegel's approach to 'the politics of recognition' and the contemporary debate over 'the politics of distribution versus the politics of recognition in Burns (2012). For some earlier reflections on Hegel, justice and recognition see Burns (2006).

Chapter 3

Natural Law in Aristotle's *Rhetoric*

Is the Concept of Natural Law to be Found in the *Rhetoric*?

There is at least some evidence that as early as the fifth century BCE one branch of the Sophistic movement in ancient Athens was already developing what are recognisably natural law arguments, as a means of criticizing the existing social and political order. Some of this evidence is provided by Aristotle, first in his discussion of natural law in his *Rhetoric,* and second in what he says about slavery in the *Politics.* As the arguments of these two parts of the *corpus* of Aristotle's writings are closely connected to one another, I shall discuss them both in this chapter.

In his *Rhetoric* Aristotle makes a distinction between the concept of 'special' or 'particular' law (*nomos idios,* νομος ιδιος) and that of 'general' or 'universal' law (*nomos koinos,* νομος κοινος). He associates the former with 'that written law under which each community lives' and the latter with 'those unwritten ordinances, which seem to be acknowledged on all hands' (Aristotle, 1995h: 1368bl–10, 2178). He suggests that this general or universal law is 'the law of nature', whereas special or particular law is that 'which each community lays down and applies to its own members' (Aristotle, 1995h: 1368bl–10, 2178). He also suggests that this general or universal law is a higher law than special or particular law. It is associated with the principles of a 'greater equity and justice'. This higher law is 'permanent and changeless', simply because 'it is the law of nature'. As opposed to this, he says of written laws that they 'often do change' (Aristotle, 1995h: 1375a25–35, 2190). At first sight, a reading of these passages seems to indicate that in the *Rhetoric* Aristotle acknowledges that there is indeed some higher law, which might legitimately be described as 'natural law' or the 'law of nature', and which might be used by individuals as a critical standard to evaluate the social conventions or the positive laws of the society in which they live.

In order to illustrate what he means by the concept of natural law, Aristotle refers to the writings of Sophocles, Empedocles and Alcidamas. The characteristic features which, according to Aristotle, are associated with the concept of natural law by his contemporaries and immediate predecessors are apparent from what he says about their views. There are three such features. It is not entirely clear whether Aristotle thinks that all three features are present in the works of each one of these authors. In the following account I shall assume that he does think this. First, Sophocles, Empedocles and Alcidamas maintain that the principles of natural law are universal, in the sense that they apply to all human beings, in all societies everywhere. Hence, according to Aristotle, these three thinkers consider the fundamental principles of ethics to be 'natural' in the specific sense in which he himself understands this term. Second, these authors argue that the principles of natural law are timeless or eternal. They are ethical principles which remain valid always, no matter what the circumstances. Sophocles, Empedocles and Alcidamas claim that the fundamental principles of ethics are not merely conventional, a product of a particular society at a particular time. Third, Aristotle asserts that these authors take the view that the principles of natural law provide a yardstick for the evaluation of existing institutions and the customs and practices associated with them.

It is for one or other of these three reasons that Aristotle argues that Sophocles, Empedocles and Alcidamas all employ the concept of natural law in their writings. For example, he claims that in a well-known passage from Sophocles' *Antigone* (lines 450–460), Antigone (and hence according to Aristotle also Sophocles) 'clearly means, when she says that the burial of Polyneices was a just act in spite of the prohibition' of her uncle Creon, that being timeless in its application, the ethical principle legitimizing her action 'was just by nature'. He further suggests that what Empedocles is claiming 'when he bids us kill no living creature', saying that 'doing this is not just for some people while unjust for others', is that such a principle, being universal in its application, is again just by nature. Finally Aristotle asserts that when Alcidamas says that 'God has left all men free; nature has made no man a slave' what he means by this is that slavery, being ethically wrong for all human beings (at all times everywhere), is something which in this case is not just but rather *unjust* by nature. As Aristotle understood him, Alcidamas evidently maintained that the institution of slavery contradicts the principle of equity, which is the most fundamental principle of natural justice. This principle states that those who are equal ought to be treated equally in relevantly similar circumstances. The difference between Alcidamas and Aristotle is that, according to Aristotle's account of his views, Alcidamas took the view that all human beings *are* as a matter of fact equal, whereas in his defence of slavery in the *Politics* (though not elsewhere) Aristotle did not.

A number of commentators have taken the remarks which Aristotle makes about natural law or 'the law of nature' in the *Rhetoric* at their face value. According to these commentators, the *Rhetoric* may be regarded as a reliable source for Aristotle's own views on the subject of natural law (Barker, 1969 [1948]: xxxiv; Bryce, 1901: 566-68; Friedrich, 1963: 23; Hamburger, 1951:

39, 65; Kelsen, 1973a: 135; Ritchie, 1894: 191, 1916: 30; Sigmund, 1971: 9–10; Salmond, 1895: 127; Strauss, 1974: 156; von Leyden, 1985: 84; Watson, 1966: 66; Wormuth, 1948). This also appears to be Fred Miller Jr.' s view, at least some the time (Miller Jr., 1991: 281, 284–5, 297, 302–3, 305–6). At one point Miller does acknowledge that 'the examples of Alcidamas, Empedocles and Antigone' referred to by Aristotle 'seem intended to illustrate the notion of natural law from familiar sources, rather than to identify specific precepts which Aristotle himself endorses' (Miller Jr., 1991: 283). It should, however, be noted that the understanding of natural law which Aristotle attributes to Alcidamas, Sophocles and Empedocles and which, here at least, Miller appears to concede that Aristotle himself did *not* hold is the same as the one which Miller himself attributes to Aristotle elsewhere.

The commentators just referred to maintain that the *Rhetoric* provides evidence in support of the view that Aristotle himself is a natural law theorist who would have been sympathetic to the natural law arguments which he claims to have discerned in the writings of Sophocles, Empedocles and Alcidamas. In my view, however, this interpretation of Aristotle's attitude towards natural law in the *Rhetoric* is mistaken. As other commentators have argued, and as the title of the work suggests, the arguments to which Aristotle refers to in the *Rhetoric* are nothing more than strategic devices, or debating points, to which students of rhetoric might plausibly appeal if they wish to argue a particular case, whatever the intrinsic merits of that case might be. None of these arguments, therefore, are ones which Aristotle himself takes at all seriously (Corbett, 2009: 230; Guthrie, 1971a: 124–5; Irwin, 1996: 142; Kelsen, 1973c: 149; McIlwain, 1932: 19; Strauss, 1974: 81; Ritchie, 1916 [1894]: 29–32; Salomon Shellens, 1959: 79–81; Yack, 1990: 221, 224–6, 1993: 145–9). F. F. Wormuth, for example, has claimed that this work 'is intended to teach rhetoricians to plead cases'. In it Aristotle 'offers arguments on both sides of the question', and this fact alone makes the work 'of doubtful value as evidence of Aristotle's opinions' (Wormuth, 1948: 53–4). Similarly Terence Irwin has said that given 'the purpose of the treatise' there is 'no reason to suppose that these must be Aristotle's own beliefs and assumptions'. Rather, to the contrary, 'we might expect persuasive arguments' of the kind alluded to by Aristotle in the *Rhetoric* 'to rely quite often on ethical beliefs and assumptions that Aristotle himself rejects' (Irwin, 1996: 142). This view seems to me to have a particular application to what Aristotle has to say about 'natural law' arguments there.

Perhaps the strongest formulation of this view of the significance of the *Rhetoric* for our understanding of Aristotle's own views is that of D. G. Ritchie. According to Ritchie, Aristotle refers to the *nomos koionos* 'as a generally received notion' which may be used as 'a rhetorical commonplace: "No case, talk about the law of nature and quote the *Antigone*" ' (Ritchie, 1916 [1894]: 91). As Ritchie also says, elsewhere, 'the principle "No case: talk about the law of nature" ', certainly appears to be a 'more lofty suggestion than "No case: abuse plaintiff's attorney"'. For Aristotle however it is, Ritchie insists, 'equally a rhetorical device' (Ritchie, 1916 [1894]: 31; also Bernadete, 1975: 9). Ritchie takes care to emphasize the significance of Aristotle's reference to the views of Alcidamas on slavery in this context. As we have seen, Aristotle cites what he suggests to his readers is Alcidamas's anti-slavery position as being an example of an appeal to the concept of natural law in recent political argument and debate. But, as Ritchie correctly maintains, it is evident that this is a position which Aristotle himself 'certainly did not hold'. Hence, according to Ritchie, it is clear that the views which Aristotle expresses about natural law in the *Rhetoric* are 'no evidence of his own opinion as a philosopher, but only of current opinion among his contemporaries' (Ritchie, 1916 [1894]: 30).

Both D. G. Ritchie and Bernard Yack have drawn attention to an interesting passage in Aristotle's *Topics* which touches on the issue of whether he himself endorses the notion of natural law as he understands it in his *Rhetoric* (Ritchie, 1916 [1894]: 32; Yack, 1993: 148–9). In the passage in question Aristotle criticizes those who think that we can and should think of the relationship between natural law and civil law, or between natural justice and political justice, by using the metaphor of 'correspondence' or 'reflection'. Aristotle states that sometimes 'the law', that is to say 'political justice', is wrongly said to be the 'measure or image of the things which are by nature just' (Aristotle, 1995a: 140a6–15, 236).[1] However, he goes on, 'such phrases are worse than metaphor', for 'metaphor does make what it signifies to some extent familiar because of the likeness involved', whereas, Aristotle continues, 'this kind of' argument 'makes nothing familiar', for 'there is *no* likeness in virtue of which the law', or political justice, may be said to be 'a measure or image' of anything, let alone of the principles of natural justice. So, Aristotle concludes, 'if a man says that the law is literally a measure or an image, he speaks falsely; for an image is something produced by imitation, and this is not found in the case of the law' (Aristotle, 1995c: 140a6–15, 236). In connection with the views expressed in this passage, Ritchie maintains that 'to call law an image is, so far as I can see, very like the notion of positive human law being a copy or reflection of the Law of Nature' (Ritchie, 1916 [1894]: 32). In this passage from the *Topics*, then, it might be suggested that Aristotle rejects the understanding which, in his view, Alcidamas, Sophocles and Empedocles had of the relationship which exists between natural justice and political justice, or between natural law and civil law. He rejects 'natural law theory' as he thought it was then understood, or as his predecessors had understood it.

Aristotle also, therefore, might be said to have rejected in advance what was later to be the Stoic understanding of the relationship which exists between civil law and natural law. For, according to Cicero in his *De Officiis*, the Stoic view was that 'civil law' is in general copied from nature. As Cicero puts it, 'the civil law is not necessarily also the universal law; but the universal law ought to be also the civil law' (Cicero, 1956 [1913]: III, XVII, 69, 339–40).

Cicero maintains that when a society fails to legally proscribe an action which is intrinsically unjust what this shows is that the positive law of this society is not as accurate an 'image' or representation of the law of nature as it might have been and ought to have been. He argues that, for this very reason, the system of positive law in question might be said to be imperfect. He concedes that 'we possess no substantial, life-like image of true law and genuine justice' (Cicero, 1956 [1913]: III, XVII, 69, 340). Nonetheless, he insists that 'even as it is', that is to say imperfect, this law can be said to be 'drawn from the excellent models which nature and truth afford' (Cicero, 1956 [1913]: III, XVII, 69, 340). In this respect, therefore, the later Stoic understanding of the relationship which exists between natural law and positive law is quite different from that of Aristotle himself, although it is similar to the view which he attributes to Sophocles, Empedocles and Alcidamas.

It should however be noted that, even so, the Stoic view, or rather Cicero's understanding of it, appears to have emerged as a consequence of an engagement with the views of Aristotle. For in the same passage Cicero echoes the views expressed by Aristotle in his *Nicomachean Ethics* about the discipline of politics generally, when he says that, so far the principles of natural law are concerned, all that we possess is 'a mere outline sketch' rather than knowledge of the substantive details (Cicero, 1956 [1913]: III, XVII, 69, 340). The difference between Cicero and Aristotle here is that Cicero seems to have thought that it is possible in principle that we *could* have genuine 'knowledge' of the substantive details relating to the application of the principles of natural law whereas, as we have seen, Aristotle denies that this is possible. That is why he says in the *Nicomachean Ethics* that the principles of natural justice are in one sense at least changeable.

We may conclude from this that the concept of natural law or the law of nature is indeed to be found in Aristotle's *Rhetoric*. Moreover, Aristotle also has a name of linguistic expression which he uses to designate this concept, namely the Greek *nomos koinos*, which translates literally into English as 'universal law' but which, as Aristotle explicitly states, is considered by some to be the 'law of nature'. In his opinion, the concept of natural law is one which is employed by political radicals like Alcidamas. However, Aristotle does not himself endorse this concept as it was then understood by his contemporaries and immediate predecessors. Nor does he approve of their use of it in political argument and debate. On the contrary he is extremely critical of those who do use it in that way, because in his view when they do so their purpose is invariably to criticize existing society, its laws and social institutions, for example the institution of slavery.

In the light of what was said about Aristotle's own doctrine of natural law in Chapter 1, this implies that although Aristotle did himself endorse the concept of natural justice or law in some sense, nevertheless in his view this concept ought not to be associated with a belief in the existence of a higher standard of justice which might be used to critically evaluate existing society, its laws and its institutions. Rather, to the contrary, in Aristotle's own thinking it is to be associated with an attempt to *defend* those institutions against their critics, including those whose critique rests upon an appeal to the very same idea, albeit understood in a different way. Thus the argument between Aristotle and his political opponents was an argument over or around the notion of natural law. It was a struggle for control of the meaning of the concept, within which each side sought to appropriate the concept for its own political purposes.

It is not clear whether Aristotle would have extended this criticism of existing natural law theorizing amongst his predecessors to Plato also, whose views are not mentioned at this point in the *Rhetoric*. Given that he agreed with Plato regarding some things, especially the issues of the natural inequality of human beings and the importance of the principle of geometrical or proportional as opposed to strictly arithmetical equality, one might think that he would not do this. On the other hand though, as we shall see in Chapter 4, Plato does seem to have thought that the there is a principle of justice inhering within the order of nature which might, in certain circumstances, be used to criticize existing social and political institutions. One suspects that Aristotle would have objected to this idea just as much if it were found in the writings of Plato as he would if it were found anywhere else.

Aristotle and the Anonymous Opponents of Slavery

It is well known that in his *Politics* Aristotle offers a defence of slavery (Aristotle, 1995h: 1253b15–1255b15, 1989–1992).[2] It is, he says, clear 'that some men are by nature free, and others slaves, and that for these latter slavery is both expedient and right' (Aristotle, 1995h, 1255a1–2, 1991). At the same time, however, Aristotle also observes in the *Politics* that there are at least some people 'who take the opposite view' to his own. He concedes that amongst his contemporaries and immediate predecessors there were those who maintained that there is no one who is by nature a slave and who insisted that slavery could *not* be defended on the grounds that it is either expedient or right.[3] According to Aristotle, this group of thinkers affirmed 'that the rule of a master over slaves is contrary to nature, and that the distinction between slave and freeman exists by convention only, and not by nature; and being an interference with nature is therefore unjust' (Aristotle, 1995h: 1253b20–23, 1989). Given these remarks from the *Politics*, Richard Kraut's recent claim that Aristotle's defence of slavery should be seen as a reply to certain unnamed opponents who maintained that slavery 'is an unjust institution, lacking a basis in nature and depending entirely upon force for its existence' is not at all surprising (Kraut, 2002: 278; see also Garnsey, 1999: 64–6, 76–7, 238–9.). What *is* surprising is the fact that this interpretation of Aristotle's text has actually been contested by some commentators, for example by Bernard Yack. According to Yack, Aristotle's remarks should *not* be taken as implying that his adversaries were opposed to slavery on moral or any other grounds. On the contrary, they were in favour of it. Rather, in Yack's view, what Aristotle's opponents rejected is the idea that slavery could be defended by arguing that it is a natural institution. As Yack presents it, the view of Aristotle's opponents in this ancient debate was that slavery *could* be morally justified, but in a manner different from that suggested by Aristotle, by appealing to the idea of 'convention' rather than to that of 'nature' (Yack, 1993: 139). In my opinion this interpretation of the issue at stake in the ancient debate on slavery is inconsistent with the wording of the text of Aristotle's *Politics* cited earlier (Aristotle, 1995g: 1253b20–23).

It is true that Aristotle does not name these anonymous opponents of slavery in the *Politics*. Nevertheless, as Moses Finley has noted, his comments there clearly imply the existence of a body of writings 'which denied that slavery was a natural institution' (Finley, 1983: 120). Indeed, elsewhere, having just cited the Roman jurist Florentinus, who maintained that 'slavery is an institution of the *ius gentium* (law of nations) whereby someone is subject to the *dominium* of another, contrary to nature', Finley observes that this view 'and even sharper formulations' of it could 'be traced back to the Sophistic literature of the fifth century BC, and, in a less formal way, to Greek tragedy' (Finley, 1981: 104). Similarly, G. E. M. de Sainte Croix once observed that for readers of the *Politics* today they are 'the unnamed thinkers of the fifth and fourth century' who are said by Aristotle to have declared that slavery 'was contrary to nature and wrong' (de Sainte Croix, 1983: 422). And Malcolm Schofield has argued, more recently, that these remarks suggest that in Aristotle's opinion such anti-slavery ideas were 'nowadays supposed true' by a significant number of Athenian citizens at the time when the *Politics* was written (Schofield, 1990: 8, 23). Indeed, Gilbert Murray once claimed that the view that slavery is contrary to nature 'was held by most Greek philosophers' in the Fourth Century (Murray, 1913: 138), although he does not say whether, in his view, the philosophers in question also thought that, for this very reason, slavery is unjust.

However, establishing the identity of Aristotle's adversaries in this ancient debate is by no means an easy task. As Fred D. Miller Jr. has pointed out, although it certainly does exist, 'the evidence for early criticism of slavery' is, nonetheless, 'admittedly scarce and tentative' (Miller Jr., 1997: 109). For example, despite his acknowledgement of the existence of these anonymous opponents of slavery, Sainte Croix could not name any of the possible candidates. As he once put it, 'the only identifiable Greek' author 'I know in whom we find a reflection of the argument that slavery can be "contrary to nature" is Philo, the Hellenised Jew who wrote at Alexandria during the first half-century of the Christian era' (de Sainte Croix, 1983: 422; see also Garnsey, 1999: 80–85, 240). Similarly, although he did not actually deny their existence, Moses Finley also acknowledged that relevant passages from the writings of these ancient critics of slavery are 'hard to find in the surviving literature' (Finley, 1983: 120). Indeed, Finley could think of only one classical author whose candidacy for membership of this group rests on more than a mere possibility, the tragic poet Euripides.[4]

Perhaps because of this problem of identification, and despite Aristotle's clear testimony to the contrary that such a group did in fact exist in ancient Athens, a number of commentators have felt confident enough to deny outright that *anyone* at all was opposed to slavery in the ancient world – including presumably, though in my view somewhat implausibly, the slaves themselves. As Neal Wood and Ellen Meiksins Wood have rightly claimed, although it 'is impossible to determine' what 'the slaves themselves thought' of their own situation, it would 'be childish to think that they were in any way satisfied with their condition of bondage' (Wood and Wood, 1978: 49). Indeed, although inconsistently with the views he expresses on the subject elsewhere, de Sainte Croix once maintained that 'virtually no objection was ever raised in antiquity to slavery as an institution' (de Saint Croix, 1983: 284). Malcolm Bull has asserted that 'no one appears to have advocated the abolition of slavery in the ancient world' (Bull, 1998: 99). And Joseph Vogt has argued that fifth-century Greeks accepted slavery 'without reservation' and that 'no one in antiquity would have found fault with such a system'. Indeed, in his view, they 'could not imagine' a life without slaves. This was true, Vogt maintains, even of 'the most enlightened minds' (Vogt, 1974a: 3, 13, 24, 192). Arguing along the same lines, R. G. Mulgan once claimed that Aristotle, like '*all* ancient Greeks', had 'little conception of individual or human rights, of obligations which are due to individuals because they are individual human beings' (Mulgan, 1977: 33). And Malcolm Schofield has argued that *no* Athenian would 'have supposed that it was obvious that human beings had equal rights simply as much as they were human' (Schofield, 1996: 833). Nor presumably, in Schofield's view, would any Athenian have considered slavery to be morally wrong because it conflicts with a universally valid ethical principle stating that all human beings are by nature equal. These extreme claims are also echoed by Moses Finley, when he says (inconsistently) that 'how completely the Greeks always took slavery for granted as one of the facts of human existence is abundantly evident to anyone who has read their literature' (Finley, 1981: 97); that in classical antiquity 'everyone was agreed that the institution must be preserved' (Finley, 1983: 121–22); and that 'nothing illustrates more perfectly' than this literature the complete 'inability of the ancient world to imagine that there could be a civilized society without slaves' (Finley, 1981: 104–5).[5]

The claims just cited are all strong claims – claims which suggest that there is a tendency for some commentators to assume that the belief that any ancient Greek writer was, or even could in principle have been, opposed to slavery on ethical grounds *must* be historically anachronistic. According to this line of reasoning, it seems obvious that any such judgment necessarily involves our reading back into the past the egalitarian ethical values of the modern era. It is clear however, in the light of the evidence provided by Aristotle's explicit remarks on this subject in the *Politics*, that this assumption of historical anachronism, together with the exaggerated claims associated with it referred to above, are not in fact supported by the available historical evidence. It may be difficult for us now to identify these anonymous opponents of slavery in ancient Athens but, assuming that Aristotle is a reliable source, we can surely be confident that they did at least exist. And we can also infer how, according to Aristotle, they argued when they criticized the institution of slavery.

An obvious starting point for anyone interested in speculating about the identities of Aristotle's adversaries in this debate over the rights and wrongs of slavery is Aristotle's other writings, especially the *Rhetoric*, an examination of which does prove fruitful. For example, as we have seen, it is in this text that Aristotle refers to the Sophist Alcidamas, a pupil of Gorgias, in this connection; although, admittedly, the reference is highly compressed. Aristotle simply refers his readers to what 'Alcidamas says in his Messianic Oration . . . [etc., etc]'. It is, in my view, extremely interesting that when citing the views of Alcidamas in the *Rhetoric* Aristotle does not consider it to be necessary to present his selected quotation in full. Presumably he thought that the views of Alcidamas on the subject of slavery were so well known at the time that it was not necessary for him to do so. Given our own lack of familiarity with the writings of Alcidamas this omission would undoubtedly have been a problem for anyone today who is interested in the interpretation of Aristotle's views on natural law. We are, however, extremely fortunate because a later scholiast, commenting on the *Rhetoric*, took the trouble to complete the unfinished sentence for us. The scholiast tells us that the original words of Alcidamas to which Aristotle is referring in this incomplete sentence were: 'God has left all men free; nature has made no man a slave' (Aristotle, 1995i: 1373b5–20, 2187; see also Gagarin and Woodruff, 1995: 276). E. R. Dodds once claimed that these remarks of Alcidamas constitute 'the first explicit condemnation of slavery which has come down to us' from the ancient world (Dodds, 1973a: 101; see also Schlaifer, 1968: 200).

Aristotle does not mention Alcidamas by name in the *Politics*, but in the light of the remarks from the *Rhetoric* cited above, it is difficult to believe that he did not have Alcidamas in mind when talking about the 'anonymous opponents of slavery' there. Although whether he correctly represents the views of Alcidamas, or indeed those of Empedocles and Sophocles, is of course another matter entirely. For present purposes, however, the important point to note is that Aristotle appears to have thought that these ancients opponents of slavery, whoever they were, did employ the concept of natural law or 'the law of nature', even if they did not possess a linguistic expression with which to designate that concept.

Despite the exaggerated claims made by some commentators referred to earlier, the existence of at least some intellectuals in classical antiquity who we might legitimately suppose were opposed to slavery on moral grounds, and specifically on the grounds that it is unjust because it conflicts with the 'law of nature', understood in an ethical sense, is something which has been noted by a significant number of others.[6] In addition to Alcidamas the list of possible thinkers who are usually associated with this 'anti-slavery' position includes the names of Euripides (485–406 BCE), Antiphon (480–411 BCE), Hippias, Lycophron and (later) Philemon. Euripides, for example, puts into the mouths of one of the characters in his *Phoenician Women* the view that 'nature gave to men the law of equal rights' (Euripides, 1972: 538, 254). And in his play *Ion* he has another character state that 'it's only the name of slave that carries disgrace with it; in every other point a loyal slave is as good as a free man' (Euripides, 1967: 854, 61).

As Margaret Reesor has noted, 'the concept of natural law', understood in the ethical sense, was probably used by both Antiphon and Hippias' (Reesor, 1951: 9). Antiphon, for example, is recorded as having made the remarkable assertion that 'by nature there is nothing at all in our constitutions to differentiate foreigners and Greeks'. In his view, 'we can consider those natural qualities which are essential to all human beings and with which we are all equally endowed, and we find that in the case of all these qualities there is nothing to tell any of us apart as foreigner or Greek. For we all breathe the air through our mouths and nostrils, laugh when our minds feel pleasure or cry when we are distressed; we hear sounds with our ears; we see with our eyes thanks to day light; we work with our hands, and walk with our feet' (Waterfield, 2000: 264; also Gagarin and Woodruff, 1995: 245). In short, it appears that Antiphon held that all human beings are by nature equal in at least some fundamentally important and ethically significant respects. This casts doubt on the claim, made for example by C. H. McIlwain, that 'the idea of the equality of men is the profoundest contribution of the *Stoics* to political thought' (McIlwain, 1932: 115). It suggests that it is not with the Stoics that the notion of the natural equality of mankind came into existence. It also suggests that the transition from the thinking about questions of ethics and politics that we find in classical Athens to that later associated with Stoicism is not as radical or discontinuous as some commentators think. I say more about this issue in the Conclusion.

It may be suggested that it is precisely because Antiphon thought that certain existing laws and conventions conflicted with the requirements of this principle of natural equality that he maintained that 'most things that are just according to law' are in fact 'inimical to nature' (Gagarin and Woodruff, 1995: 245–6). Given these remarks it is not too surprising that Robin Waterfield has argued that Antiphon should be considered to be a fifth-century Athenian 'radical' who championed the claims of 'nature' over those of law and convention. According to Waterfield, Antiphon arrives at conclusions which, for this reason, 'would have seemed highly shocking and unusual' to his contemporaries' (Waterfield, 2000: 259; see also Sabine, 1973a: 43; Saunders, 1977–78). It must be conceded, as T. J. Saunders has noted, that there is heated debate around the issue of how these remarks of Antiphon should be interpreted (Saunders, 1977–78: 215). It is true that some commentators, including Glen R. Morrow, have associated them with the views of Plato's Callicles (Morrow, 1948: 26–7; see also Gagarin, 2002), and hence with a form of nihilistic 'anarchism' (Furley, 1981). For example, R. B. Levinson has claimed that Antiphon was an 'advocate of self-regarding egoism' or an 'evangelist' for 'self-regarding expediency'. It is behaviour of that kind which Antiphon considered to be both 'natural' and contrary to 'law'. According to Levinson, then, Antiphon had no moral beliefs at all. On the contrary, like Callicles (as his views are usually understood), Antiphon's philosophy of life was 'founded', Levinson claims, 'on the wreck of morality' (Levinson, 1953a: 144–6). Nor is Levinson alone in thinking this. For example D. J. Furley has claimed that for Antiphon the important distinction is 'not between justice as obeying the law and justice as following nature, but rather between justice always construed as obedience to the law, and respect for the claims of nature' (Furley, 1981: 83). Furley insists that in the surviving fragments Antiphon 'is not proposing a different justice' based on nature but, rather, 'opposing justice' itself 'to nature' (Furley, 1981: 84). There is, Furley insists, 'no trace' in the fragments of Antiphon 'contrasting natural justice' to 'legal justice'. Indeed, according to Furley, 'the epithet "legal"', when characterizing justice is, for Antiphon, 'strictly redundant' (Furley, 1981: 86).[7]

According to Saunders, however, other commentators have taken a very different view, reading Antiphon's criticisms of law to be 'essentially ethical' and therefore 'not anarchistic' at all, at least not in the nihilistic sense of the term. Saunders himself agrees with this 'ethical' reading of Antiphon. In his opinion, Antiphon's 'attack on existing laws is made, *not* on the grounds that they are laws' only, but rather on the grounds that the laws in question 'are hostile to nature' (Saunders, 1977–78: 227). He suggests therefore that Antiphon was not opposed to *all* laws, but only to those laws which he considered to be contrary to nature. In Saunders' opinion, then, there is a big difference between the views of Antiphon and those of Plato's Callicles precisely because Antiphon did subscribe to the notion of a 'law of nature', understood in an ethical sense, whereas Plato's Callicles does not. A similar view is also taken by Martin Ostwald, who has suggested that 'it is by no means clear' that Antiphon's polemic involves a 'complete rejection of all *nomoi*'. On the contrary, Ostwald maintains, 'there are good reasons to believe that the attack is not directed at *nomoi* as such' but, rather, at those who 'in attributing too absolute a value to their own *nomoi*, fail to consider the fact that *phusis* accords no higher rank to one society or ethnic group over another' (Ostwald, 1990: 301). Indeed according to Gerard Pendrick, although he himself does not accept it, the ethical 'natural law' reading of Antiphon represents 'the consensus view' amongst modern commentators (Pendrick, 2002: 61).[8]

Such views have also been attributed to Hippias. According to Plato, in his *Protagoras* Hippias was of the opinion that 'by nature like is kin to like, but custom is a tyrant over human beings and forces many things on us that are contrary to nature' (Plato, 1952 [1924]: 337d–338b, 180–83; see also Waterfield, 2000: 255; Gagarin and Woodruff, 216). Similarly, Xenophon in his *Memorabilia* presents his readers with a dialogue between Hippias and Socrates, in which Socrates defends the traditional view that justice is a matter of following the laws or *nomoi* of one's own *polis* and Hippias responds by suggesting, to the contrary, that justice is a matter of obeying the 'unwritten laws' (αγραφοι νομοι, *agraphoi nomoi*) of the Gods (Ehrenberg, 1954b; Ostwald, 1973). This is what led Joseph Vogt to the conclusion that Hippias 'postulated the existence of natural justice, and declared that it was contrary to such natural justice for one man to be the master of another' (Vogt, 1974a: 14). It is true that, as Xenophon represents his views, Hippias does not connect this notion of an 'unwritten law' with the idea of a 'law of nature', as Aristotle was later to do in his *Rhetoric.* Nor does Aristotle name Hippias in the *Rhetoric* as being one of his predecessors who employed the concept of natural law. Nevertheless, given what Plato and Xenophon say about Hippias and his beliefs, it is not at all surprising that some modern commentators have concluded that he was indeed an early advocate of the notion of a 'law of nature', construed in an ethical sense. W. K. C. Guthrie, for example, has claimed that Hippias was one of those 'fifth century supporters of the unwritten laws' who were 'on the side of *physis* against the limitations and errors of positive *nomoi*' (Guthrie, 1971a: 118).

Lycophron, also, is alleged to have maintained that 'the beauty of high birth (*eugenia*) is not evident; its nobility exists only in the word' (Gagarin and Woodruff, 1995: 275). And Philemon is said to have claimed, in words which echo those of Alcidamas, that 'even if someone is a slave, he has the same flesh; by nature no one was ever born a slave' (Schofield, 1990: 5; Brunt, 1993: 351; Schlaifer, 1968: 200). It is remarks like this that led Karl Popper to go so far as to make the exaggerated claim that there was a veritable 'anti-slavery movement' in fifth-century Athens, a movement which he alleges 'came very close to abolishing slavery at this time' (Popper, 1969b: 43; also Havelock, 1964: 350; and, for the contrary view, Levinson, 1954: 141–67). According to Popper, there is 'very strong evidence that the fifth-century Athenian movement against slavery was not confined to a few intellectualists like is Euripides, Alcidamas, Lycophron, Antiphon, Hippias, etc., but that 'it had considerable practical success' (Popper, 1969b: 278–79). Popper, Eric Havelock and more recently Peter Garnsey have all argued that if those who opposed slavery were completely unsuccessful in their efforts to influence popular opinion it would be difficult for us to explain why conservatively minded thinkers like Aristotle, who defended this institution, should have felt it necessary to attempt to discredit them and their opinions (Popper, 1969b: 278–79; Havelock, 1964: 7; Garnsey, 1999: 12, 76–7, 239; see also Strauss, 1968b). As Garnsey has put it, Aristotle certainly thought that this critique of slavery 'was sufficiently dangerous to warrant a counter attack' (Garnsey, 1999: 77; also 238–39). Indeed, in Garnsey's opinion, this was the principal motivation behind Aristotle's attempt to develop a theory of natural slavery in the *Politics* (Garnsey, 1999: 12).

George Cambiano has made a systematic attempt to refute the claim that we can be confident that Alcidamas, Antiphon, Euripides, Hippias and Lycophron are the opponents of slavery to whom Aristotle is referring in the *Politics* (Cambiano, 1987: 24–5, 30–1, 37–9). However, Cambiano does not suggest an alternative list of possible candidates of his own. At the same time, though, neither does he question the veracity of Aristotle's assertion that there was indeed a group in ancient Athens which criticized slavery because it is contrary to nature and unjust. In Cambiano's work, therefore, the problem of identifying the ancient opponents of slavery is simply left hanging. The approach adopted by Cambiano is certainly a cautious one, which may seem refreshing to some if it is compared with the somewhat cavalier attitude adopted by Popper when talking about the same subject. Nevertheless, it seems to me that Cambiano is excessively cautious. No doubt each of these diametrically opposed judgments about the presence or absence of anti-slavery ideas in fifth-century Athenian politics, and the degree of support which these ideas received, is exaggerated. As Levinson notes, Popper's claim is seriously weakened by the fact that he does not actually provide his readers with the 'very strong evidence' to which he refers when making it. Nevertheless, it seems to me that the testimony of Aristotle, in the *Politics* and the *Rhetoric*, suggests that even if Popper was exaggerating when he claimed that there was an 'anti-slavery movement' in fifth-century Athens, it might still legitimately be argued that on the issue of the justice or injustice of slavery Alcidamas was not a completely isolated figure. As H. C. Baldry has maintained, it does not seem unreasonable to suppose that there were at least '*some* thinkers at this time whose views on the subject were more advanced than were those of most Greeks for generations to come' (Baldry, 1965: 39; see also Garnsey, 1999: 76–7, 238–9). It may be true, as Baldry concedes, that 'it was only a small minority – perhaps only a few outstanding intellects – who moved by various paths in the opposite direction to the mainstream of contemporary opinion towards the idea of the human race as a unity' (Baldry, 1965: 24), but again that is hardly the point. The important point, here, is that Aristotle explicitly indicates in his *Politics* that in his rejection of slavery Alcidamas did not stand alone. He was not the only one who condemned slavery as both contrary to nature and unjust, and who (at least implicitly) based that condemnation on the principle that all human beings are by nature equal. The testimony provided by the *Rhetoric* suggests that, as Aristotle understood them, ancient opponents of slavery such as Alcidamas took the view that the moral law which asserts that, because they are equals, all human beings ought to be treated equally, possesses a 'natural' and not a merely 'conventional' character. According to these thinkers, therefore, this principle constitutes a universally valid ethical truth.

It may well be the ideas associated with this particular branch of the Sophistic movement which Paul Sigmund had in mind when he claimed that, contrary to the conventional understanding of the ethical views associated with Sophism, nature was 'regarded as a source of norms' by at least some of the Sophists, and that in the fifth century BCE this group of Sophists came to challenge 'the prevailing identification of existing laws with justice and nature' (Sigmund, 1971: 2–3, 5–6; also Zeller, 1997: 80, 86, 89–90). If there is anything at all in this argument it appears that, as Aristotle seems to have thought, and contrary to the claims of Eric Havelock (Havelock, 1964: 6, 9–13, 17–20, 26–9, 32), at least some of the Sophists were not relativists but objectivists so far as questions of ethics are concerned (Classen, 1981). Indeed, to the extent that this group of Sophists thought that there are objective ethical principles (or principles of natural law) which are eternally and universally valid, they adopted a position very similar to that later adopted by Plato and Aristotle in the fourth century – the crucially important difference between the two being, of course, that these early advocates of natural law disagreed with their more illustrious successors regarding the question of how the ethical concepts associated with these principles are to be interpreted and applied, and hence also regarding the practical political significance of any commitment to the idea of such a natural law.

More important for our present purposes, however, the existence of this group of thinkers supports the view that even in the fifth century BCE some educated Athenians had already begun the process of uniting the concepts of *physis* and *nomos* in a manner which commentators like W. K. C. Guthrie and G. L. Morrow have associated with the fourth century only. The members of the alleged fifth century 'anti-slavery movement' referred to by Popper appeal (at least implicitly) to the idea of natural justice, or to a natural law within the sphere of ethics and politics. They suggest that it is possible for existing conventions to be critically evaluated by contrasting them with the requirements of this natural law. Indeed, as Guthrie himself and others have pointed out, the critical attitude of this group of thinkers towards the institution of slavery indicates the presence in fifth-century Athens of a universalist, cosmopolitan, rationalist and humanitarian approach to questions of ethics and politics, of the kind which was later to be associated with the natural law theory of the Stoics (Guthrie, 1971: 2, 118; see also Baldry, 1965: 39-45; Ritchie, 1916 [1894]: 25, 30; Schlaifer, 1968: 169–71; Zeller, 1997: 86, 89–90).

There is, then, evidence to support the view that already in Athens in the fifth century BCE there were at least some intellectuals who employed what are recognizably natural law arguments to defend their claim that, as again Guthrie puts it, 'distinctions based on race, noble birth, social status or wealth, and institutions such as slavery, had no basis in *nature* but were only by *nomos*' (Guthrie, 1971: 118). These were, Guthrie points out, 'revolutionary ideas of incalculable potency' (Guthrie, 1971: 118). Long ago Sir Ernest Barker described the proponents of these ideas as a 'radical school' of later Sophists which had 'divorced nature from convention' and which, as a result, had 'become revolutionary in its tenets' (Barker, 1960a: 86, 253). Similarly, D. G. Ritchie also once argued that these radical views about the equality of all human beings represented 'an attack on the very basis of ancient society' (Ritchie, 1895: 25-6). It is for this reason, it may be conjectured, that Aristotle was so opposed to them in his *Politics*.

Aristotle and Sophocles' *Antigone*

If one looks at the literature which discusses the history of the concept of natural law one often finds this history being traced back as far as the political thought of the ancient Greeks in the fifth century BCE, and especially to the following famous lines from the *Antigone*:

> That order (χηρυξαs) did not come from God. Justice,
> That dwells with the gods below, knows no such law.
> I did not think your edicts (χηρυγματα) strong enough
> To overrule the unwritten unalterable laws (νομιμα)
> Of God and heaven, you only being a man.
> They are not of yesterday or today, but everlasting,
> Though where they came from, none of us can tell.
> Guilty of their transgression before God
> I cannot be, for any man on earth.
> Sophocles, *Antigone* (450–461) (Watling, 1970, 138)

This passage is often used as evidence to support the claim that the idea of natural law as it came to be understood by Cicero and the Stoics, as a higher principle of universally valid, absolute justice by means of which individuals might critically evaluate the positive laws of the particular society in which they live, does not actually originate with them at all, but is clearly to be found in the earlier political thought and experience of classical Greek civilization, even before Plato and Aristotle, in the Athenian democracy under Pericles during the fifth century BCE. It is here, or so it is alleged, that the 'initial baptism' of the concept of natural law in Saul Kripke's sense is to be discerned (Kripke, 1988: 96). For example, according to Jacques Maritain, the concept of natural law goes back 'to the great moralists of antiquity and its great poets, particularly Sophocles'. For Maritain, 'Antigone is the eternal heroine of natural law, which the ancients called the unwritten law' (Maritain, 1942: 78). Similarly,

George H. Sabine has claimed that Sophocles' 'identification of nature with the law of God' in the *Antigone*, combined with his contrast 'of convention with the truly right' was 'destined to become almost a formula for the criticism of abuses, a role in which the law of nature has appeared again and again in the later history of political thought' (Sabine, 1973a: 42–3). Sabine maintains that the distinction between φυσις and νομος or nature and convention which (in his view) lies at the heart of the play provides Antigone, as an individual, with an argument to justify her conscientious disobedience to the laws of her *polis*. Sabine tells us that in the fifth century BCE, 'as frequently it has done since', this distinction comes to 'form the defense of the rebel, in the name of a higher law, against the standing conventions and the existing laws of society' (Sabine, 1973a: 42–3).[9]

This natural law reading of Sophocles' *Antigone* has a very long pedigree. As both Gerard Watson and B. M. W. Knox have noted, it can be traced back to Aristotle's *Rhetoric*. In an article on the early history of natural law Watson concurs not only with what he takes to be Aristotle's claim in the *Rhetoric* that 'the law of nature entitles us on occasion to ignore the narrow prescriptions of particular law codes', but also with Aristotle's alleged further claim that it 'was on this' that Antigone 'based her well known response to Creon's decree in the play of Sophocles'. Watson claims that according to Aristotle, Antigone 'knows that she is not speaking of law in the ordinary sense', that is of traditional or customary law, but rather of conscience, or 'the individual's consciousness of what is due to him (*sic*) in a particular situation' (Watson, 1966: 67). The Aristotelian source of this view of the origins of the concept of natural law, and indeed of this particular interpretation of Sophocles' *Antigone*, has also been emphasized by Knox, who has rightly observed that 'the ancient authority for treating Antigone's speech as a formulation of "natural" law' (an interpretation which Knox himself rejects) is Aristotle, and specifically Aristotle's *Rhetoric* (Knox, 1983: 96–7).

It is arguable, then, that it was Aristotle who first claimed that the significance of Sophocles' *Antigone* is that for some people (perhaps not Aristotle himself) it symbolically represents the conflict between natural law and positive law, or the conflict between φυσις and νομος, which was the subject of heated debate in fifth-century Athens. As we have seen, in the *Rhetoric* Aristotle refers explicitly to the *Antigone* in this context. In particular, he cites the lines quoted above, in which Antigone argues that it was right for her to bury her brother Polyneices despite the fact that such an action had been forbidden by an edict of her uncle, King Creon, and hence by human positive law. According to Aristotle, the reading of the *Antigone* in which he is interested maintains that the reason which Sophocles puts into the mouth of Antigone to justify her act of disobedience is that it was 'just by nature'. It was, therefore, an action which ought to have been performed 'in spite of the prohibition' in question (Aristotle, 1995i: 1373a10–15). As Aristotle himself puts it in the *Rhetoric*, for those who read the *Antigone* in this way 'there is a certain natural and universal right and wrong, which all men divine, even if they have no intercourse or covenant with each other'. Aristotle then goes on to illustrate this point by using the example of the *Antigone*: just 'as', he says, 'in Sophocles, Antigone is found saying that, in spite of the interdict, it is right to bury Polyneices, this being naturally right' (Aristotle, 1995i: 1373b10–15).

However, the natural law reading of the *Antigone* which Aristotle discusses in the *Rhetoric* is open to obvious criticism. For although there certainly was a debate in the fifth century between the defenders of the respective principles of *physis* and *nomos*; and although it is also correct that Sophocles' *Antigone* might be interpreted as representing, through the characters of Antigone and Creon, the symbolic confrontation of divine or unwritten law with human law, understood specifically as an edict or enacted decree; nevertheless there is no reason why these two things should be connected together so that the divine or unwritten law to which Antigone appeals in the play becomes identical with the principle of *physis* whilst the written law or enacted decree of Creon becomes identical with the principle of *nomos*. Certainly, there is no evidence from within the play itself which supports such an identification. As a number of commentators have pointed out, what is most conspicuous about the play is the fact that Antigone does *not* refer explicitly to the laws of the gods as being laws of nature. Bernice Hamilton, for example, rightly insists that in the play Antigone 'is in fact appealing from made law to sacred custom', which, later on, was 'so often to be confused with natural law'. It is true, Hamilton acknowledges, that for Antigone (and no doubt for Sophocles) 'divine justice' is 'immutable and everlasting'. In Hamilton's opinion, however, what is especially significant about the play is the fact that 'the word "natural" does not appear' anywhere in the passage which is usually cited in support of the view that Antigone's argument involves an appeal to natural law (Hamilton, 1965: 38). This is also the view of Paul E. Sigmund. Sigmund points out that in the *Rhetoric* Aristotle cites *Antigone* in support for what appears to be a claim that there is such a thing as an 'eternal and unwritten law'. He also notes that Aristotle goes on to identify this unwritten law with the natural law. In Sigmund's view, however, Aristotle is quite wrong to do this. For it is evident that 'the actual issue – the burial of a brother – involves a religious and ceremonial law rather than an appeal to nature' (Sigmund, 1971, 10).[10]

It could be argued, then, that in the *Antigone* Sophocles does not have his central character say anything which suggests that the divine law which commands her to bury her dead brother is one which is natural in the specific sense usually associated with the concept of natural law, and in the sense in which Aristotle understands the term in the *Rhetoric*. For this is usually thought of in the Stoic manner, as implying an appeal to a universally valid, cosmopolitan principle of justice, which is discoverable by the faculty of reason and which is considered to be applicable to all human beings at all times and in all places. But there is no evidence in the play itself which would support our going beyond the view that for Antigone (and perhaps also for Sophocles) it is the immemorial laws, customs and traditions of the particular community of which one happens to be a member, which are considered to be sanctioned by the gods and therefore divine.

It is not unreasonable to consider the relevance of Sophocles' own political beliefs for any attempt to interpret the political message of the *Antigone*. As I have noted, some commentators agree with the view, referred to by Aristotle, that Sophocles subscribed to the basic assumptions of natural law theory. On this view, Sophocles was a humanist and a cosmopolitan thinker, who was committed to the idea that there are certain universally valid principles of justice which are valid for all human beings in all societies everywhere (Baldry, 1965: 31–2, 37; Barker, 1960b: 65; Havelock, 1964: 26–7; Vogt, 1974b: 1–2; Whitman, 1951). Other commentators, however, have argued against this assessment of Sophocles' political outlook. For example, Victor Ehrenberg, Karl Popper and Francis Wormuth have all maintained that so far as the key debates in fifth-century Athenian politics are concerned Sophocles' position was essentially aristocratic, backward looking and again fundamentally religious, rather than democratic, forward looking and secular or philosophical. According to these commentators, despite Aristotle's suggestion to the contrary, Sophocles would not in fact have been at all sympathetic towards natural law arguments of the sort which are discussed in the *Rhetoric*, or towards the humanist assumptions with which such arguments are usually associated (Ehrenberg, 1954a: 25, 64, 138, 140, 153, 163–6; Popper, 1969a: 185, 299; Wormuth, 1948: 54).

From this point of view, the natural law interpretation of the *Antigone* referred to by Aristotle secularizes Sophocles' approach to politics and therefore ignores completely the overriding importance which Sophocles attaches to religion and to the role of the gods in human affairs. It fails to take into account Sophocles' hostility to the idea, usually associated with Presocratic philosophy, that mankind might be able to provide an entirely rationalistic account of the world generally, and specifically of human society – an account within which the gods have no part to play (Ehrenberg, 1954a: 23–8). Indeed, as C. Segal has argued, Sophocles' intentions in writing the *Antigone* might be construed as an attempted qualification of 'the rational optimism of the fifth century "enlightenment"' (Segal, 1964: 63). For this reason Francis Wormuth has rightly insisted that 'the unwritten law of Sophocles' in the *Antigone* is in fact 'the complete opposite of M. Maritain's natural law'. In Wormuth's view, Sophocles employed the concept of 'unwritten law' (αγραφος νομος, *agraphos nomos*) as 'a conscious symbol of opposition to the new humane and rationalistic spirit' presented by more radical figures such as the poet Euripides in fifth-century Athenian politics (Wormuth, 1948: 54; also Vogt, 1974b: 17). Mario Attilio Levi has noted that for Sophocles it is invariably the faculty of 'reason', to which philosophers generally attach so much importance, which is the root cause of all human pride or *hybris* and which represents the fundamental 'stumbling block to mankind' when it comes to establishing solutions to the fundamental questions of ethics and politics (Attilio Levi, 1965: 111; also Ehrenberg, 1954a: 65–6; Segal, 1964: 63).

An important piece of evidence for those who maintain that Sophocles was a humanist is the famous 'ode to man' which Sophocles puts into the mouths of the chorus in the *Antigone* (335–375), and which begins with the lines: 'Wonders (δεινα) are many on earth, and the greatest of these | Is man'. There then follows an impressive list of mankind's achievements, including not only the development of language but also equally impressive developments in navigation, agriculture, in social organization and in politics. However, as a number of other commentators have pointed out, what those who appeal to this ode in defence of their view that Sophocles is a humanist fail to notice is the sting which he puts into its tail. The Greek word which Sophocles uses here to capture the more positive aspects of man's historical development and which is so often translated as 'wondrous' is δεινοτερον. But there is an ambiguity about this term. For it can also be translated as 'awful' or 'dangerous'. For these commentators the ode is in fact a warning to the audience that in the end man remains a relatively insignificant part of the divine order of the cosmos.[11] Great though the development of human knowledge and capacities has been, nevertheless man must use this knowledge wisely and no one should get ideas 'above his station'.

For Sophocles the overriding principle in ethics and politics appears to have been something like that of 'my station and its duties'. Each one of us must respect the principles in accordance with which the cosmos has been divinely ordered. In so far as these principles have an application to politics, this implies that we must respect the institutions, customs and traditions of our own *polis*, for these also have been divinely ordained and sanctioned. Whoever fails to respect these things suffers from the sin of *hybris*. More than one commentator has argued that this is one of the principal political concerns of Sophocles, not only in the *Antigone* but also in *Oedipus Rex* (Attilio Levi, 1965: 111; Bernadete, 1975: 29–30; Lesky, 1978: 95; Torrance, 1965: 269–327; Winnington-Ingram, 1980: 118–19). This concern for hybris explains the lines which Sophocles employs to bring the ode to man to a conclusion: 'O wondrous subtlety of man, that draws | To good or evil ways! Great honour is given | And power to him who upholdeth his country's laws | And the justice of heaven. | But he that, too rashly daring, walks in sin | In solitary pride (hybris) to his life's end. | At door of mine shall never enter in | To call me friend' (365–75) (Sophocles, 1970: 136).

The concept of humanism is closely related to the question of whether all human beings are by nature equal, which was one of the key political questions in Periclean Athens. The answer that the ancient Athenians gave to this question determined their attitude towards both democracy and slavery, the two dominant institutions in their social and political life in the fourth and fifth centuries. We have seen that the institution of slavery, in particular, was the subject of some debate at this time (Aristotle, 1995h: 1253b15–1255b15, 1989–1992; Cambiano, 1987; Saunders, 1984; Schofield, 1990: 23–7). It is arguable that this question of the natural equality or inequality of human beings, and hence of the rights and wrongs of slavery, is logically connected to the further question of whether there is such a thing as natural law. For the concept of natural law can be associated with the idea that there is at least one universally valid ethical principle which is applicable to all human beings in all times and in all places. As Aristotle implies in his *Rhetoric*, the claim that such a natural law exists appears to make no sense at all unless we assume that all human beings are indeed by nature equal. It is for precisely this reason that, in the *Rhetoric*, Aristotle cites the Sophist Alcidamas, together with both Sophocles and Empedocles, as an example of someone who adopts a natural law approach to questions of ethics and politics. As Aristotle understood him, Alcidamas appears to have maintained that the institution of slavery contradicts rather than conforms to the principle of equity, which is the most fundamental principle of natural justice. This principle states that those who are equal ought to be treated equally in relevantly similar circumstances. The difference between Alcidamas and Aristotle, as again Aristotle appears to have understood him, is that Alcidamas took the view that all human beings *are* by nature equal, and therefore that slavery is necessarily unjust, whereas Aristotle did not.

It is fruitful to link a discussion of the politics of Sophocles' *Antigone*, and especially Sophocles' attitude towards the concept of natural law, with these fifth-century political debates, and especially the debate over slavery. Was Sophocles a humanist in the sense that, like Alcidamas, he too believed in the natural equality of all human beings, and hence that slavery is wrong because it conflicts with the requirements of a fundamental principle of natural law? One of the figures singled out by Karl Popper as being a humanist in this particular sense, and consequently another fifth-century opponent of slavery, is the poet Euripides. At the same time, however, Popper specifically contrasts Euripides' attitude towards slavery with that of Sophocles who was, he claims, adamantly opposed to it. According to Popper, Sophocles response to Euripides was to insist that it is wrong that 'the lowly born should flourish, while the brave and nobly born are unfortunate' (Popper, 1969a: 299). This assessment of Sophocles' attitude is also held by Robin Waterfield, who uses Sophocles, in particular, as an example of someone who was opposed to the doctrines of fifth-century political radicals such as the Sophist Antiphon. According to Waterfield, it is Antiphon and *not* Sophocles who was an ardent 'champion of nature over law and convention'. He arrived at what can only be described as 'remarkable conclusions for a Fifth Century Greek', conclusions which, 'however familiar in today's liberal and pluralistic western societies, would have seemed highly shocking and unusual' to contemporaries such as Sophocles.

For as we saw earlier, and arguably against those who thought like Sophocles, Antiphon maintained, in the words of Waterfield, that 'natural law is so much more essential than man made law'; that 'there is nothing essential or natural to distinguish Greeks from foreigners'; and that 'all such distinctions', including therefore the distinction between master and slave, 'are matters of convention' only. Waterfield maintains that Sophocles' position with respect to this particular issue was in fact 'exactly the opposite' of that of Antiphon. For in Sophocles' opinion 'men are born different', that is to say unequal, and it is law which in some cases 'makes them similar' and hence in one sense at least equal, although only artificially so (Waterfield, 2000: 259).

Much the same view is also taken by Robert Schlaifer. According to Schlaifer, despite the fact that 'already attacks on the institution [of slavery] were commencing' in fifth-century Athens, nevertheless in his earlier plays Sophocles 'follows the lead of Aeschylus and makes the slave roles unsympathetic' (Schlaifer, 1968; 114). Sophocles' attitude towards slavery is captured nicely, albeit obliquely, by the following passage from his *Tereus* in which he has the Chorus say: 'There is one human race. A single day brought us all forth from our father and mother. No man is born superior to another. But one man's fare is a doom of unhappy days, another's is success; and on others the yoke of slavery's hardship falls'. According to H. C. Baldry, Sophocles' intention in this passage was to indicate to his audience the fact that he disapproves of slavery. Consequently, these words 'express the egalitarian and unifying spirit' which Baldry associates with the writings of at least some intellectuals in fifth-century Athens, including as we have seen the poet Euripides (Baldry, 1965: 37). In my opinion, however, this interpretation of Sophocles is implausible. It may be conceded that there were indeed a number of intellectuals at this time who were opposed to slavery on humanitarian grounds. We have this on the authority of Aristotle. However, it is by no means clear that Sophocles should be counted amongst their number, as Aristotle appears, to the unwary reader, to be suggesting in his *Rhetoric*. An alternative reading of this passage indicates that Sophocles' intention is not at all to condemn the institution of slavery, but rather on the contrary to condone it. On this alternative reading, Sophocles takes the view that the existence of slavery is a mystery, a matter of man's inscrutable fate - something which cannot be explained rationally at all, and certainly not if we make the erroneous assumption that all human beings are by nature equal. Nevertheless, this is an institution which must certainly be accepted. For existing as it has done from time immemorial, slavery is a product of the inscrutable will of the gods. It is the consequence of divine intervention in human affairs.

The central conflict which Sophocles dramatically represents in the *Antigone* might indeed, as Aristotle observes, be seen as a conflict between two different types of ethical principle or law. In my view however these are not natural law and civil law, but what today we would refer to as customary law and statute law (each of which is a type of positive law in the sense in which the term 'positive' is traditionally understood by students of natural law theory). One of the weaknesses of the natural law interpretation of the *Antigone* is the fact that it fails to appreciate the importance of this distinction for our understanding of the political issues which Sophocles is seeking to dramatize in the play. We may illustrate this point by returning again to the 'ode to man'. It will be recalled that at one point in the ode Sophocles has the chorus say that 'Great honour is given | And power to him who upholdeth his country's laws | And the justice of heaven' (365–370) (Sophocles, 1970: 136). So far as the interpretation of the ode is concerned, Victor Ehrenberg has rightly claimed that everything depends here on the phrase 'country's laws' (Ehrenberg, 1954a: 62; Hester, 1971: 27; Kitto, 1977: 157; Knox, 1983: 112.). Once we have made a conceptual distinction between customary law and statute law, the ambiguity of the reference to 'his country's laws' (or alternatively to the 'laws of the land') in these lines is readily apparent. What exactly, according to Sophocles, are the laws which should be upheld by the citizens of a particular *polis*? Are these the customary laws associated with ancient tradition, as defended by *Antigone*, or are they rather the statute laws associated with the edicts and decrees of a modern political ruler such as Creon or the nascent Athenian democracy? It is arguable that this is the main conflict which Sophocles is seeking to dramatize within the play. This is the nub around which the conflict between Antigone and Creon turns. A number of commentators have observed that, from Antigone's point of view, Creon's command forbidding the burial of Polyneices is not actually a law at all. According to Antigone, Creon's commands are nothing more than edicts or decrees (χηρυγματα). They are not laws (νομιμα) in the strict sense of the term. It is for this reason that Antigone insists that she is under no ethical obligation to obey them (Blundell, 1989: 128; Conklin, 1997: 136; Lane and Lane, 1986: 168; Santirocco, 1980: 183–4; Segal, 1964: 46–7).

On this reading of the *Antigone*, the political message which Sophocles wished to communicate to his fifth-century audience is the overriding need for constitutional government and the 'rule of law'. Sophocles was warning his audience about the two main dangers which might possibly threaten the established social and political order of fifth-century Athens. These dangers are tyranny on the one hand and anarchy on the other. Tyranny derives from *hybris* and the lawless actions of unrestrained political rulers, for example Creon. Anarchy also arises from *hybris*, and from the equally lawless actions of rebellious subjects, for example Antigone. In particular, one of the concerns which Sophocles appears to have had in mind when he wrote the play is the possibility of tyrannical rule even by those who have been democratically elected. Sophocles is especially concerned about what Aristotle was later to refer to as the 'tyranny of the majority' in democratic political systems like that of fifth-century Athens (Aristotle, 1960, 103, 141, 197–9, 253, 275, 305). It could plausibly be argued that in the *Antigone* Sophocles is anxious to point out that even in a democracy the 'ancient constitution' and the rule of law with which it has traditionally been associated ought to be respected by all alike – both by the rulers and by the ruled. L. A. MacKay has claimed that it is by no means an accident that Creon is presented by Sophocles, at least initially, as 'not a vulgar tyrant, but a democratic leader' (MacKay, 1962: 169). Creon is a legitimate ruler whose authority is acknowledged by all Theban citizens. As C. Segal has rightly observed, from this point of view the *Antigone* is 'almost certainly a statement about the nature and ideals' of fifth-century Athenian democracy. To be more precise, it is about the weaknesses of Athenian democracy – and, by implication, the limitations of democracy itself as an abstract system of government (Segal, 1964: 63).

On this reading of the *Antigone*, as Alvin Gouldner has pointed out, the divine law to which Antigone appeals is associated with the customs and historical traditions of ancient Thebes (Gouldner, 1965: 226). It has nothing to do with reason or nature, at least not in the sense in which Aristotle understood these terms. Antigone's principal argument in the play in defence of her act of disobedience to the edict of her uncle Creon is that the edict in question conflicts with this ancient customary law, which she considers to be divinely sanctioned. From Antigone's point of view, although prior to this edict Creon's status as the legitimate ruler of Thebes was certainly not in question, nevertheless by refusing the ancient rites of burial to her brother Creon is indeed acting from *hybris* and in a tyrannical manner. He is a ruler who is refusing to respect the principle of the rule of law associated with the customs and traditions of the *polis* over which he has inherited authority. Antigone does not, therefore, claim that Creon's edict is unjust because it is unnatural. She claims rather, as Charles Maurras once argued, that his edict is unjust because it is unconstitutional (Steiner, 1984: 186–7). Antigone's argument is primarily an historical argument, to which so far as we know Sophocles himself would have given his qualified approval. This is not to say that Sophocles would have gone so far as to condone Antigone's action – only that he would have been sympathetic to the spirit of the argument which she uses to justify it.

Given what is known about Sophocles' own political beliefs, the claim that he would indeed have been sympathetic towards Antigone's argument justifying her disobedience to the edict of Creon makes no sense at all if Antigone is considered to be a champion of natural law who rejects the historical conventions associated with the existing social and political order of the society in which she lives because she is committed to a cosmopolitan ethical ideal which she considers to be universally valid for all human beings. If the reading of the play referred to by Aristotle were correct then it would be as difficult to understand any sympathy which Sophocles might possibly have had for Antigone as it would be to understand that of Hegel – who at one point, as is well known, refers to Antigone as 'the heavenly Antigone', the 'noblest of figures that ever appeared on earth' (Hegel, 1968: 441). In the terminology of the Hegelian philosophy, as Chris Arthur has pointed out, Antigone does not reflect the standpoint of *Moralität*, or that of natural law. Rather, she reflects the standpoint of *Sittlichkeit* and of the ethical duties associated with her particular station in Theban society (Arthur, 1990: 35; also Blake Tyrell and Bennett, 1998: 18). Antigone's attitude to the situation in which she finds herself is not at all, as the natural law interpretation of the *Antigone* erroneously suggests, that of an isolated individual wrestling with the demands of her own conscience and standing in opposition to existing customs and conventions. On the contrary, her attitude at least (if not her action) is entirely typical for someone in her position in ancient Greek society.

It could plausibly be argued that, as in the case of the Hegelian philosophy, the purpose of Sophoclean tragedy is to present to the audience what is basically a theodicy. It is, as Lowes-Dickinson has rightly observed an attempt on Sophocles' part 'to "justify the ways of God to Man"' and therefore to promote in his audience an attitude of reconciliation towards the world generally, and towards their social and political world in particular' (Lowes-Dickinson, 1960: 158–9). It may be conjectured that this is the principal reason why, from a very early age, Hegel was so enthusiastic about the works of Sophocles generally and about the *Antigone* in particular – even going so far as to translate it into German when he was fifteen years old (Avineri, 1979: 2). From the standpoint of Sophocles' own political beliefs, the significance of the appeal to religion and divine law in the *Antigone* is not that it seeks to subvert the existing social and political order, as the interpretation of the play alluded to by Aristotle maintains, but on the contrary that it seeks to defend that order from the criticisms of the radical Sophists in fifth-century Athens. It was not Sophocles but his radical political opponents, the egalitarians and democrats of his day, who employed the concept of natural law in political argument and debate. Sophocles had little sympathy for the kind of abstract reasoning indulged in by the natural law theorists who are criticized by Aristotle in his *Rhetoric*. Unlike Aristotle, however, Sophocles appears to have been an extreme advocate of 'conventionalism'. His first instinct so far as questions of ethics and politics are concerned was to appeal to history and to existing customs and traditions rather than to any allegedly universally valid principles of natural law. It would appear, then, that if Aristotle's intention when he wrote the *Rhetoric* was to attribute such a view to Sophocles, or to suggest that Sophocles himself endorsed the natural law reading of the *Antigone* which he discusses there, then he was very much mistaken. I shall discuss the issue of whether Aristotle did in fact make such an error of interpretation in the concluding section of this chapter.

Was Aristotle the First Natural Law Theorist?

If we wished to write a history of the concept of natural law where should we begin? One obvious response to this question would be to say that the origins or, as Saul Kripke would put it (Kripke, 1988: 96), the 'initial baptism' of this concept are to be found in the writings of the members of Popper's alleged 'anti-slavery movement' in fifth-century Athens, many of the ideas of which have unfortunately not been handed down to posterity, being preserved only partially and in fragments. But this can hardly be an adequate response taken on its own, if only because we cannot be sure that later writers who have contributed to the history of the concept of natural law were even aware of the existence of these radicals and their revolutionary ideas. As the institution of slavery was not in fact abolished at the time they represent, as E. R. Dodds once observed, one of history's 'failures' (Dodds, 1973c). For this reason they have fallen victim to what in a different context E. P. Thompson has referred to as 'the enormous condescension of posterity' (Thompson, 1975: 13). For many people today, just like the slaves whose natural or human rights they might be said to have been defending, they are figures who, to adapt a phrase of Sheila Rowbotham's, remain hidden from history (Rowbotham, 1973; see also Daube, 1972: 52–3). Interestingly, Eduard Zeller has linked the ideas of the political radicals under discussion with early Greek feminism. As he puts it, 'no doubt the movement for the emancipation of women in the last third of the fifth century, for which we have only the indirect evidence of Aristophanes and Euripides, was also connected with this development in the theory of natural law' (Zeller, 1997: 89).

A second obvious response to the question of where we should locate the origins of the concept of natural law would be to claim that, at least so far as posterity is concerned, it is Aristotle who gave birth to this concept as it was to be understood by later generations. It is Aristotle who in his *Rhetoric* was the first major thinker to associate the concept of 'unwritten law' as we find it, for example, in the writings of a fifth-century author like Sophocles, and especially in the *Antigone*, with that of 'nature' and who thereby transformed it into the concept of natural law as this is now commonly understood. From this point of view, it is the reading of Sophocles' *Antigone* which Aristotle presents in the *Rhetoric*, together with what he has to say there about the views of Empedocles and Alcidamas, which was one of the sources of the later, Stoic conception of natural law.

It seems to me, though, that this second claim is obviously incorrect. For there is a difference between the concept of natural law and the word or name which in a particular language is used to designate or express that concept. In my view, the most that could be said for this second claim is that Aristotle indirectly suggested a possible name for the concept of natural law – one which did not 'catch on' amongst his successors. This, and not the concept itself, was his contribution to the later history of political thought. Indeed, this would also appear to be Aristotle's own view. For (rightly or wrongly) he suggests that his predecessors, Sophocles, Empedocles and Alcidamas, all possessed the concept of natural law or the law of nature as he understood it. And yet it is also clear that in Aristotle's view, unlike himself, none of these earlier thinkers had a name for this concept.

There are two things about Aristotle's discussion of rhetorical arguments in the *Rhetoric* which are of particular interest to anyone interested in the history of the concept of natural law. The first is that according to Aristotle rhetoric is concerned with 'modes of persuasion' the purpose of which is to appeal not to the reason, but to the emotions of the listener (Aristotle, 1995i: 1355a1–5, 2153; 1355b25–30, 2155; 1356a10–15, 2155). This is important because it implies that the rhetorical arguments in question are the only means available for getting the listener to accept the speaker's point of view. In other words, Aristotle does not consider these arguments to be good arguments. They are arguments which will not withstand examination. If this idea is related to what Aristotle has to say about natural law in the *Rhetoric* then the appropriate conclusion seems to be that Aristotle is not at all neutral regarding the intrinsic merits of those arguments which involve an appeal to the idea of natural law, as some commentators suggest (Salomon Shellens, 1959: 80–1; Yack, 1990: 225–6). He is, rather, extremely critical of such arguments, precisely because he considers them to be nothing more than mere rhetorical devices. Aristotle's reason for citing the works of Sophocles, Empedocles and Alcidamas in the *Rhetoric* is to provide his readers with some classic examples a bad argument of this type.[12] It is not entirely clear whether Aristotle thought that these three authors themselves used bad arguments of this kind, or whether he thought that it was their later readers (his own contemporaries) who did so.

The second thing of relevance to students of the history of natural law in Aristotle's *Rhetoric* is the fact that according to Aristotle effective rhetorical arguments must appeal to 'received opinions' or 'notions accepted by everybody' (Aristotle, 1995i: 1377b1–20, 2193–4; 1355a25–30, 2154). This is important because it indicates that when he wrote the *Rhetoric* Aristotle evidently took the view that a belief in the existence of natural law, and the employment of this concept by the Athenians of his own day in political argument and debate, was widespread. It suggests for example that, for Aristotle, Sophocles' *Antigone* was of interest, not because of the uniqueness or originality of the appeal to the idea of natural law which (allegedly) it contained, but rather because it represented a spurious argument which Aristotle considered to be politically influential amongst his contemporaries and immediate predecessors in fourth- and fifth-century Athens. (Again, however, it is not clear whether Aristotle seriously intended to attribute such an argument to Sophocles himself.) On this view, as Guthrie has noted, when discussing the notion of an unwritten 'law of nature' in the *Rhetoric* 'Aristotle is simply repeating notions already familiar in the heyday of the Sophists' (Guthrie, 1971: 125).

We may conclude from this that although Aristotle does refer explicitly to the concept of natural law or a law of nature in his *Rhetoric* there is no case for claiming that it was he who actually introduced this concept to the history of political thought. Aristotle may arguably have suggested a possible name for it, but as he himself acknowledges he certainly did not invent the concept. We may also conclude that the concept of natural law, which appears to have originated in the writings of small number of thinkers in Athens in the fifth century BCE, had within a period of roughly 100 years become a commonplace amongst the educated Athenians of the fourth century. C. H. McIlwain has observed that when discussing arguments which appeal to the concept of natural law in the *Rhetoric* Aristotle was primarily concerned with the 'practical effect on a large popular jury' of arguments which make this appeal rather than with the intrinsic merits or demerits of the arguments themselves. But, as McIlwain also points out, it is 'none the less significant that he should have thought that such an appeal might secure a popular response' from an Athenian jury. According to McIlwain, it is clear that 'there must have been a fairly widespread popular acceptance of these views' at the time 'if it was ever advisable to appeal to them in addressing a jury of some hundreds of Athenians' (McIlwain, 1932: 19). Indeed, Robin Waterfield has noted that arguments of this sort had 'gained enough currency in Athens by the end of the Fifth Century for it to be found necessary to pass a law forbidding references to unwritten laws in court' (Waterfield, 2000: 252). It may be conjectured that it is because of the increasing use which was being made of the concept of natural law that a specific label eventually came to be provided for it in the Greek language. Quentin Skinner has rightly suggested, 'the surest sign that a group or society has entered into the self-conscious possession of a new concept is that a corresponding vocabulary will be developed' which can be used to 'pick out and discuss the concept with consistency' (Skinner, 1995: 8).

It was, presumably, precisely because of the potentially radical political implications of the concept of natural law, combined with the fact that Aristotle considered the acceptance of this notion in the Athens of his day to be so widespread, which made him so anxious, both in his *Rhetoric*, as in his *Politics*, to register his opposition to the way in which thinkers like Alcidamas, Antiphon and Hippias employed this concept in political argument and debate. Aristotle sought to defend the existing social order in Athens against the challenge which was posed to it by the 'modern' political assumptions of Athenian democracy, above all the idea of the natural equality of all human beings subscribed to by Alcidamas and the anonymous opponents of slavery in the fifth and early fourth centuries to which he refers in Book 1 of the *Politics*.

This is not to say, however, that Aristotle rejected the concept of natural law completely. For, as we have seen, it can be argued that in his *Nicomachean Ethics* Aristotle presents his readers with an alternative, much more uncritical and basically conservative, natural law theory which differs markedly from that of his Sophist opponents and which is logically compatible with his Aristotle's acceptance in the *Politics* of the legitimacy of existing customs and traditions, especially the institution of slavery. Julia Annas has argued that one of Aristotle's 'most unfortunate legacies' is the fact that his name has often been 'unfairly' associated with 'reactionary political attitudes which have appealed to nature' in order to 'uphold existing inequalities in society, such as slavery and the subordination of women' (Annas, 1996: 731). So far as slavery, in particular, is concerned it does not seem to me to be at all unfair to attach some such label to Aristotle, although the word 'conservative' would perhaps be a more appropriate one to use than 'reactionary' in this particular context.

Aristotle's Attempted Appropriation of the Concept of Natural Law

As a proposed 'interpretation' of Sophocles' *Antigone,* the reading which Aristotle offers in his *Rhetoric* does not withstand scrutiny. It might, as Gabriella Remow has suggested, be characterized as a 'blunder' (Remow, 2008: 586). Aristotle does indeed, as Remow also suggests, appear at first sight to 'bungle' his discussion of the 'law of nature' by employing this particular example (Remow, 2008: 587). This raises the question of why Aristotle made what appears to be such an obvious mistake, given his stature as a philosopher, and given also the fact that he himself distinguishes between 'particular law' and 'universal law' in the *Rhetoric,* and claims that it is only the latter which constitutes the 'law of nature', whereas the law to which Antigone appeals appears to be of the former kind only (Aristotle, 1995i: 1373b1–1373b6, 2187). In the light of these considerations, it seems most unlikely that the reason why Aristotle presented his readers with this reading was because he had simply misunderstood Sophocles' text. We need not assume that Aristotle did himself subscribe to the natural law reading of the *Antigone* to which he refers in the *Rhetoric.* However, if we assume for the sake of the argument that he *did,* then I agree with Remow that it is not sufficient simply to point out that he made an interpretive error. Rather, as Remow puts it, 'we need a better explanation of why Aristotle interpreted *Antigone*' in this way (Remow, 2008: 586). Similarly, if we make the counter-assumption that Aristotle did not himself endorse this interpretation then we need a plausible explanation of why, nevertheless, he thought it was important to introduce it to his own readers. In pursuit of such an alternative and better explanation it is fruitful to deploy the conceptual framework introduced in the Introduction to the present work, in particular the distinction made there between those readings of texts which are 'interpretations' and those which are 'appropriations'.

Before applying these concepts to Aristotle's reading of the *Antigone,* it should first be noted that there is a difference between embracing a particular reading of a text as a plausible 'interpretation' of it, on the one hand, and endorsing the ideas which are associated with that reading on the other. Two readers might agree that a certain reading of a text, for example the natural law reading of the *Antigone*, is a valid interpretation of it and yet nevertheless disagree with one another about the value of the ideas (in this case the idea of natural law) which are associated with that reading. For one of them might endorse those ideas whereas the other might reject them. The relevance of this for Aristotle's remarks about Sophocles' *Antigone* is obvious. It is possible in principle that both Aristotle and his political opponents subscribed to the same natural law interpretation of Sophocles' text and yet that they disagreed with one another regarding the value of the conception of natural law which they claimed could be found within it. For example, Aristotle's opponents might have enthusiastically endorsed that particular conception of natural law, whereas Aristotle himself rejected it.

We can be fairly confident that Aristotle did reject the kind of natural law thinking which he associated with this reading of the *Antigone*. However, this leaves open the different question of whether he considered this reading to be the correct (or even a plausible) interpretation of Sophocles' text. Did he or did he not believe that Sophocles deploys the concept of natural law in the *Antigone*? If he did believe this, then he was guilty of the interpretive 'blunder' referred to by Remow noted above. If he did not, then we must consider why he thought it important to refer to this reading at all in the *Rhetoric*, given that he rejected the type of natural law thinking which is associated with it.

In my view, although it is certainly possible, nevertheless it is unlikely that Aristotle was in fact guilty of an error of interpretation when he connected Sophocles' *Antigone* to the notion of the 'law of nature' in his *Rhetoric*. It is far more likely that Aristotle made this connection deliberately and that the reason for this is because he was interested in the ideas which, according to this reading, can be found in the play – ideas which in his opinion were politically significant because they were not only undesirable but also influential amongst the Athenian citizens of his day.

We are now in a position to invoke the conceptual apparatus introduced earlier. It will be recalled that, on this view, there are a number of different possible approaches that one might adopt when reading texts. In particular, it is possible either to offer an interpretation of a text, in which case one ought to be faithful to the intentions of its author; or alternatively one might seek to appropriate the text, or the ideas contained within it, for purposes of one's own, completely setting aside the intentions of the author as being of no interest. Bearing this distinction in mind, let us now turn to consider the natural law reading of Sophocles' *Antigone* to which Aristotle refers in the *Rhetoric*. The crucial question here is whether this reading is best seen as a (deeply flawed) interpretation of Sophocles text, on the one hand, or as an attempted appropriation of it on the other? In the light of the above discussion, it seems to me that it is far more plausible to think of this reading as an attempted appropriation rather than an (incorrect) interpretation of the *Antigone*. Indeed, as a proposed interpretation, the natural law reading arguably presents us with the opposite of the truth, because it reverses the intentions which Sophocles appears to have had when writing the play. From being the ardent defender of existing customs and traditions, Sophocles is presented on this reading as being one of their staunchest critics. But in either case, whether it is an appropriation or an interpretation of Sophocles' text, the reading of the *Antigone* referred to by Aristotle does in effect 'read into' the play ideas which although they were certainly historically available to Sophocles, and indeed to which he alludes elsewhere in his writings, are not actually of concern to him in the *Antigone* at all.

It is arguable, then, that the natural law reading of the *Antigone* which Aristotle refers to in the *Rhetoric*, whether or not he endorsed it himself, is best seen as an appropriation of Sophocles' text and not as an interpretation of it. Aristotle's engagement with this reading might be characterized as a political act. It was a contribution to one of the great political debates of the day in Athenian politics. Thus it can be seen as part of an attempt to counter, or neutralize, the way in which the concept of natural law or 'the law of nature' was currently being employed by his contemporaries, including the 'anonymous opponents of slavery' referred to in the *Politics*. It may be conjectured that it was not Sophocles, but rather these opponents, who were Aristotle's main target; and it is possible, of course, that it was they and not Aristotle who first thought of reading Sophocles' text in this way. On this view, when he wrote the *Rhetoric* Aristotle's intention was twofold. In the first place, it was to offer his readers an account, not of Sophocles' *Antigone* and the ideas which it contains, but rather of the way in which those ideas had been appropriated by his political opponents, the natural law theorists of his day. In the second place, it was to oppose the specific form of natural law reasoning associated with this reading by dismissing it as being nothing more than empty rhetorical persuasion.

One might say here that Aristotle and his opponents were engaged in a conflict around and over the meaning, not only of Sophocles' text, but also of the concept of natural law – a conflict in which both parties were seeking to appropriate this concept for their own political purposes. So far as the text is concerned, I suggested in the Introduction that, it is fruitful in this context to think of this conflict as a 'struggle for recognition' in the sense in which Hegel employs the term in his *Phenomenology*. This can be seen as a struggle for ownership or control of the text and its meaning which took place between the author of the text and one of its readers, in this case between Sophocles and Aristotle. So far as the concept of natural law is concerned, this was a struggle around and over the meaning of the concept which took place between Aristotle and his political opponents, a struggle within which both sides sought to appropriate the concept for their own particular cause. To speak metaphorically, the decisive issue in this struggle was that of who was to be the 'master' and who the 'slave' so far as the meaning of either the text or the concept was concerned? According to this view, advocates of the natural law reading of the *Antigone* had no interest in the issue of whether their reading constituted an accurate or faithful account of the meaning of the text as it was understood by its author. They set aside as being of no importance the issue of the intentions which its author, Sophocles, had when writing it. The irony of Aristotle's suggestion in the *Rhetoric* that it was his radical political opponents who employed the concept of natural law in a merely rhetorical manner, whereas he himself employed the same concept elsewhere in the pursuit of objective ethical truth, is readily apparent – especially (but not only) to those of a Nietzschean or Poststructuralist philosophical persuasion.

Notes

1 According to Ritchie, the Greek phrase is ο νομος μετρον η εικων φυσει δικαιον. (Ritchie, 1895: 32). Ritchie notes that 'what is meant by this is left obscure' because 'Aristotle does not discuss this alternative'. Ritchie goes on to surmise that what Aristotle had in mind was 'probably that law determines what is otherwise vague'.

2 See also Ambler, 1987; Bodéüs, 1996: 86–99; Brunt, 1993; Dobbs, 1994; Fortenbaugh, 1991; Garnsey, 1999 [1996]: 11–13, 64–6, 75–7, 107–27; Miller Jr., 1991: 296–7, 1997: 108–9; Schlaifer, 1968 [1936]; Schofield, 1990; Smith, 1991.

3 For discussion of this ancient debate on slavery, and of who Aristotle's opponents within it might have been, in addition to the works listed earlier see also Cambiano, 1987; and Saunders, 1984.

4 For the suggestion that Euripides was opposed to slavery on these grounds see also Appleton, 1927; Baldry, 1965: 35–7; Barker, 1960a [1918]: 87–8; Conacher, 1998; Murray, 1913: 137–9; Sabine, 1973a: 42–3; Synodinou, 1977; Vogt, 1974a: 15–23.

5 A similar inconsistency is also to be found in the writings of Alvin Gouldner and Joseph Vogt. See Gouldner, 1965: 24, 28–31, 190–1; Vogt, 1974a: 3, 13, 24, 40.

6 See Baldry, 1965: 2, 24, 39–45; Barker, 1960a: 73–9, 86–7; Cartledge, 1993: 41–3, 122–4, 126–7; Dodds, 1973c: 99–102; Gouldner, 1965: 28–31, 190–1; Havelock, 1964 [1957]): 348–9; Popper, 1969b: 69–70, 187, 236, 278–9, 299; Sabine, 1973a: 39–44; Saunders, 1984: 25–36; Schlaifer, 1968: 199–201; Schofield, 1990: 5, 23–7; Vogt, 1974a: 14–25, 40; Wood and Wood, 1978: 62–3, 78.

7 For a similar view see also Gagarin, 2002: 69, 72, 73; Luria, 1926; Morrow, 1948: 26–7; Nill, 1985: 53, 56; Pendrick, 2002: 60–61, 64, 320–21, 323, 343, 346, 351, 367.

8 For the 'natural law' reading of Antiphon see also Merlan, 1950: 161–6; Moulton, 1972; Reesor, 1987; Reesor, 1951: 9, fn. 1; and Sinclair, 1959: 70, 74, 78. For further references see Pendrick, 2002: 61, fn. 115, 320–23, 346, 354–55, 367.

[9] See also Aubenque, 1980: 152; Baldry, 1965: 31–2; Barker, 1948: 312–13, 1960a: 65, 1960b: xxiii; Bloch, 1986: 113–15, 120, 122, 254; Bryce, 1901: 565–6; Destrée, 2000: 220; Gough, 1967: 9; Guthrie, 1971: 22; Joachim, 1951: 154–5; Robson, 1935: 193–4; Rommen, 1998: 11; Segal, 1964: 47; Sigmund, 1971: 9–10; Vogt, 1974b: 1–2; Watson, 1966: 67; Weinreb, 1987: 21–3.

[10] See also Bernadete, 1975: 9; Foriers and Perelman, 1973: 15; Knox, 1983: 98; Lowes-Dickinson, 1960: 158–9; McKirahan, 1994: 411; Morrow, 1948: 18–20, 25; Strauss, 1968a: 80; Wormuth, 1948: 52, 54–5.

[11] See Dodds, 1973b; 8; Ehrenberg, 1954a: 64; Ferguson, 1972: 167–8; Goheen, 1951: 53, 141; Hester, 1971: 26–7; Knox, 1983: 127; Santirocco, 1980: 181–2; Segal, 1964: 52–3, 66; Shephard, 1947: 46–8.

[12] For the view that Aristotle's attitude towards rhetoric is more nuanced than that suggested above, that he distinguishes between different types of rhetorical argument, and that his attitude towards such arguments is not always or entirely negative see Coleman, 2000: 65–9; Miller Jr., 1991: 281; and Skinner, 1996: 121–2, 256–7. For a valuable collection of essays on Aristotle's *Rhetoric* generally see Rorty, 1996.

Chapter 4

Aristotle and the Nature Versus Convention Debate

In this chapter I shall say something about the origins of the concept of natural law, as that concept arose out of the famous 'nature versus convention debate' in ancient Athens (Barker, 1960a [1918]: 74–6; Beardslee, 1918; Burnet (1897); Guthrie, 1971: 55–134; Kerferd, 1981c; Heinimann, 1945; Long, 2005: 412–30; Sabine, 1973a: 42–5). I shall argue that the nature versus convention debate is decisive for our understanding of Aristotle. It provides the necessary background context for understanding Aristotle's political thought because, as we saw in Chapters 1 and 2, Aristotle's ideas are best seen as a contribution to it. In the course of the discussion I shall have something to say about Plato. This is necessary because of his importance for our understanding of the issues associated with the nature versus convention debate, and hence for our understanding of Aristotle's attitude towards those issues.

It will be recalled that I suggested at the end of Chapter 2 that Aristotle attempted to steer a 'middle course' between the two extremes of 'conventionalism', on the one hand, and 'naturalism' as it had been understood by his predecessors (including Plato) on the other. Alternatively, one might say that Aristotle offered a theoretical synthesis of these two opposed theoretical positions. I hasten to add, however, that this third approach should in my view be located firmly within the camp of 'naturalism'. It was a modified form of naturalism, associated with a new way of thinking about the concept of natural law, rather than a departure which is so great that Aristotle's thought should not be considered to be a form of naturalism at all. In effect, as we have seen, Aristotle sought to redefine the concept of naturalism, forcing a rethink of what (in his view) a politically acceptable form of the doctrine must involve. He sought to appropriate the doctrine of naturalism and the concept of natural law for political purposes of his own.

The Historical Background

Prior to the scientific or philosophical revolution in roughly the sixth and the first half of the fifth centuries BCE it seems not to have occurred to anyone to separate and contrast the notions of *physis* and *nomos* from one another. In a world dominated, intellectually, by myth and religion everything was considered to be divine. The disenchantment of the world associated with the Greek 'enlightenment' which occurred in this period led to the development of the concept of *physis* as a secular concept having to do with an impersonal world of nature which was constant and unchanging and susceptible of being rationally understood. At the same time this development also opened up the possibility of drawing a contrast between the world of 'nature', understood in this sense, and that of human affairs, especially the spheres of ethics, law and justice. The available empirical evidence suggested to some that the world of human society, especially in the area of moral values, is unlike the natural world because it is dominated by the principles of variation and change. The regulating principle of human society was taken by those who argued in this way to be *nomos*, that is to say, 'law' or 'convention', the concept of which was, therefore, considered to have a meaning which was directly opposed or antithetical to that of 'nature' or *physis*.

The question of the origins of the concept of natural law, understood specifically in the moral or ethical sense, needs to be considered against this background. This concept combines together two component elements, the concepts of *physis* and *nomos*, into one complex concept, that of a *nomos tes physeos*, a phrase which so far as we know appears for the first time in the writings of Plato, in the critique of Sophism which he develops in his *Gorgias* (Plato, 1996 [1925]), 482c–483e, 384–7). It is evident that, historically, it would have been impossible to combine these two concepts together until they have actually first been distinguished from and contrasted with one another. Consequently, it would make no sense to claim that the ancient Greeks possessed the concept of natural law at the time when their way of thinking about the world generally was dominated by concepts associated with mythology and religion. At the same time, however, it is also clear that as soon as the two concepts of *physis* and *nomos* had been contrasted with one another this could be said to have immediately and contemporaneously opened up the theoretical possibility of their being combined together into the complex concept of a *nomos tes physeos* or 'natural law'.

Anyone who argued in this way at the time would in effect be maintaining that, despite appearances to the contrary, the permanence, order and stability which some of their contemporaries associated solely with the natural world are *also* to be found in the world of human affairs, especially in the spheres of ethics, justice and law. Such a person would be claiming that there is indeed such a thing as a natural law in the spheres of ethics and politics. They would be asserting that there are certain principles of morality or justice which are universally valid, timeless and unchanging, and the existence of which can be discerned behind or beneath the empirically observable flux which is associated with the moral and legal systems of different human societies. They would also be arguing that the ethical imperatives associated with this natural law have nothing to do with mythology or religion; in short, that this secular natural law is *not* to be identified with divine law or the unwritten law of the Gods. Thus, for example, Leo Strauss has suggested, citing Aristotle as a case in point, that for those who think this way 'it is possible to admit natural right without believing in particular providence or in divine justice proper' (Strauss, 1974 [1953]: 94). Indeed it may be suggested that not only is it possible to do this, it is in fact necessary to do it. For a law the understanding of which could not be separated conceptually from the idea of that which is divine could not properly speaking be said to be a 'natural' law.

As we saw in Chapter 3 this rules out the possibility that Sophocles' *Antigone* might be considered to be a source for the notion of natural law. It also implies that the pre-Socratic thinker Heraclitus, writing at the turn of the sixth and fifth centuries BCE, did not possess the concept of natural law in the sense in which the term is used here either. For, as T. A. Sinclair has noted, Heraclitus was of the opinion that law in general is 'a universal principle of divine origin' and that 'all human laws are nourished by one divine law' (Sinclair, 1959: 30, 48). It is sometimes suggested that Heraclitus's 'divine law' is a forerunner of the Stoic conception of natural law (Long, 1975). There is evidently some truth in this. Given that they endorsed the notion of Pantheism, the Stoics took the view that the law which they considered to be natural is also a law which is divine. According to the understanding of the concept of natural law presented here, however, the Pantheism of the Stoics, and hence also any religious or theological associations which the concept of natural law might have in Stoic philosophy, are not an essential component of the Stoic conception of natural law, insofar as it is a conception of *natural* law. From this point of view, as J. L. Adams has noted, because within Stoic philosophy 'the distinctions of classical philosophy are ignored' and 'reason, nature and God become almost synonymous terms', it follows that Stoicism exhibits a 'retrograde tendency' in the history of the concept of natural law; a step backwards from the purely secular understanding of natural law held by the fifth-century Sophist thinkers who first developed it (Adams, 1945: 110).

It is arguable that the logical possibility that someone might argue in this way and suggest that the two separate concepts of *nomos* and *physis* be combined into just one concept, that of a *nomos tes physeos* or a 'natural law', was opened up from the very first time that any ancient Greek intellectual made the assertion that justice or law is something which is merely or entirely conventional. For it is the denial of this view which, when its logical implications are fully unpacked, leads theoretically to the development of the notion of natural law. W. K. C. Guthrie, for example, has asserted that it was at the point when some ancient Athenians committed themselves to the 'denial of the absolute status of law and moral values, or any place for them in the permanent nature of things' that 'the stage' was 'set' for the ensuing controversy 'between the two' sides in the 'nature versus convention debate' (Guthrie, 1971a: 60). Similarly, Gerald Watson has rightly claimed that 'the very contrast of *nomos* and *physis* had from the beginning suggested an ideal state of affairs where the two would coincide' (Watson, 1996: 237). However, to point this out is simply to record what is a purely theoretical possibility. There still remains the important question of whether in fact the two concepts of *nomos* and *physis* did come to be combined in this way and, if so, when? Did this combination take place in the fourth century with Plato, or did it occur earlier, in the fifth century, amongst the Sophists? It should be clear from what I said in the last chapter that I incline to the latter view.

The Nature Versus Convention Debate

So far as the nature versus convention debate itself is concerned, there are a number of questions that need to be considered. First, did such a debate take place in ancient Athens? Second, if there was such a debate, what exactly was it about? Third, if there was such a debate, who participated in it? And fourth, if such a debate did indeed occur, when exactly did it occur? The first question appears to be relatively uncontentious. There is a widely held consensus that a nature versus convention debate did in fact occur in ancient Athens. No doubt this contention could be challenged. However, I do not propose to do that here. What I do wish to suggest, though, is that at least some doubt might be cast on the claim that there was just *one* such debate, and hence also on the claim that we can talk about *the* nature versus convention debate in ancient Athens. Indeed it is arguable that there was not one but *two* (closely related) debates in classical Athens, each of which might be characterized as a disagreement over the respective merits of *physis* or 'nature', on the one hand, and *nomos* or 'convention' on the other.[1] One important consequence of this is that there has been some confusion and/or disagreement between commentators, just as there was amongst the ancient Greeks, in relation to our second question, that is the question of what *the* nature versus convention debate is supposed to have been about? Similarly, the answers to questions three and four are also open to dispute. There is disagreement amongst commentators over the issues of who the participants within it actually were, and about when the nature versus convention debate is supposed to have occurred.

For the participants in the first of the two debates referred to above, the question at issue was that of 'moralism' versus 'immoralism' or 'nihilism'. An important source here is Plato's *Gorgias*, in which Socrates defends the former point of view against Callicles, who defends the latter (Plato, 1996 [1925]), 482c–483e, 384–7). In this first debate immoralists such as Callicles criticized not just existing moral laws and the duties associated with them, but *all* moral laws, and hence also the very idea of morality. Indeed Paul Shorey has claimed that the views expressed by Callicles constitute 'the most eloquent statement of the immoralist's case in European literature' (Shorey, 1933: 154;

see also Dodds, 1959b: 266; Kerferd, 1981b: 118).[2] Their opponents, on the other hand, defended the claims of morality generally, although not necessarily those of existing moral customs and conventions. Within this first debate it was the immoralists who based their criticisms of the very idea of morality, and therefore also of existing laws and conventions or *nomoi,* on an appeal to the notion of *physis* or nature.

In the second nature versus convention debate, on the other hand, the question at issue was a different one. In this case the disagreement was between the advocates of moral relativism or conventionalism, on the one hand, and moral objectivism or universalism on the other. Here it was the conventionalists, for example Protagoras, who defended existing laws and customs, whereas it was objectivists or universalists such as Socrates who criticized those laws and conventions, basing their critique upon an appeal to nature, or to the idea of a justice or law which is natural, which they considered to be applicable in all societies at all times and in all places, and therefore (by implication) to all human beings.

Although these two debates are related to one another, nevertheless they are not identical, and should not be confused or conflated with one another, as Heinrich Rommen has done (Rommen, 1998 [1947]: 7–8). To do this is to wrongly identify nihilism and ethical relativism. However there is an important difference between these two doctrines. For nihilists reject the standpoint of morality altogether (in this case because they consider it to be contrary to the dictates of nature), and insist that there is nothing at all which anyone *ought* to do or refrain from doing. According to them, any effort by moralists to persuade others that there are such things as moral rules or laws which ought to be followed, and duties associated with them, is a rhetorical manoeuvre the purpose of which is to manipulate those who are taken in by it. In all cases the point of appealing to morality is to get others either to do or to refrain from doing things which are in the interests of the moralists who make the appeal in question. From the standpoint of their nihilist critics, then, moralists employ 'the language of morals' insincerely and for self-interested reasons. Relativists, on the other hand, do not reject the moral point of view altogether and are happy to accept that individuals living in particular societies at particular times do indeed possess certain moral duties (and arguably even certain rights), which are associated with the laws or conventions of the society in which they happen to live. What they deny is that there are any moral principles which might be said to be 'natural' in the sense that they are universally applicable and objectively valid, applying in all societies everywhere. It is a mistake, therefore, to identify these two debates about the respective merits of nature versus convention with one another. Such an identification makes it impossible for us to distinguish between nihilism and a relativism. It also makes it more difficult for us to establish what the protagonists, in what is erroneously referred to as *the* nature versus convention debate, were arguing about.

A very good example of this conflation, although in this case one hesitates to describe it as confusion, is to be found in Plato's *Laws*, which is an important source of information for modern commentators who are interested in the nature versus convention debate. Plato refers there to *a* 'school of thought' in ancient Athens, by which he meant his opponents the Sophists, which maintained that government 'has very little to do with nature' and is 'artificial' or 'largely a matter of art'. According to Plato's account, this group of thinkers considered laws to be like 'the gods', namely 'fictions' or 'artificial concepts corresponding to nothing in nature'. Consequently the laws of different societies 'vary very widely, according to the different conventions' which as a matter of fact people happen to 'agree on'. According to this school of thought therefore, Plato goes on, 'there is no *natural* standard of justice at all', for men 'are always wrangling about their moral standards and changing them', and in their view 'every change introduced becomes binding from the moment it's made, regardless of the fact that it is entirely artificial, and based on convention, not nature in the slightest degree' (Plato, 1981 [1926]: X, 889–890, 310–17).[3]

This account of the nature versus convention debate in the *Laws* indicates that what Plato saw as being the decisive feature of his opponents' position in that debate, and what he most objected to, was the Sophists' commitment to ethical relativism. On the other hand, though, Plato goes on in the same passage to make the quite different point that his Sophists opponents *also* maintain 'that anything that one can get away with by force is absolutely justified', because a '"true natural life"' is essentially nothing more than a 'life of conquest over others, not one of service to your neighbours as the law enjoins' (Plato, 1981 [1926]: X, 889–90, 310–17). In short, he associates Sophism with nihilism. This further claim, that his Sophists opponents actually advocated a life of moral 'lawlessness', implies that in Plato's opinion there is no difference at all between being a relativist and being a nihilist or an immoralist. It is not clear why Plato took this view. For, as Richard Norman has observed, 'the view that morality is conventional rather than natural does not necessarily entail a rejection of morality' (Norman, 1990 [1983]: 10). One can only assume that Plato did this because he thought (wrongly) that moral relativism is necessarily associated with, or inevitably leads to, nihilism.

As is clear from the *Laws*, the participants in the second nature versus convention debate were interested in the question of whether law and justice are natural or whether they are merely conventional, and hence historically relative, varying from society to society. Those who held the former position maintained either that there are certain principles of justice or law which can in fact be found in the legal systems of all societies everywhere, or alternatively that there are certain principles of justice or law which are valid for or applicable to all human beings everywhere. Understood in this way, the nature versus convention debate is, as Leo Strauss has claimed, a 'basic controversy in political philosophy', because the participants within it are addressing (and disagreeing with one another) about a fundamentally important question, namely: 'Is there' such a thing as "natural right" or "natural law"?' (Strauss, 1974 [1953]: 93). It is, therefore, impossible to talk about the nature versus convention debate, understood in this second sense, without exploring the relationship which exists between that debate and the history of the concept of natural law – just as it is impossible to account for the emergence of the concept of natural law without discussing the nature versus convention debate. The writings of Plato are an important source of information regarding both of these debates. Those of Aristotle have to do more with the second than the first. Of particular importance here, of course, are those passages in Aristotle's works, discussed in Chapters 1 to 3, which touch on the issue of natural justice or law. Before turning to discuss the views of Aristotle in connection with the second nature versus convention debate, however, I shall say something about the contribution which Plato made to both of them.

Plato and the First Nature Versus Convention Debate

One of Plato's concerns in the *Gorgias* is the first nature versus convention debate referred to above, although the views expressed by the character Callicles in his engagement with Socrates do have implications for any assessment of Plato's position within the second debate also. What are the views which Plato puts into the mouth of Callicles? At one point in the dialogue, when considering the beliefs of those who reject 'the moral point of view', and whose conduct is devoted entirely to the pursuit of their own self-interest as they understand it, Plato has Callicles say that such men 'follow nature – the nature of right – in acting thus; yes, on my soul, and follow the law of nature' (νομον γε τον της φυσεως) (Plato, 1996 [1925]), 482c–483e, 384–7). A number of commentators have claimed that, so far as we know, this is the very first time that the phrase *nomos tes physeos*, or 'natural law', is used in the history of Western philosophy (Guthrie, 1971: 118; Morrow, 1948: 42; Maguire, 1947: 151; Striker, 1987: 83; Taylor, 1949 [1908]: 117; Watson, 1966: 66, 1996: 218).

Let us consider further the beliefs of Callicles as they are presented by Plato. I have said that Callicles is an 'immoralist' or a 'nihilist'. By these terms I mean someone who does not look at the world from what is usually referred to as 'the moral point of view' and whose thinking, when it comes to deciding which course of action is to be taken either by oneself or others, does not employ terms or concepts which are usually associated with 'the language of morals', especially the concepts which are expressed by the English words 'duty' and 'right' (Baier, 1966 [1958]; Hare, 1963 [1952]). Most commentators see no problem in employing expressions such as 'the moral point of view', the 'language of morals', 'moralism', 'immoralism', and so on, when discussing the ethical and political thought of the ancient Greeks; although, some do claim that it is not appropriate to employ such expressions in this context. They maintain that anyone who does so is guilty of historical anachronism (Ball, 1988: 2, 4, 6, 21, 145–49; MacIntyre, 1998 [1967]: 1).[4]

The basic thrust of Callicles' approach to questions of ethics and politics in the *Gorgias* is to deny both that a life of morality or of 'justice', as this term was commonly understood in fifth-century Athens, is something which is natural to human beings and also, by implication, the related view that there is any such thing as natural justice or natural law, understood in the ethical sense. For Callicles to act in accordance with what passes for justice conventionally in *any* society would be to act 'contrary to nature'. In his view, the 'law of nature' (*nomos tes physeos*) necessitates that human beings are devoted entirely to the pursuit of their own self-interest as they understand it and have no concern at all for the well-being of others. I note in passing that, in his *The Will to Power*, Nietzsche also considers Callicles to be an immoralist (Nietzsche, 1968: 429, 233–34). There Nietzsche says with approval of the Sophists generally that they were 'realists' who 'have the courage, which all strong spirits have, to recognize their own immorality' (see Dodds, 1959: 389; also Dodds, 1973c: 105).

It is true that Nietzsche does not mention Callicles specifically by name in this passage, alluding directly only to the 'realist' attitude adopted by the Athenian envoys in the Melian Dialogues described by Thucydides, who are usually thought to have set aside all consideration of morality in their dealings with the inhabitants of the island of Melos. However, as more than one commentator has noted, it is difficult to believe that Nietzsche would have wished to exclude Callicles when making this judgement about the Sophist attitude towards morality. According to E. R. Dodds, for example, 'it seems evident that in this large generalization' Nietzsche also 'has in mind men of the stamp of Callicles', as well as thinkers such as Thrasymachus, and the fact that Nietzsche 'considered Callicles a spokesman for "the Sophists" is made clear in his lectures on Plato' (Dodds, 1959: 389; see also Hobbs, 2000: 151).

Some commentators have objected to the suggestion that the views which Plato puts into the mouth of Callicles in the *Gorgias* are those of a nihilist or an immoralist. After all Plato's Callicles *does* employ 'the language of morals'. He argues that an appeal to nature demonstrates that 'it is *right* that the better man should prevail over the worse and the stronger over the weaker' (Plato, 1994: 483b–e, 65–6). As Plato presents his views, Callicles evidently does consider himself to be some kind of moralist.[5] However, like Plato, I find the reasoning which lies behind this view unconvincing. Plato suggests that Callicles and others like him who also use the language of morals in this way do not understand the meaning of the words they are using and continually contradict themselves. It is, perhaps, for this reason that Plato employs the literary device of having Callicles explain his own ideas by using what many Athenians would have considered to be a self-contradictory expression, namely *nomos tes physeos*. Modern commentators who take the remarks which Plato places in the mouth of Callicles literally, as an expression of an alternative type of morality do not sufficiently appreciate this point. Moreover, there is a tendency for them to think of Callicles as if he were a real person and not a fictitious character in a work of literature.

If we accept that it was indeed Plato who first employed a phrase (*nomos tes physeos*) which might be thought to express the concept of natural law, this raises two important questions, which (contrary to the views of some commentators) are not necessarily connected to one another. The first is whether this implies that Plato himself can be seen as a natural law theorist. The second is whether Plato was the first ancient Greek to employ the concept of natural law in political argument and debate. I shall consider these two questions in turn, the first in the remainder of this section, and the second later in the chapter.

So far as the first question is concerned, it is arguable that Plato's employment of the expression *nomos tes physeos* in the *Gorgias* does not necessarily imply that Plato himself endorsed the concept of natural law. One obvious reason for this is that Plato places this expression in the mouth of Callicles and not Socrates. It is clear, however, that Plato does not approve of the views of Callicles, and indeed appears to be intent on ridiculing them (and him) by demonstrating their logical absurdity. As W. K. C. Guthrie has noted, 'in this first appearance of the phrase "the law of nature", it is used as a deliberate paradox' (Guthrie, 1971: 104). Another reason is that in any particular language exactly the same word or phrase might be used to designate two quite different concepts. Consequently, linguistic considerations of this kind are not by any means decisive when it comes to answering the question whether Plato himself endorsed the concept of natural law. Plato's employment of the phrase *nomos tes physeos* demonstrates this point very well. For it is clear that Plato's Callicles (and presumably, therefore, also Plato himself) does not mean by this expression what the later Stoic thinkers or indeed perhaps any natural law theorist properly so-called means by it, and that it designates or expresses a quite different concept from that of natural law understood in a moral or ethical sense. Callicles could, *not* therefore, be said to embrace the doctrine of naturalism as this stands opposed to conventionalism in the second nature versus convention debate. As E. R. Dodds notes, the doctrine advocated by Callicles ought 'not to be confused with "natural law" ' in anything like 'the Stoic sense'because it is not a moral rule. Indeed 'as Socrates shows later it amounts to domination by instinctive appetites' (Dodds, 1959: 268; also Guthrie, 1971: 104).

Although it is certainly true, then, that the notion of a *nomos tes physeos* is associated with Callicles in Plato's *Gorgias*, nevertheless its meaning in that particular context is quite different from the meaning which it would have for the advocates of the claims of nature as against those of convention, according to the second understanding of what the nature versus convention debate was about referred to earlier (Guthrie, 1971: 104; Striker, 1996: 212). It may be suggested, then, that so far as the question of whether Plato himself endorses the concept of natural law in an ethical sense is concerned we should not attach too much importance to the occurrence of the expression *nomos tes physeos* in the *Gorgias*.

It is, presumably, because Plato did not employ the concept of *nomos tes physeos* to express his own views, but only when identifying a view which he himself rejected, that G. P. Maguire has maintained that 'the term "natural law" is *not* Platonic' (Maguire, 1947: 151). Against this, however, it might be argued that, given that it was Plato who appears to have first used it, then it must be conceded that in one sense at least the term evidently *is* Platonic. Moreover, even if Plato did not employ this *term* in order to express his own beliefs, and even if the phrase *nomos tes physeos* could not for that reason be said to be Platonic, nevertheless there may be other reasons for thinking that Plato's own system of political thought could legitimately be said to rest upon a commitment to the concept of natural law. As John Wild has observed, 'even though the *terms* used' by Plato when expressing his own views 'may be different', nevertheless 'the *concept* could be present' (Wild, 1953: 135).

Plato and the Second Nature Versus Convention Debate

There are three reasons for attributing the notion of an ethical natural law to Plato, even though he did not have a linguistic expression to designate it; even though he employed the expression *nomos tes physeos* to express a quite different concept; and even though, when he used this phrase in the *Gorgias*, Plato's intention was evidently to ridicule the ideas of the person with whom he associates it. The first is that in the passage from the *Laws* where he provides an account of the nature versus convention debate Plato attributes to his opponents the Sophists the view that 'there is no *natural* standard of justice at all', for men 'are always wrangling about their moral standards and changing them', and in their view 'every change introduced becomes binding from the moment it's made, regardless of the fact that it is entirely artificial, and based on convention, not nature in the slightest degree' (Plato, 1981 [1926]), X, 889–890, 310–17). But this remark implies of course that those like Plato who rejected the Sophist view as it is presented in the *Laws* must have been committed to denying the truth of the assertion that 'there is no natural standard of justice', and hence to affirming the truth of its opposite.

The second reason is that Plato's political thought generally rests on the idea that a life of justice under law is something which is natural for human beings. It is an expression of their nature. Someone who thought in this way ought not to have been (and surely would not have been) critical of the idea of a 'natural law' or a 'law of nature', understood specifically in an ethical sense, provided some appropriate linguistic expression could be found to express it. Indeed, T. A. Sinclair has claimed that provided it is appropriately understood the idea of an ethical *nomos tes physeos* is not logically self-contradictory at all, and there would have been no inconsistency in Plato's own thinking if he had himself endorsed it. According to Sinclair, in such circumstances, the concepts of *physis* and *nomos* would be 'seen to be different, but *not* to be mutually exclusive' (Sinclair, 1959: 90). It is true, however, that Plato did not himself think that this is possible.

According to this line of reasoning to maintain, as Plato does against Callicles, that a life or morality of justice is natural, is but a very short step from arguing that there is indeed such a thing as natural justice. Thus, for example, Glenn R. Morrow has argued on these grounds that although it is true that there is a sense in which the expression *nomos tes physeos* could not strictly speaking be said to be 'Platonic', nevertheless it is clear that Plato *did* both possess and endorse the concept of natural law, or at least that of natural justice, precisely because his critique of Callicles is based on the assumption that, far from being 'contrary to nature', a life or morality or justice is natural for all human beings (Morrow, 1948: 42).

As I suggested in the Introduction, it seems clear that in his debate with the Sophists Plato was more concerned with the nature of justice or with the concept of justice than he was with natural justice or the concept of natural justice. He does not, for example, talk about natural justice as a type or species of justice, as distinct from other types or species of justice which might be said to stand alongside it or be related in some way to it. However, as Glenn R. Morrow has observed, it is arguable that according to Plato natural justice and the nature of justice, or the idea of justice, are one and the same. In Morrow's words for Plato 'natural justice *is* the Idea Justice'. Thus in his view '"justice itself" and "natural justice" mean the same thing' (Morrow, 1948: 31). I note in passing that much the same might also be said of Aristotle, and indeed even of Cicero. For this same ambiguity is also to be found in the famous passage form Cicero's *De Republica* which is invariably cited by commentators discussing Cicero and the concept of natural law (Cicero, 1966 [1928]), III, XXII, 33, 210–11).

The third reason for associating Plato with the concept of natural law has to do with the remarks which Plato puts into the mouth of Socrates, when debating with Callicles in the *Gorgias,* about the Pythagorean notion of geometrical equality and its relationship to the concept of justice. There Plato has Socrates criticize the views of Callicles in the following way. 'We can', Socrates argues, 'win happiness only by bending all our own efforts and those of the state to the realization of uprightness and self-discipline, not by allowing our appetites to go unchecked, and, in an attempt to satisfy their endless importunity, leading the life of a brigand'. Men like Callicles 'who adopts the latter course' are, Socrates claims, 'incapable of social life'. For 'we are told on good authority', he continues, 'that heaven and earth and their respective inhabitants are held together by the bonds of society and love and order and discipline and righteousness [*dikaiosune*], and that is why the universe is called an ordered whole or cosmos and not a state of disorder and license' (Plato, 1975: 508a, 117–18).

The connection between the views expressed here by Plato and those of the Pythagorean School is widely acknowledged (Adams, 1945: 106; Dodds, 1959: 20, 337–38; Fideler, 1988 [1920]: 36–7; Guthrie, 1971: 151; Greene, 1948: 234; Maguire, 1947: 160–62; Sinclair, 1959: 124–5). Indeed, what is particularly interesting about these remarks is that this is one of the few occasions where Plato suggests that justice is a cosmic principle inhering within the order of the universe, rather than something which is solely a human phenomenon. It is, in other words, a part of the natural order of things. However it is arguable that someone who thinks that justice is natural, in this particular sense of the term, must also believe that there is such a thing as natural justice. Moreover, given that there is a close relationship between the notion of justice and that of law, it follows that these remarks can be seen as an implicit endorsement of the idea of natural law, understood in an ethical sense. From this point of view, there is indeed a moral law or a principle of natural justice which is the inherent within the a cosmic system of order. There is a law of nature in a quite different sense from that which Plato had in mind when he put the expression *nomos tes physeos* in the mouth of Callicles.

It may be suggested, then, that there is an sense in which Plato's system of political thought may be said to rest upon a commitment to the notion of an ethical natural law, even if he did not employ the phrase *nomos tes physeos* to express that concept. Given this, it is not surprising that a number of commentators have argued that Plato's own political thought rests on a commitment to the notion of natural law, and indeed that Plato was the founder of the natural law tradition because it is in his writings that the concept of natural law, understood in its ethical sense, first clearly emerges. J. W. Salmond, for example, has argued that 'one of the chief objects of the *Republic* is to demonstrate the reality of a natural justice of which conventional justice is but an imperfect image or shadow' (Salmond, 1987: 126–7). And Michael Bertram Crowe has claimed that we find in Plato's writings 'almost all the elements of the fully formed theory of natural law as it was to appear in the Stoics and those who came after them' (Crowe, 1977: 17). Nor is it at all surprising therefore, Crowe continues, 'that it has been argued by some commentators that the natural law really begins with Plato, rather than with the

Stoics, who are usually given the credit of having been the first to formulate the doctrine' (Crowe, 1977: 17). Similarly Glenn R. Morrow has argued that 'it is plausible to suppose' that Plato's philosophy 'was an important factor in the formulation of the Stoic doctrine of the Law of Nature', and indeed that it was Plato, and not any of his predecessors, who 'laid the foundations for the Stoic conception of natural justice (Morrow, 1947: 17, 29; see also Friedrich, 1955; Levinson, 1953a; Maguire, 1947; Morrow, 1948; Ostwald, 1977; Salmond, 1897: 126–7; Sigmund, 1971: 2–9; Weinreb, 1987: 32; Wild, 1953: 38, 62, 103, 134–36).

This way of thinking about natural law constitutes one important point of similarity or continuity between the philosophy of Plato and that of later Stoicism. It therefore counts against the view of those commentators who argue that the transition from the political thought of classical Athens and that of Stoicism should be thought of in terms of the principle of discontinuity. I shall say more about this issue in the Conclusion. For the present it will suffice to draw attention to other similarities also. Marcus Aurelius (121–180 CE), for example, endorsed what might be termed the Platonic-Pythagorean notion of a 'cosmic order' of things in which everything has its 'place' alluded to by Socrates in the *Gorgias* (Plato, 1996 [1925]: 507–8). In his view, 'universal nature's impulse was to create an orderly world' (Marcus Aurelius, 1984: VII, 75, 119). For Marcus Aurelius, the bond which unites all things in the universe into a definite system of 'order' is the 'dependence' of one thing upon another (Marcus Aurelius, 1984: VI, 38, 99). In this cosmic order all 'are working together for the same end' and therefore, albeit in different ways, 'contributing their share to the cosmic process' (Marcus Aurelius, 1984: VI, 42, 101–2). In this cosmic 'society' there is a definite division of labour within which 'to one man falls this share of the task, to another that', and of course, as with Plato, Marcus Aurelius thinks that if one person were to 'interfere' with this cosmic order of things by attempting to do another's job then both 'disorder' and injustice will inevitably follow (Marcus Aurelius, 1984: VI, 43, 101).

It is true that there are also important differences between Plato's thought and that of the Stoics, not least regarding the issues of the natural equality of all human beings. However, whatever disagreement might exist between them about other issues, Plato and the Stoics were in agreement that there is an ethical law of nature which provides a higher standard of morality or justice which the laws of human societies ought to imitate or reflect; and which could, therefore, in certain circumstances be used to critically evaluate existing laws and institutions. As we shall see, this is a view which was emphatically rejected by Aristotle. This brings us to the second question referred to earlier, namely, was Plato the first person to argue, along these lines, that there is such a thing as natural justice or law?

Was Plato the First Natural Law Theorist?

In answer to the first of the two questions raised earlier I have argued that, quite irrespective of his employment of the phrase *nomos tes physeos,* Plato's political thought *can* be seen as resting upon the notion of natural law, understood in an ethical sense. Thus Plato himself embraced the doctrine of naturalism and was a staunch critic of conventionalism. But was Plato the first ancient Greek to do this? Is it in the writings of Plato that we can locate the origins or the emergence of the concept of natural law, as some commentators have argued? It should be obvious from what I said in the preceding chapter about the ideas of some of the Sophists (including Alcidamas, Antiphon, Hippias and Aristotle's 'anonymous opponents of slavery') that in my view the answer to this question is 'no'.

In this connection there is a view which I propose to subject to critical examination, and which is most clearly formulated in the writings of Glenn R. Morrow (Morrow, 1948: 17–20, 23–5, 27–8; but see also Strauss, 1968a: 80, 1974 [1953]: 93; Guthrie, 1971: 118–19; Myres, 1975 [1927]: 255). Morrow argues that the concept of natural law is to be found for the first time only in the writings of Plato and not before. In his view, therefore, the second nature versus convention debate referred to above took place not in the fifth century, but in fourth-century Athens. Moreover, it took place between the Sophists and Plato. Within this debate it is the Sophists who were unanimously committed to conventionalism and embraced the standpoint of ethical relativism, whilst it was Plato who was the first person we know about to oppose them, claiming that because a life of justice is natural for human beings there must be such a thing as natural justice or natural law. If we were to take seriously Morrow's suggestion that the concept of natural law first emerges in the writings of Plato then we would have to accept that there was no debate at all surrounding the respective merits of *physis* and *nomos* in fifth-century Athens *before* Plato, nor could there have been. For it is a logical requirement for the existence of any debate that there should be two sides to it which stand in opposition to one another. In Morrow's view, however, this was not the case in Athens in the fifth-century BCE. Or, more accurately, we do not have good enough reasons for thinking that this *was* the case. For at that time, Morrow claims, there was only one side to the story, the conventionalist side. It was Plato who presented the argument for the other side, associated with the doctrine of naturalism. However he did so only in the fourth century.

What is especially interesting about this view for present purposes is its implicit claim that there was unanimity among the Sophists in the fifth century, before Plato challenged their views, over the merits of conventionalism. Morrow suggests that, so far as we know, nobody in Athens before Plato possessed the concept of natural justice or law. Consequently he also suggests that there was no nature versus convention debate (in the second sense above) at all in the fifth century. Plato's discussion of the second nature versus convention debate in the *Laws* should not, therefore, be taken as a report of a debate which occurred between his predecessors in fifth-century Athens. Rather it should be seen as constitutive of that debate. It represents the very first occurrence of the nature versus convention debate, understood in this second sense.

This view, which is advanced by Morrow and others, relies heavily on the fact, upon which most commentators are agreed, that the linguistic expression *nomos tes physeos* is used for the first time by Plato, in his *Gorgias*. It is precisely because we do not find this phrase, or any equivalent linguistic expression, in the extant writings prior to Plato that Morrow claims that there are no good reasons for us to suppose that in fifth-century Athens before Plato any earlier Greek thinker possessed, let alone endorsed, the concept of natural law. According to this view, then, we cannot be confident that anyone in ancient Athens, before Plato, had thought of combining the two notions of *physis* and *nomos* together so as to produce the complex concept of natural law. Indeed, given the available empirical evidence, there is good reason to believe that before Plato nobody had thought of doing this. W. K. C. Guthrie, for example, has maintained that in ancient Greek political thought 'a verbal association of 'unwritten laws' with *physis* only occurs, among extant sources, in fourth-century authors' and, again, that 'the first use of the actual term' is in Plato's *Gorgias* (Guthrie, 1971: 18–19). Leo Strauss has claimed that in the fifth century before Plato 'the notion of "natural law" would have been considered to be 'a contradiction in terms' (Strauss, 1968a: 80). A. E. Taylor has argued that it is here in Plato's *Gorgias* that we find 'the first occurrence' in the 'extant literature' of 'the ominous phrase "Law of Nature"' (Taylor, 1949 [1908]: 17). And Morrow himself claims that no phrase which 'implies a connection between *nomos* and *physis*, is clearly attested in the extant literature of the Fifth and early Fourth Centuries, outside the writings of Plato' (Morrow, 1948: 19; see also 20–8). Indeed, Morrow agrees with Guthrie and Strauss that 'the Stoic phrase νομος φυσεως would probably have sounded strange and even paradoxical to the cultivated Athenian of the Socratic age' (Morrow, 1948: 19–20; see also Kroger, 2004: 916; Sinclair, 1959: 50; and Weinreb, 1987: 944, fn 105).

How might this view be criticized? One possible criticism is that Morrow and the other commentators cited above who agree with him are wrong to identify words with concepts. Morrow assumes that if it cannot be shown empirically that someone employed the phrase *nomos tes physeos*, or an equivalent linguistic expression, in fifth-century Athens then we are not justified in claiming that anybody at that time possessed the concept of natural law in the ethical sense (Morrow, 1948: 19; Maguire, 1947: 151). This is why he maintains that the concept of natural law is found for the first time only in the writings of Plato. However it is arguable that this assumption is excessively restrictive. One reason for thinking this is that, as we saw in the preceding chapter, it is possible for a member of a particular linguistic community to possess a concept even if there is no short-hand label or name within the language of that community to designate the concept in question. It is possible, as Terence Ball has noted, that 'one may possess a concept', or come to possess one, 'without having a word to express it' (Ball, 1988: 16; Skinner, 1995 [1989]: 7–8). Indeed, John Wild has suggested that arguments like Morrow's focus solely on 'philological considerations' which are 'hardly relevant to the theory itself'. For, Wild insists, 'even though the *terms* used may be different' nevertheless 'the *concept* could be present' (Wild, 1953: 135). Wild uses this argument to defend his claim that the concept of natural law can be found in the writings of Plato, and that it was Plato rather than the Stoics who was the founder of the natural law tradition (Wild, 1953: 38, 62, 103, 134–36). It is clear, however, that if Wild's reasoning on this point is valid then it applies in principle, not just to Plato, but to Plato's fifth-century predecessors also. It is possible therefore to argue against Morrow that the question of whether we can demonstrate that there were any Athenian intellectuals in the fifth century who employed the phrase *nomos tes physeos,* or an equivalent, is not decisive for any attempt to establish whether they possessed the concept of natural law, for there might be other reasons for thinking that they possessed this concept. In short, there could be alternative ways of establishing whether or not there was indeed a debate over the respective merits of nature versus convention in fifth-century Athens prior to and independently of Plato.

Morrow rightly suggests that a 'notable transformation' in the meaning of 'one or both' of the concepts of *physis* and *nomos* had to take place 'so as to permit their union' in the later 'Stoic doctrine' of natural law (Morrow, 1948: 19–20). So far as *physis* is concerned, this term came to be associated, in the doctrine of naturalism, with the idea of a universally valid 'higher' moral law. In the case of *nomos* this term came to lose the necessary association which it formerly had with that of custom or convention. In my view, however, it would be more accurate to say that, although such a process of conceptual transformation was indeed required before the concept of natural law in its ethical sense could emerge, there is no decisive reason to suppose that this only happened in the philosophy of the Stoics.

When exactly, therefore, did this happen? Morrow suggests that this act of combination must have occurred, not in the Fifth, but 'some time in the Fourth Century' (Morrow, 1948: 19–20). It is not clear whether he thinks that this process of conceptual change or innovation took place within, or independently of, the writings of Plato. Given Plato's own employment of the phrase *nomos tes physeos* in the *Gorgias,* which suggests that he considered this phrase to be self-contradictory, it might seem that in Morrow's view this development took place independently of Plato. However the broad thrust of Morrow's argument supports the conclusion that, in his opinion, Plato himself was the driving force behind it. Against this view, however it is arguable that this shift in meaning of the notions of *physis* and *nomos* actually occurred before Plato, in the fifth century, amongst the Sophists, not all of whom were conventionalists.

A logical implication of the views expressed by Morrow on this subject is that, in his opinion, *all* of the Sophists were conventionalists. According to Morrow we are justified in identifying Sophism with conventionalism. Moreover, we are also justified in maintaining that conventionalism was not simply the dominant view in fifth-century Athens, but the *only* view adopted by Athenian intellectuals prior to Plato. Morrow suggests that this is the only safe conclusion at which to arrive, given the available historical evidence, and providing we limit ourselves to the issue of whether, so far as we know, the phrase *nomos tes physeos*, or some equivalent linguistic expression has or has not been employed. In his view, although 'the distinction between natural and legal justice' does appear in the writings of Plato and Aristotle, nevertheless there is 'not sufficient evidence' that it had in fact 'been formulated by their predecessors' (Morrow, 1948: 27). Indeed, despite his more cautious claim at one point that 'there is little evidence' to support the view that fifth-century Athenian intellectuals even 'thought in terms of "natural justice," ' let alone that 'they succeeded in formulating an explicit theory of it', it is difficult to avoid the conclusion that in Morrow's judgment there is no evidence at all to support this view. Given this it is not at all surprising that Morrow insists that Callicles, in Plato's *Gorgias*, must be thought of as a literary character and not a real person. For 'if Callicles was a real person and actually expressed himself' in the terms attributed to him by Plato, then we would, Morrow concedes, have 'an instance of an attempt *prior* to Plato to unite the concepts of nature and justice' (Morrow, 1948: 30). Given that Morrow is an advocate of the view that it is Plato himself who unites these two concepts for the first time, it is not surprising that he emphasizes the fact that 'we know nothing about this Callicles other than what Plato's dialogue contains', and that 'it may well be' that he is nothing more than 'a dramatic fiction' (Morrow, 1948: 30).[6]

A number of other commentators have also identified Sophism and conventionalism (Friedrich, 1963: 13; Havelock, 1964 [1957]: 6, 9–13, 17–20, 26–29, 32; McIlwain, 1932: 395; Strauss, 1974 [1953]: 93). For example, Eric A. Havelock associates what he calls ancient Greek 'liberalism' with the Sophism and a commitment to ethical relativism or conventionalism and an emphasis on history rather than abstract reason or metaphysics (Havelock, 1964 [1957]: 6, 9–13, 17–20, 26–29, 32). C. J. Friedrich also identifies Sophism and conventionalism (Friedrich, 1963: 13). Indeed one commentator, Joseph Ober, has gone so far as to suggest that, not just the Sophists, but *all* Athenian intellectuals in 'classical Greece' prior to the Stoics were conventionalists or, as he puts it, 'legal positivists' (Ober, 1995: 395). I note in passing that C. H. McIlwain has claimed that the ultimate source for this identification is the writings of Plato and Aristotle, which (given their hostility to Sophism) raises the issue of whether their accounts of it 'may be trusted' (McIlwain, 1932: 395).

The views of Leo Strauss on this subject are of particular interest. Strauss has pointed out that although the 'discovery' of the 'fundamental distinction between nature and convention' in the fifth and sixth centuries is certainly a '*necessary* condition for the emergence of the idea of natural right' some time thereafter, nevertheless it could not be said to be 'its *sufficient* condition' (Strauss, 1974 [1953]: 93). For it is logically possible, of course, that 'all right might be conventional'. Or rather (more accurately) Strauss should perhaps have said that it is logically possible that there was unanimous agreement amongst the Athenians who discussed this issue in the fifth century prior to Plato that 'all right is conventional'. If this were indeed the case then, Strauss suggests, this would explain the fact that it is only in the writings of Plato that we find, for the very first time an expression of the concept of natural law in its ethical sense. On this point, then, Strauss seems to have concurred with Morrow and the other commentators cited above.

In his *Natural Right and History*, Strauss maintains that conventionalism was the view which 'prevailed' amongst Athenian intellectuals 'prior to Socrates' (Strauss, 1974 [1953]: 93). However, the precise meaning of this assertion is unclear. It is possible that what Strauss had in mind when he made it is that conventionalism was the unanimously accepted view in fifth-century Athens, and that this was so precisely because it had in fact not occurred to anyone before Plato that there might be certain principles of right, justice or law which are natural rather than conventional. Alternatively, however, Strauss might have had in mind the somewhat different, and to my mind far more plausible, claim that conventionalism 'prevailed' in ancient Athens in the fifth century because, although there were at least some thinkers who rejected it, insisting that there is indeed such a thing as natural right or natural law, nevertheless the view of these thinkers was a minority view. There is a significant difference between these two different interpretations of Strauss's views. However, given that Strauss agrees with Morrow that in the fifth century the expression 'natural law' would have been considered to be a contradiction in terms, then it seems that, despite his employment of the word 'prevailed' in the passage cited above, Strauss actually endorsed the first of these two interpretations and not the second. That is to say he held what I consider to be the implausible view that there was indeed unanimity around the doctrine of conventionalism in fifth-century Athens.

It should be emphasized that the explicit or implicit claim, made by Morrow, Strauss and others, that there was unanimity over this issue in fifth-century Athens, together with their suggestion that the reason why this unanimity existed is because before Plato it did not occur to anyone that there might be such a thing as natural justice or natural law, *is* an implausible one. My reason for thinking this is because simply to formulate the question 'is justice or law conventional?' entails the possibility that someone might offer a negative answer to it. However, it is difficult to see how one could possibly explain what is meant by the claim that justice or law is not conventional without invoking the idea of a justice or law which is 'natural'. For the terms 'natural' and 'conventional', in this context, are correlative in meaning. To say that justice and law are natural is precisely to say that they are *not*-conventional, and vice versa. Moreover once this question has been asked, and the theoretical possibility that it might be answered either positively or negatively has been raised, it is highly improbable that literally everyone in ancient Athens who considered it and who had an opinion about it would have agreed that the answer to it should be 'yes' rather than 'no'. In short, the doctrines of naturalism and conventionalism are logically related to one another and stand or fall together. If there were any thinkers at all who could legitimately be said to have been conventionalists in fifth-century Athens, and it is generally conceded that there were, then this implies that there could in principle have been at least some other thinkers who endorsed the opposing naturalist approach to questions of ethics and politics. And once we have conceded that this is a possibility then the balance of probabilities indicates that as a matter of fact there were at least some people who *did* think in this way, even though the amount of evidence testifying to their existence is undeniably small. We can also, of course, speculate about how they are likely to have argued. Moreover, this speculation is in fact supported by the little historical evidence which is available to us, including that provided by Plato in his remarks about the nature versus convention debate in the *Laws*.

Against Morrow, then, it may be suggested that there is at least some evidence that a second debate over the respective merits of nature and convention did indeed take place within the Sophist movement in the fifth century before Plato, and that the passage from Plato's *Laws* cited earlier was intended as an account of the arguments employed by the two opposing sides in this debate as well as being a contribution to it. For example, the view which Plato puts into the mouth of his character Callicles in the *Gorgias* appears not to have been novel and did not originate with Plato himself. Indeed, it is strikingly similar to that of the Athenian envoys at Melos as recounted by Thucydides in his *History of the Peloponnesian War*. According to Thucydides, the envoys argued that 'of the gods we believe, and of men we know, that by a necessary law of their nature they rule wherever they can' (Thucydides, 1952: V, LXXXIV–CXVI, 155–79). This view is much the same as that defended by Callicles. It could not, therefore, be said to have been created *de novo* by Plato himself. Rather, it is best seen as reflecting what Plato considered to be an insidious a current of thought prevalent in some circles in the Athens of his day. However, it is not clear why we should think any differently about what Plato has to say about the naturalism side of the second nature versus convention debate in the *Laws*. These remarks might also be seen as a report on views currently held by others, rather than an original contribution to the debate made by Plato himself.

This conclusion has implications for our understanding of Sophism. As we saw in the last chapter, there is at least some evidence that the Sophists movement in the fifth century was internally divided, and that not all of the Sophists were conventionalists. Consequently, there is also some evidence to support the view that already in the fifth century there were thinkers who possessed the concept of natural justice or law, even if they did not have a short-hand linguistic expression to designate it. Moreover it is arguable that those of the Sophists who adopted the standpoint of naturalism prefigured in a striking way the later argument of Plato, maintaining not only that a life of justice is something which is natural to man, but also (by implication) that there are certain principles of natural justice or natural law which all human beings ought to follow. Where they disagreed with Plato is over the issue of the natural equality of all human beings. The ideas of Plato can be seen as a critical response to or engagement with, but not an outright rejection of, the arguments of this naturalist wing of the Sophistic movement, at least some of the assumptions of which (though not all) Plato evidently shared.

It is worth pointing out in this connection that Morrow is somewhat hesitant about his own suggestion that the doctrine of naturalism is first clearly formulated in the writings of Plato. For at one point he acknowledges that there might have been some thinkers in fifth-century Athens who were not nihilists and who, when they appealed to nature as against convention, appear to have been making moral claims associated with an endorsement of the concept of an ethical natural law. There is, he concedes, a 'pronounced vein of cosmopolitanism and even humanitarianism in some of the surviving fragments of this controversy' (Morrow, 1948: 27). It is for this reason that G. B. Kerferd has maintained that although it is true that for some Sophists the 'antithesis of *nomos* and *physis*' was intended to be 'destructive of *nomos*', nevertheless the reason for holding this view this was not the same for all Sophists. It appears that some of the Sophists were nihilists who, like Plato's Callicles, took the view that all justice and law are 'contrary to nature'. According to Kerferd, however for others the 'appeal from *nomos* to *physis*' involved a 'recognition of *physis*' as being 'in some way prescriptive' and hence a 'source of values' (Kerferd, 1981: 114, 128). Similarly, Paul E. Sigmund has claimed that nature was 'regarded as a source of norms' by at least some of the Sophists (Sigmund, 1971: 2). Indeed Heinrich Rommen once went so far as to claim (implausibly) that 'the Sophists' (or more accurately some of them), by contrasting 'what is naturally right with what is legally right', were able to attain even at this 'early date to the notion of the rights of man and to the idea of mankind' (Rommen, 1998 [1947]: 7–8).[7]

As I suggested in Chapter 3 it is arguable that it is here in the extant fragments associated with the 'radical' wing of the Sophist movement and not in the writings of the Plato (or Aristotle, or the Stoics) that, in the words of W. K. C. Guthrie, we can locate 'the birth of the concept of natural law' (Guthrie, 1971: 118). In Guthrie's view, it is the members of this branch of the Sophistic movement, with their 'altruistic championship of *physis* against *nomos*' who first gave birth to 'ideas of equality, and of cosmopolitanism and the unity of mankind' which were later to be associated with Stoicism and the Stoic conception of natural law (Guthrie, 1971: 118; see also Baldry, 1965: 39–45; Dodds, 1973a: 105; Vogt, 1974a: 2). The significance of this was not lost on G. H. Sabine, who long ago argued, against the position later defended by Morrow and others, that 'the critical Athenian of the Fifth Century was quite aware that his society had its seamy side and the critic was prepared to appeal to natural right and justice as against the adventitious distinctions of convention' (Sabine, 1973a: 42–3). Sabine appreciated very well that an important corollary of this view is that a 'humanistic reaction' must have taken place 'in Greek philosophy' some time 'about the middle of the Fifth Century B.C' (Sabine and Smith, n.d. [1929]: 15). This 'change of interest', Sabine claimed, led to a consequent 'transformation' of the way in which the 'distinction between nature and convention', and hence also the concept of natural law itself had hitherto been conceived. After this transformation the conceptual distinction between 'nature' and 'convention' came to be thought of in a quite different way, as a distinction not between immoralism and moralism, as in the case of the first nature versus convention debate, but rather between 'that which has permanent and universal human interest and that which has merely external and superficial importance' that is to say, between 'the unchanging principles of human conduct', which were thought of as being 'moral or naturalistic', on the one hand, and the 'varying practices of customary morals, law and religion' on the other. It was in this revised sense that, according to Sabine, the distinction between *nomos* and *physis* 'was made current by the Sophists' in the second half of the fifth century. Moreover, Sabine argued, it is clear that those of the Sophists who opposed conventionalism at that time embraced a naturalistic doctrine which, because of its 'radical contrast between some sort of ideal life and the requirements of established law and morals', must have been a 'powerful solvent of traditional morality' (Sabine and Smith, n.d. [1929]: 15).

It is arguable, then, that both of the nature versus convention debates referred to at the beginning of this chapter took place in Athens in the fifth century BCE and that this does have implications for our understanding of Sophism. Some of the fifth-century Sophists, like Protagoras, were ethical relativists or conventionalists. However their views were opposed by two other groups of Sophists – a fact which alone demonstrates the dangers of attempting to generalize about what '*the* Sophists' thought. As William Chase Greene, has put it, 'it is now realized that the Sophists were united more by a common profession' than by 'any common doctrine'. It is, therefore, 'fallacious, to speak of "the Sophistic point of view"' (Greene, 1948: 222; see also Adams, 1945: 102).

The members of the first group of Sophists who rejected conventionalism were nihilists, like the character Callicles in Plato's *Gorgias*. As G. H. Sabine notes, in the opinion of Plato the nihilism of Callicles 'was the logical upshot of the Sophists teaching'. However, Sabine goes on, Callicles' view was 'not, of course, the doctrine taught by *every* Sophist' (Sabine and Barney-Smith, n.d. [1929]: 15). For the members of the second group of Sophists which rejected conventionalism also rejected nihilism. This group included Antiphon, Hippias and others, all of whom were advocates of naturalism or natural law theorists.

So far as Plato himself is concerned, we may say that in the fourth century he made a contribution to *both* of these debates over the respective merits of nature and convention. In his intervention in the first debate, he agrees with the critics of nihilism and sides with conventionalists such as Protagoras against Callicles. W. K. C. Guthrie has noted that Plato's attitude (as exemplified through the character Socrates) towards Protagoras in the *Protagoras* is much less hostile than his attitude towards the nihilist Callicles in the *Gorgias*. As Guthrie says, 'although he [Protagoras] might deal in relatives, where Socrates and Plato sought for absolutes, his moral teaching was far from reprehensible'. According to Guthrie, although Protagoras shared 'the general Sophistic belief that law and morality are the product of convention', he was nevertheless not their critic but 'their champion' (Guthrie, 1970 [1956]: 21–2). In his intervention in the second debate, Plato goes on in turn to criticize Protagoras's commitment to conventionalism or ethical relativism and insists that there are certain principles of natural justice which are objective or universally valid, and hence applicable to all human beings in all societies everywhere.

Contrary to the view held by some modern commentators, however, it is arguable that Plato was not in fact the first person to argue in this way. Although Plato was indeed the first person to employ the expression *nomos tes physeos*, or law of nature, albeit somewhat idiosyncratically, there is at least some evidence to support the view that he was not the first person to possess the concept of natural law. This suggests that in comparison with the views of his fifth-century predecessors Plato's views are closest to those of the Sophist natural law theorists, who he might be said to have in a sense followed. Plato's problem, of course, was that of differentiating his own position from theirs, especially given that in their thinking the concept of natural justice or law is associated with that of the natural equality of human beings. We shall see below that this was a problem for Aristotle also.

Aristotle and the Nature Versus Convention Debate

Aristotle's writings, especially his *Rhetoric* and *Nicomachean Ethics*, are an important source of information regarding the second of the two nature versus convention debates referred to earlier. In these texts Aristotle provides his readers with an account of the views of his predecessors in fourth and fifth century Athens. But what he says there about the nature versus convention debate, and about the concept of natural law, is also of importance for anyone who wishes to engage with Aristotle's own ideas. If it were asked whether it is useful to relate the political thought of Aristotle to the nature versus convention debate, understood in the second of the two senses indicated above and, if so, how might this be done, my answer to the first of these questions would be a decisive 'yes'. Indeed, I would go further and claim that familiarity with the debate in question is an essential pre-requisite for understanding Aristotle's ethical and political thought, which should be seen as a contribution to it. As I argued in Chapters 1 and 2, Aristotle's ideas are best seen as an attempt to steer a via media between the two opposing positions in the debate, naturalism and conventionalism, by combining them in to some kind of theoretical synthesis.

This is also the view of a number of other commentators. John Morrall, for example, has claimed that Aristotle's political thought was inspired by 'his desire to overcome the antithesis made by many Sophistic thinkers of the fourth and fifth centuries BC between law and nature (the famous *nomos-physis* controversy)' (Morrall, 1977: 82). Leo Strauss has suggested that Aristotle was seeking to avoid 'the Scylla of "absolutism" and the Charybdis of "relativism"' (Strauss, 1974 [1953]: 162).[8] W. A. Robson has argued that Aristotle 'steadfastly refrained from setting up an antithesis between nature and convention' (Robson, 1935: 201–2). A. A. Long has accepted that 'one could probably categorize Aristotle's overall theory of law as one that steers a middle course between nature and convention' (Long, 2005: 423). And Jean Roberts has argued recently that 'Aristotle's dialectical method is well illustrated by his contribution to the by then traditional nature-convention (*nomos-phusis*) debate'. According to Roberts, Aristotle 'claims that there is some truth on both sides, that is, that justice is *both* natural *and* conventional'. At the same time however Roberts also maintains, in my view wrongly, that for Aristotle natural justice provides 'a standard which any actual law should not violate' (Roberts, 2005 [2000]: 345). If this were true then it would follow that, for Aristotle, justice would be entirely 'natural' rather than something which is both natural and conventional. In short, Aristotle's intellectual and political project is to develop what Harold J. Berman has in a different context referred to as an 'integrative jurisprudence', that is to say a legal theory which seeks to integrate what are usually considered to be the two opposed positions of naturalism and conventionalism (Berman, 1993a: 1993–94). What the commentators just cited do not do, however, is clarify the details of this Aristotelian project by explaining just what this theoretical synthesis involves. What is required here is an account, which I attempted to provide in Chapter 1, of Aristotle's understanding of the relationship which exists between natural justice, legal or conventional justice and political justice; or between natural law, positive law and civil law.

Although, as we have seen, numerous commentators have argued that Aristotle is best seen as attempting to find a theoretical 'third way' between the two extremes of naturalism and conventionalism, not all of them have done so. Rather, like Fred Miller Jr., some have interpreted Aristotle as an advocate of the doctrine of naturalism, whereas others, like Hans Kelsen, have understood him to be a conventionalist. This disagreement which exists between modern commentators over the issue of whether Aristotle is a naturalist or a conventionalist has occurred partly because of the fragmentary character of the available historical evidence which has come down to us and partly because of the obscurity and consequent ambiguity of the remarks which Aristotle makes about this particular subject, especially the passage in Book V, Chapter 7 of the *Nicomachean Ethics* which I analyzed in Chapter 1. Moreover, as we saw in Chapter 2, there is evidence in Aristotle's writings to support *both* interpretations despite the fact that they appear to flatly contradict one another. This is one reason for thinking that Aristotle's ethical political thought require some kind of theoretical 'reconstruction'. Each of these interpretations attaches importance to certain passages the significance of which is dismissed or downplayed by the other. Given this disagreement it is perhaps not too surprising that W. K. C. Guthrie has suggested that Aristotle's views are logically inconsistent with one another and that there was an ongoing 'conflict between Platonist and Sophist' in Aristotle's 'own mind' (Guthrie, 1971: 123). In other words, according to Guthrie, Aristotle actually took *both* 'sides' in the debate at different times, and perhaps even at the same time. In short, his views on this subject are self-contradictory. In my view, however, this alleged contradiction is more apparent than real, and is resolvable once the necessary conceptual distinctions have been made.

How might Aristotle's own contribution to the second nature versus connection debate referred to earlier best be understood, in relation to the two extremes of conventionalism and naturalism? The traditional understanding of the Sophists is that they maintained that all justice is conventional. From this point of view, the existing social and political order in ancient Athens and the rule of law associated with it did not have the divine or religious sanction which it had traditionally been thought to possess, for example by writers such as Sophocles. It will be recalled that in the passage in the *Laws* where he offers an account of their views Plato states that the Sophists maintained that, like the laws, so also the gods are nothing more than 'fictions', or 'artificial concepts corresponding to nothing in nature'. In the context of fifth-century Athenian politics, therefore, the views of these Sophists were perceived by Aristotle to have radical political implications. They were considered to be subversive of the existing social and political order. Like Plato, Aristotle is best seen as an opponent of this doctrine. He should not, therefore, be understood as a conventionalist or as an ethical relativist. On the contrary, one of his aims in the *Ethics* is to provide a refutation of the claim made by some Sophists that there is no such thing as natural justice and that all justice is merely conventional. I am, therefore, in agreement with Richard Bodéüs when he says, in his discussion of natural justice in the *Nicomachean Ethics*, the argument of which underpins his *Politics*, that 'Aristotle's purpose is to refute the opinion of those who hold that positive right is strictly "legal", that is to say, a matter of "convention"' (Bodéüs, 1999: 80). On the other hand, however, Aristotle does not go to the opposite extreme and advocate that justice is in its entirety something which is either natural or rational. In particular he is opposed to the view that the principles of natural justice or law can provide a rational or ahistorical standard by means of which the system of political justice of any society might be criticized. For in the context of Athenian politics, such a doctrine would have been just as radical as that of his Sophist opponents. It could be employed for example, and indeed arguably was so employed by the 'anonymous opponents of slavery', to criticize that particular institution. Rather, Aristotle seeks to combine the ethical and legal conventionalism of one group of Sophists with the idea of a universally valid natural justice or law held by another group into a third doctrine which, in his view, possesses the strengths of each and the weaknesses of neither of these two opposed positions.

I suggested earlier that Aristotle's position in the nature versus convention debate is best thought of as a third approach, which is basically a theoretical synthesis of, or a compromise between, the more extreme positions associated with it. However, it might be asked, in what sense *could* Aristotle's position be said to be a theoretical synthesis of the two opposed positions of naturalism and conventionalism? For if Aristotle did indeed endorse the notion of natural justice or law, and is therefore rightly considered to be a 'natural law theorist', then it appears to make no sense at all to claim that he attempted to steer a middle course between the standpoint of naturalism and that of conventionalism. Does it not follow from this that he embraced the doctrine of naturalism, and that he rejected that of conventionalism outright? Did he not agree with his predecessors that there is indeed such a thing as an ethical 'law of nature', and hence that the position adopted by the conventionalists is just wrong? The answer to this question is a simple one. It is that Aristotle agreed with certain features of the doctrine of naturalism as it had hitherto been understood but not with others.

The suggestion that Aristotle's political thought attempts to steer a *via media* between the two extremes of naturalism and conventionalism appears to imply that Aristotle did not take sides within the debate as it was then understood. Rather, he sought to distance himself from both sides, precisely because he considered them both to be extreme. However things are not quite so simple as this, for a number of reasons. First it is arguable that there is a sense in which it is just not possible to compromise between the two sides in the second nature versus convention debate as Aristotle understood it. For given the fundamental question at issue in that debate either one accepts that there is such a thing as natural justice or law or one does not. In my view, therefore, there is an obvious sense in which Aristotle certainly *did* take sides in this debate. For in Book V, Chapter 7 of the *Ethics* he emphatically affirmed the existence of natural justice or law. *Pace* Kelsen, therefore, Aristotle was definitely not a conventionalist. If the question 'Is Aristotle a naturalist or a conventionalist?' were posed in a straightforward 'either-or' form (although it should not be) then the answer to it would have to be that he embraced the doctrine of naturalism and rejected that of conventionalism. Nor is there any inconsistency involved in asserting both that Aristotle took sides in the nature versus convention debate and that his views constitute a theoretical synthesis of, and therefore a compromise between, the two extreme positions within it which were taken by his predecessors. In short, Aristotle's own position in the debate does constitute a form of 'naturalism'. This particular version of the doctrine of naturalism, however, differed significantly in certain respects from that of Aristotle's predecessors, including Plato.

Aristotle evidently agreed with Plato over some issues, especially Plato's rejection of an extreme version of the doctrine of conventionalism, and hence also of Sophism as that doctrine is often understood. C. H. McIlwain was at least partially right when he said that Aristotle 'takes a position on this question' which is 'not fundamentally different from Plato's'. According to McIlwain, the answer which Aristotle gives to 'the greatest of all the questions about justice' is 'in the main' the 'same answer that Plato also gave to the Sophists'. McIlwain correctly argues that Aristotle 'was as much concerned as Plato in proving against the Sophists' that justice is 'no mere variable human device, but rather a natural and universal characteristic of man as man'. There are undeniably points of *dis*agreement between Plato and Aristotle with respect to a number of significant issues, not least questions of metaphysics, but this is not one of them. So far as their respective attitudes towards the second nature versus convention debate are concerned, as McIlwain argues, what is important to Aristotle 'as much as to Plato' is 'the fundamental fact' of the '"natural" character' of justice (McIlwain, 1932: 395–97). As Lloyd L. Weinreb has put it, 'having to make a choice, Aristotle undoubtedly sided with Plato against the Sophists' (Weinreb, 1987: 34). However, Aristotle's version of naturalism was of a peculiar kind, and in certain respects significantly different from that of Plato. In short although Aristotle agreed with those of his predecessors who embraced naturalism about some things, nevertheless he disagreed with them about others.

So far as the agreements are concerned, like the advocates of naturalism who preceded him Aristotle accepted that there is such a thing as natural justice or law. He accepted that the hallmarks of natural justice or natural law are that it possesses the features of timelessness and universality, and also considered those actions which are forbidden by natural justice or law to be essentially unjust or intrinsically wrong. It is the nature of these actions that they are wrong or unjust, always and everywhere. This alone is sufficient to establish Aristotle's credentials as a natural law theorist rather than an ethical relativist or conventionalist.

This view that Aristotle's ethical and political thought is best seen as a certain type of naturalism, and therefore a contribution to natural law theory, is also supported by a consideration of his metaphysical beliefs. As we saw in Chapter 2, Aristotle makes a distinction between that in an individual substance which is 'essential' and that which is 'accidental'. It is not difficult, however, to connect the notion of natural justice or law, as he understood it, with the former, and legal or conventional justice with the latter. For Aristotle if a political constitution is indeed an individual 'substance', in the sense in which he talks about such things in his *Metaphysics*, then what is of essential importance about it are the principles of natural justice or law which underpin it, which are shared with all other constitutions everywhere, rather than the accidental characteristics which Aristotle associates with its particular historical existence and which vary legitimately from constitution to constitution.

So far as the disagreements between Aristotle and the natural law theory of the Sophists are concerned, although Aristotle certainly did embrace some form of naturalism what he did *not* accept is the idea, which he associated with naturalism as it was then understood, that the law of nature is a yardstick or higher standard of justice which might be employed to critically evaluate the principles of political justice (civil laws) of a particular *polis* and its constitution. Rather than seeing the principles of natural justice or natural law as being component elements of (and therefore inhering immanently within) the principles of political justice, which in Aristotle's view is how they should be seen, his predecessors thought (as Plato did) of those principles as existing or subsisting separately from and in a sense outside or above the system of political justice of any particular *polis*. In other words, they subscribed to a transcendent rather than an immanent conception of natural law. As I argued in Chapter 1, to attribute such a view to Aristotle would be to misunderstand completely his view of the relationship which exists between the principles of natural justice and those of political justice or between natural law and civil law.

It may be conjectured that it is for this reason that, in Aristotle's opinion, the employment of the concept of natural law by his predecessors had objectionable radical political implications, whereas his own did not. Despite endorsing the concept of natural justice or natural law, then, Aristotle also argued that in the final analysis the standard or rule which determines the ethical duties of the individual citizens of any *polis* are the principles of political justice, or the civil laws, associated with the constitution of that polis. In this respect, therefore, Aristotle's political thought makes a major concession to the doctrine of conventionalism or ethical relativism. Indeed, as we have seen, some commentators, including Hans Kelsen, have claimed that Aristotle was not a naturalist at all, but rather an out-and-out conventionalist with views very close to those which are usually associated with Sophism (Guthrie, 1971: 53;

Kelsen, 1973c: 122–36, 1957b: 125–36; Kroger, 2004: 917; Morrall, 1977: 98–9; Yack, 1990: 216). W. K. C. Guthrie, for example, went so far as to conclude that 'on the subjects in which the Sophists were primarily interested, Aristotle's standpoint was in many ways closer to theirs than to Plato's' (Guthrie, 1971: 53). This seems to me, however, to be an exaggeration.

It follows from the above that if we do attempt to locate Aristotle's ethical and political thought against the context of the nature versus convention debate in fifth-century Athens then Aristotle may be said to have not just one but *two* groups of Sophists opponents. The first group includes the advocates of conventionalism, whereas the second includes those who, in Aristotle's view, were committed to the doctrine of naturalism, and hence to the idea of natural justice or natural law, understood in a sense which Aristotle considered to be objectionable. Aristotle was opposed to conventionalism because, in his view, this doctrine undermined the existing social and political order by depriving it of any rational or philosophical justification. On the other hand though, in Aristotle's opinion, the opposite point of view, the naturalism or 'natural law theory' which he also rejected, tended to undermine the existing social and political order for a different reason. It did so because it was excessively rationalistic and far too inflexible. It set up a critical standard of justice, which it alleged to be 'natural' and therefore superior to the laws and customs of particular societies or *poleis* precisely because it is the highest standard of justice. Its proponents argued that if existing customs, laws or institutions do not conform to the requirements of the 'universal law' or the 'law of nature' then individuals might legitimately claim that they are contrary to nature and therefore unjust. To Aristotle this form of extreme naturalism was just as objectionable as the doctrine of conventionalism. Again, as we have seen, it could be and was used by 'the anonymous opponents of slavery' referred to by Aristotle in the *Politics* to criticize that particular social institution.

Few commentators have properly understood Aristotle's views on the relationship between natural law, positive law and civil law. One of those who has done so is Hegel (Burns, 1995, 1996, 1998b). Another is Sir Ernest Barker. As Barker rightly puts it, for Aristotle 'that the law is natural does' not 'preclude the agency of man in creating law', for Aristotle 'refuses to make an antithesis between nature and art'. We must, Barker insists, 'distinguish between the naturally and the legally just, not however as antithetical, but as supplementary to one another' (Barker, 1959: 327). Pierre Aubenque also appreciates this point. Like Barker, Aubenque acknowledges that for Aristotle 'law (*nomos*) is not opposed to nature (*physis*)' (Aubenque, 1980: 147). Aubenque rightly suggests that when Aristotle contrasts that which is 'natural' with that which is 'legal' or 'conventional', what he has in mind is 'a distinction rather than an opposition, since natural justice, given its generality, needs to be particularized', and for Aristotle this is the task of conventional justice or positive law (Aubenque, 1980: 154). Readers familiar with Hegel's *Philosophy of Right* will recognize the similarity between Aubenque's account of Aristotle's understanding of the relationship which exists between natural law and positive law and Hegel's pronouncement in his *Philosophy of Right* that although natural law is indeed 'distinct from positive law', nevertheless to 'pervert their difference into an opposition and a contradiction would be a gross misunderstanding' (Hegel, 1979: §3, 16). The affinity between the views of Aristotle and Hegel on this point is striking and, as Aubenque himself observes, by no means accidental (Aubenque, 1980: 157). Nor is the significance of this for those seeking to establish Aristotle's relationship to the natural law tradition lost on Aubenque. He understands very well that if, for Aristotle, that which is 'legal' does not and cannot stand opposed to that which is 'natural', but rather complements it, then it follows that civil law can never conflict with the requirements of natural law (Aubenque, 1980: 151).

I agree, then, with R. J. Corbett's recent suggestion that for Aristotle 'natural political justice is not a "higher" rule by which the positive law may be judged, but is instead a part of what a particular city says about what is just and unjust' (Corbett, 2009: 230). Corbett has argued that for Aristotle if by 'natural right' or 'natural law' we mean 'a standard or rule by which to judge such actions that would be a useful guide to decision-making', a 'cosmopolitan' standard of justice, then this idea has no part to play in Aristotle's political thought, as for Aristotle 'only conventional right provides such a standard' (Corbett, 2009: 250). However, it seems to me that Corbett comes very close here to suggesting, wrongly, that the notion of natural law, properly so called, has no part to play in Aristotle's political thought, and that Aristotle is best thought of as being a 'conventionalist' *simpliciter*, precisely because he endorses the principle of 'the particularity of all right' (Corbett, 2009: 250).

Corbett's analysis overlooks two things. First, for Aristotle the ethical imperatives which forbid the performance of acts such as murder, theft and adultery are principles of natural justice as well as being also, in their particularized forms, principles of political justice. Aristotle holds, for example, that it is the principle of natural justice or law forbidding the act of murder which places the citizens of a *polis* under a moral obligation to obey the principle of political justice which, in their case, declares certain acts of killing to *be* acts of 'murder'. It is not at all clear, therefore, that it can legitimately be claimed, as Corbett does, that the principles of natural justice are not a useful guide to decision making in Aristotle's ethical thought. Second, Corbett seems to be suggesting here that if the principles of natural justice or law do not provide a 'standard or rule' which is a useful guide to decision making, because this function is carried out by political justice or civil law, then it is clear that the concept of natural law can serve no useful function in Aristotle's political thought. Hence the notion can be discarded, and the few references which he makes to it in his writings, can be safely set aside. Again, however, this seems to me to overlook something important, namely the fact that for Aristotle the idea of natural justice or law has a legitimating function. In his view it is the natural justice or law which lies behind or inheres within the principles of civil law (especially but not only in the sphere of corrective justice) that makes those principles 'just', and which might therefore be said to justify them.

The suggestion that Aristotle's theoretical project was to combine the doctrines of naturalism and conventionalism presupposes, of course, that in his opinion both of these standpoints had in fact already been formulated by his predecessors. In particular, it assumes that some of the intellectuals who were the targets for Aristotle's criticism had already embraced naturalism before Aristotle set himself the task in the *Ethics* of providing his readers with an account of their beliefs. I suggested in Chapter 3 that Aristotle developed his own understanding of the concept of natural law by way of a critical engagement with the ideas of these early natural law theorists, some of whom, *pace* Morrow and others, he locates historically prior to Plato in fifth-century Athens. In his *Rhetoric* Aristotle suggests that a nature versus convention debate, understood in the second of the two senses outlined earlier, did take place in Athens in the fifth century BCE within the Sophist movement, and that some of the participants in that debate embraced a version of naturalism. It would seem, then, that Aristotle did not identify Sophism with conventionalism. He was well aware that not all of the Sophists were conventionalists, and that some of them embraced a form of naturalism which he himself rejected because of what he considered to be its objectionable political implications.[9]

On this view, then, although Aristotle's approach to questions of ethics and politics undoubtedly did attach importance to that which is culturally relative and historically particular, nevertheless this should not be thought of as over-riding his emphasis on the importance of that which is natural, rational and universal. It is fair to say, therefore, that Aristotle's theoretical synthesis of naturalism and conventionalism, as these two doctrines had hitherto been understood, did not transcend the standpoint of naturalism altogether. Rather, it should be thought of as significantly modifying that doctrine. In effect Aristotle was responsible for a shift in the understanding of what was meant by naturalism, and hence also of the concept of natural justice or law.

We saw in Chapter 1 that, according to M. Salomon Shellens, 'philosophers and historians almost invariably claim that Aristotle is the father of natural law' (Salomon Shellens, 1959: 72; see also Crowe, 1977: 19; Destrée, 2000: 220; Friedmann, 1967: 10; Friedrich, 1963: 22–23). However this is an exaggeration. Aristotle's engagement in the second nature versus convention debate can indeed be seen as having an important part to play in the historical evolution of the meaning of the concept of natural law. However, the significance of Aristotle's contribution to the history of this concept should not be misunderstood. It was not in the writings of Aristotle that the concept of natural justice or law first emerged. To claim that it was would be no more true in the case of Aristotle than it is in that of Plato.

Notes

[1] After I had written the first version of this chapter I discovered that the suggestion that there were actually two debates in ancient Athens and not just one is also made in Gisela Striker. See Striker, 1987: 79–94. I am grateful to Thornton Lockwood for drawing this to my attention.

[2] For the commonly held (and in my opinion correct, although not unchallenged) view that Plato's Callicles is a nihilist or an immoralist see also Barker, 1960 [1918]: 66–69; Field, 1930: 90; Dodds, 1959: 263–4; Foot, 2003: 150; 1994: 7; Greene, 1948: 222, 237, 239–40; Hamilton, 1975 [1960]: 10–11; Havelock, 1964a [1957]: 256–58, 260, 262, 267, 278, 288; Jaeger, 1939–45, II, 327; Kerferd, 1981b: 118; Nill, 1985: 18, 53, 56; Parry, 2004: Sinclair, 1959 [1951]: 70–76, 81, 87, 129; Striker, 1996: 211–12; Strong, 2000 [1975]: 354.

[3] W. A. Robson overlooks this passage when he claims, wrongly, that it is only with Aristotle that 'the distinction between nature and convention was clearly formulated for the first time' (Robson, 1935: 201).

[4] For a thoughtful response to this line of reasoning, to which I am sympathetic, see Warnock, 1971: 3–10.

[5] For the claim that Callicles *is* a 'moralist' of a peculiar kind see Furley, 1981: 82; Guthrie, 1971: 106; Hamilton, 1975 [1960]: 10; Kerferd, 1981b: 118–19; Pendrick 2002: 61.

[6] For the issue of the ontological status of Plato's 'Callicles' see Dodds, 1959a: 12; Guthrie, 1971: Kerferd, 1981b: 52; Shorey, 1933: 141-2; and Untersteiner, 1954: 344–5.

[7] However Rommen confuses matters, in the same passage, by citing as an example of this view Plato's Callicles and his thesis that 'might makes right'. It is arguable that this is not an ethical doctrine at all and that Plato's Callicles is a nihilist rather than an advocate of the idea of natural law in any relevant sense.

[8] Although I disagree with Strauss's further claim that the reason why Aristotle was able to avoid these two extremes is because he took the view that 'there are no universally valid rules of action'. See Burns, 2010b. It seems to me that anyone who took this view would be denying outright that there are any principles of 'natural justice' or 'natural law', something which Aristotle evidently did not wish to do.

[9] For Aristotle's understanding of and attitude towards the Sophists more generally see Classen, 1981.

Conclusion

In my concluding remarks I would like to return again to the theoretical framework introduced in the Introduction to the present work and summarize my account of its relevance for an assessment of the political thought of Aristotle so far as it touches on the concept of natural law. It will be remembered that I made a distinction there between issues relating to the meaning of texts and how this is to be established, on the one hand, and issues relating to the meaning of the concepts, like that of natural law, which are deployed by the authors of these texts (as well as by other language users in wider society), on the other. So far as the first of these issues is concerned I made a further distinction between a number of different ways in which the meaning of texts might be established, associated with the activities of interpretation, appropriation, negotiation, deconstruction and reconstruction. The first of these, interpretation, can be associated with the idea of the discovery of the meaning of a text by those who read it. It is often thought that this approach to the reading of texts is best exemplified in the work of Quentin Skinner. The second of them, appropriation, can be connected with the imposition of meaning on a text by those who read it. This approach within the discipline of philosophical hermeneutics can be found in the writings of Martin Heidegger and is often associated with the philosophy of Nietzsche and of Poststructuralism, especially (though wrongly) with the work of Jacques Derrida, and with two slogans of 'anything goes!' and 'the death of the author'. The third method of establishing the meaning of a text, negotiation, can be found in the writings of Hans Georg Gadamer, and can be associated with the idea of the reader of a text steering a 'middle course' between the extremes associated with the other two positions. We also saw that this might happen in different ways, or for different reasons.

The last method referred to, that of reconstruction, as I understand it, applies in situations where our sources are fragmentary, or the integrity of a text is at issue. It also comes into play where the pronouncements made by an author either appear to be, or really are, logically inconsistent, both between texts and within them, especially the latter. In such cases a variety of readings, each of which renders the views of a particular author internally consistent will be possible. On this view the aim of a reconstruction, or a reconstructive reading, in such cases is to seek to recover the ideas of the author of a text or texts, or to restore them to something like their original integrity, it being assumed of course that this is something which can and should be done. The ideas associated with such reconstructions are intended to be not only logically coherent but also a true and faithful account of the beliefs of the original author of a text as they were understood by the author herself or himself. The activity of reconstruction is therefore very similar to that of interpretation, and the two terms are close to one another in meaning. We also saw, however, that the notion of 'reconstruction' is employed in a different way by other authors.

Given this terminology, how are we to conceptualize the reading of Aristotle's key texts, the *Nicomachean Ethics*, the *Politics* and the *Rhetoric*, which is put forward in the present work? Certainly the intention here has been to offer an 'interpretation' in the strict sense of the term of the ethical and political thought of Aristotle, as it is laid out in these works, so far as it deals with or relies on the concept of natural law. It has not been my intention to appropriate the meaning of these texts, or of the ideas deployed within them, for purposes of my own. Although it may well be, of course, that the reader will take the view that I have not in fact succeeded in realizing my own intentions. Should that be the case then the argument developed in this book should be seen as an invalid interpretation of the political thought Aristotle rather than an attempted appropriation of it.

So far as the second issue referred to above is concerned, I suggested in the Introduction that there are a number of different ways in which we might think about the meaning of concepts and about the idea of conceptual change, both as to how it occurs and also as to why it occurs. For example, like T. S. Kuhn, Michel Foucault and the early Quentin Skinner, we can think a conceptual change as involving a 'paradigm shift' or an intellectual 'revolution', a radical shift in perception and conception associated with the complete abandonment of an old way of thinking, with its concepts and corresponding terminology, and its replacement by a new one. Or, alternatively, one might think about conceptual change along slow, evolutionary lines, as is suggested by a reading of the philosophy of the later Wittgenstein (Burns, 2011a). I also suggested in the Introduction that one way of thinking about concepts such as that of natural law is to suggest that they do not have a core or essential meaning, but rather a meaning which can be seen to evolve or change more or less rapidly over time. Those who employ the concept, who may be historically distant from one another, may nevertheless still be able to communicate with one another because there is a linguistic convention which governs the use of the phrase which expresses it in a particular natural language which they all recognize and follow. It is, however, possible for those who use this phrase at a later time to follow the relevant linguistic convention in new and creative ways. In this way the meaning of the associated concept can and does alter over time.

One way of thinking about the subject of conceptual change is to focus on the issue of the emergence of new concepts and on the process of how this comes about in a particular society at a particular time, such as for example the concept of natural law in ancient Greece. It is clear that there is a linguistic dimension to this. That is to say, part of what is involved in this process is the introduction of a new terminology, and expansion of the vocabulary employed by the members of a particular linguistic community, in the case of the concept of natural law its ethical vocabulary. However, there is a difference between talking about words and talking about the concepts with which those words are associated. There is also what might be termed a separate, conceptual dimension to this phenomenon. In some cases, for example, a new concept can come into being as a consequence of the combination of two other concepts, which may have been considered to be incompatible with one another before this act of combination took place. And the emergence of this new concept may or may not be associated with the parallel emergence of a convenient short-hand label, or linguistic phrase, in effect a 'name', by means of which it might be designated. One example of such a process of concept formation would be the emergence of the concept of 'dialectical materialism' during the nineteenth century (Burns, 2002b). Another example, as I have sought to show, is the emergence of the concept of natural law in classical Athens in the fifth century BCE.

I have suggested that, at the time when Aristotle was writing, there was a political struggle taking place in ancient Athens around the concept of natural law. The participants in this struggle sought to appropriate the concept of natural law for their own particular cause. To employ the terminology of Hegel, this was a 'struggle for recognition' relating to the ownership or control of the meaning of this nascent concept, and over the issue of how it ought to be employed in political argument and debate. At the same time this was also a conflict around the issue of which linguistic phrase should be used to express it. Aristotle's political thought can fruitfully be seen as a contribution to these struggles, which commentators sympathetic to Marxism would consider to be an early form of 'ideological warfare'.

Aristotle's involvement in this form of conceptual politics constitutes a major contribution to the history of the concept of natural law, both during the period of its emergence in ancient Greece and afterwards. This is not, however, because he was the first person, or even the first significant political philosopher, to employ the concept, either in the *Ethics* where it is expressed by the phrase *physikon dikaion*, or in the *Rhetoric*, where it is expressed by the phrase *nomos koinos* or 'universal law', which Aristotle associates with the 'law of nature'. I have suggested that not just Plato but also some of the fifth-century Sophists did this before him. Nor is it because Aristotle contributed the most popular, convenient or influential short-hand phrase by means of which this concept could be expressed. The term 'universal law' (*nomos koinos*) of the *Rhetoric* did not really 'catch on'; and the *physikon dikaion* of the *Nicomachean Ethics* is usually translated into English as 'natural justice' or 'natural right' rather than 'natural law'. Nor, finally, is it because Aristotle's efforts in this ideological or conceptual 'struggle' were particularly successful. For the way of thinking about the concept of natural law to which he was opposed, and which he sought to combat in his writings, came eventually in the writings of the Stoics and later Cicero to be the dominant one. It was to achieve hegemonic status in comparison with his own way of thinking about natural law and its relation to civil law.

Cicero is rightly considered to be a major figure in the history of the concept of natural law and, although he was not himself a Stoic, is often thought to have provided *the* classical account, not just of the Stoic doctrine, but of the idea of natural law and of 'natural law theory' *per se*, which as I have argued elsewhere is usually identified with the Stoic conception of it (Burns, 1996b). The much cited passage from Book III, Chapter XXII of his *De Republica* referred to in the Introduction to the present work is especially important in this regard. This passage is invariably cited by commentators who write about the concept of natural law and its history and is considered to be canonical. The passage from Book V, Chapter 7 of the *Nicomachean Ethics*, which was the subject of analysis in Chapter 1, on the other hand, although also widely cited, has often been misunderstood, and its status questioned. For Aristotle does not say there what many commentators expect him to say, and think that he *ought* to have said, if he really is an authentic example of someone who attaches importance to the concept of natural law.

What, then, is Aristotle's significance for the history of the concept of natural law? In my view there are two reasons for thinking that Aristotle made a major contribution to that history. The first is because he was the founder of a distinct natural law tradition, the existence of which should be acknowledged, and which ought to bear his name. Indeed an alternative and equally appropriate title for the present work would be *The Founding of the Aristotelian Natural Law Tradition*. As J. W. Harris has claimed, this Aristotelian natural law tradition, especially its Thomist version, may properly be seen as conservative if its practical consequences are compared with 'the revolutionary implications' to which natural law theory 'later gave rise' in the seventeenth and eighteenth centuries (Harris, 1980: 10; see also Berki, 1984: 107; Burns, 2000a; Eccleshall, 1978: 55; Neumann, 1957: 81, 85).

If one were to employ the terminology associated with the different political ideologies when discussing the views associated with the Aristotelian natural law tradition, then one might say that whereas Cicero and the Stoic conception of natural law are the forerunners of the individualist liberal natural rights theory of modern times, Aristotle is the founder of the conservative conception of natural law which in the medieval period is best expressed in the writings of Aquinas and in the modern era is to be found in the writings of figures such as Montesquieu, Burke and Hegel. I agree entirely with Hans Kelsen when he observes that the view that 'the interpretation of natural law is the prerogative of the authorities established by positive law' is one which serves, not to weaken but precisely 'to strengthen the authority of positive law.' Consequently, this type of natural law theory 'has, on the whole, a strictly conservative character' (Kelsen, 1957c: 150; see also Lloyd, 1959: 53). One of the aims of the present work is, by focusing on Aristotle's understanding of the relationship between natural law, positive law and civil law, to explain how and why this is the case. It should be emphasized that Aristotle's way of thinking about that relationship is inherited by those who follow him within the tradition, including the Scholastic theologians of the medieval period, notably St. Thomas Aquinas and Francisco Suarez (Burns, 2002a).

I have on a number of occasions, in the course of his book and elsewhere, drawn a parallel between the political thought of Aristotle, or the particular natural law interpretation of it presented here, and that of Hegel, who I consider to be the last great thinker working within the Aristotelian tradition, and someone whose political thought is best understood by locating it against that background (Burns, 1995, 1996, 1998b). Many hundreds of years separate Aristotle and Hegel. In the present work I have discussed the founding of the Aristotelian natural law tradition, which is also a conservative natural law tradition, in the writings of Aristotle himself. The later history of that tradition however, between the time of Aristotle and that of Hegel, and of the ideas of the many theorists who have contributed to it, has yet to be written.

Aristotle and the Stoic Conception of Natural Law

The second reason for thinking that Aristotle made a major contribution to the history of the concept of natural law has to do with the impact which his ideas had, or may plausibly be thought to have had, on the thinking of the Stoic thinkers who came after him. It is often suggested that the origins of the concept of natural law are to be found, in the period *after* Plato and Aristotle, in the philosophy of the Stoics. For example, John Wild refers to 'the accepted opinion that natural law philosophy began with the Stoics' (Wild, 1953: 62, 135; see also Ober, 1995: 395; Striker, 1987: 80–1). And Gerard Watson has observed that 'the development of the 'natural law tradition' is 'normally accredited to the Stoics' (Watson, 1966: 67). According to Watson, 'to write about natural law' in Stoicism is 'to write about Stoic morality'. For although it is true that Plato and Aristotle 'also had systems of morality', nevertheless their 'names are not linked in the way that the Stoics' are with natural law' (Watson, 1996: 218). A. A. Long also tends towards this view. He maintains that the concept of natural law only 'fully emerged' or was 'explicitly established' in 'Stoicism and in the Stoically influenced work of the Roman jurist and philosopher Cicero'. Without naming those involved, Long also concedes however that the concept did appear 'spasmodically and sketchily in earlier thinkers'

(Long, 2005: 413). Cicero, although not himself a Stoic, is of course usually considered to be of major significance in this regard. Indeed, D. G. Ritchie has gone so far as to suggest that it is only in 'Cicero's ethical teaching' that 'we find the *first* distinct formulation of the idea of the law of nature' (Ritchie, 1916 [1894]: 36); and Lloyd L. Weinreb has also claimed that 'natural law emerges distinctly' only 'in the first century B.C. in Cicero's Latin renderings of Greek Stoic philosophy' (Weinreb, 1987: 1).

It has been argued by some commentators that the political thought of the Stoics, as represented by Cicero, based as it is on the concept of natural law, was a new departure in the history of political thought and that it constituted a radical departure from the thinking of Cicero's classical Greek predecessors, especially Plato and Aristotle, within which the concept of natural law allegedly had no part to play. In his *Natural Right and History* Leo Strauss refers to the existence of such a view amongst twentieth-century commentators on the history of the concept of natural law. As Strauss puts it, commentators who hold this view maintain that there was a 'radical break' between the thought of Cicero and the Stoics and that of Socrates, Plato and Aristotle (Strauss, 1974 [1953]: 135). Strauss himself, however, appears not to have subscribed to this view. Rather he argues that one can legitimately speak in this connection of two different conceptions of 'classic natural right' (Strauss, 1974 [1953]: 135). This way of speaking suggests that in Strauss's opinion Cicero and the Stoics, on the one hand, and Socrates, Plato and Aristotle on the other, all subscribed to a particular version of the classic doctrine of natural right. Thus it suggests that Strauss himself did not think that there was a 'radical break' in the intervening period between classical and later Greek thought.

The belief that such a radical break occurred appears to have been held by Cicero himself, who states at one point that a 'gulf' divides the views of Stoics from those of the Peripatetics (Cicero, 1961 [1933]: I, VII, 16, 19). It is unclear, therefore why Strauss claims that Cicero, 'who must be supposed to have known what he was talking about, was wholly unaware of a radical difference' between, for example, 'Plato's teaching and his own' (Strauss, 1974 [1953]: 135). The view that a conceptual gulf exists between Aristotle and the later Stoic thinkers is also held by a number of modern commentators. G. H. Sabine, for example, has claimed that the ideas of Cicero must be considered to be 'closer to Kant' than they are to those of Aristotle (Sabine, 1973a: 163). Similarly, R. W. Carlyle and A. J. Carlyle once argued that 'no change in political theory is so startling in its completeness' as that which occurred between Aristotle and Cicero (Carlyle and Carlyle, 1903–36, I, 8). And G. H. Sabine and S. Barney Smith have suggested that 'between the appearance of the ideal of world empire and the ideal of the city-state a sharp line seems to be drawn'. In their view, 'if there is any point in history where the continuity of political philosophy is broken, that point is at the death of Aristotle'. It is only thereafter, they argue, 'from the beginning of the theory of natural law in the Stoic school to Cicero and Seneca', and thence 'to the modern doctrine of the rights of man' that it is possible to discern a 'continuous and unbroken development' (Sabine and Barney Smith, n.d. [1929]: 7–8). C. H. McIlwain has also argued that an important 'turning point' occurred somewhere 'in the period between Aristotle and Cicero' (McIlwain, 1932: 115).

According to this way of thinking, then, the history of political thought between the time of Aristotle and that of the Stoics is not one of smooth, continuous even development. It is rather fissured, punctuated by the principle of discontinuity. Between Aristotle and Cicero there is something like an epistemological rupture or 'coupure', which was the ethical equivalent of what the philosopher of science T. S. Kuhn refers to as a 'scientific revolution' (Kuhn, 1970 [1962]), and which can be associated with what Michel Foucault would characterize as a radical shift in 'ethical perception' or of 'the ethical gaze' (Foucault, 1993 [1963]). Quite independently of the issue of its applicability to the history of ethics in the ancient world between the time of Aristotle and that of the Stoics, what is lacking in this approach to the understanding of conceptual change is any insight into the mechanism or agency by means of which conceptual revolutions of this kind are brought about. Rather, according to both Kuhn and Foucault, like a 'Gestalt switch' they just happen. Indeed, Foucault states explicitly at one point that in his view it is not the task of an 'archaeology of knowledge' to even consider 'causal' questions of this kind (Foucault, 1994 [1966]: xii–xiii).

It should be pointed out, however, that not all commentators have taken this view about the transition, in the history of ethics, from the thought of Aristotle or of classical Athens to that of the Stoics. For example C. J. Friedrich casts doubt on the claim that there was a radical break in continuity between Plato and Aristotle, on the one hand, and Cicero on the other. In his view, 'we are not justified in treating the contrast between', say, Plato and Cicero 'as a radical one', even though 'it is at the same time erroneous to interpret Cicero and the Roman natural law as merely a copy of Platonic and Aristotelian legal thought' (Friedrich, 1963: 31). Moreover this view that the thinking of Aristotle and that of the Stoics were in certain respects similar, and therefore in a sense continuous, has classical origins. According to Cicero, for example, it was held by his former tutor, the Stoic thinker Antiochus of Ascalon. Cicero expresses surprise in his *De Natura Deorum* that Antiochus, who he says possessed a 'first rate intellect', should 'have failed to see what a gulf divides the Stoics, who distinguish between expedience and right not in name only but in essential nature, from the Peripatetics, who class the right and the expedient together, and only recognize differences of quantity or degree, not of kind, between them'. This, Cicero suggests, is not an insignificant 'verbal discrepancy' between the Stoics and Aristotle, but rather 'a fundamental difference of doctrine' (Cicero, 1961 [1933]: I, VII, 16, 19). In short, in Cicero's account of his views, Antiochus was of the opinion that the Stoics agreed with Aristotle with respect to fundamental questions of ethics. According to Cicero, Antiochus wrongly believed that Stoic doctrine and that of Aristotle were essentially the same and that the differences which exist between them were merely verbal.

The discussion of the views of Plato and Aristotle on the notion of natural justice or natural law presented earlier also casts doubt on the view that there was a radical break in the history of ethics sometime between the time of Aristotle and that of Cicero. Throughout this book, and in what remains of the Conclusion, I emphasize the points of similarity and continuity which exist between the ethical and political thought of Aristotle and that of the Stoics rather than the points of difference and discontinuity. In my view the concept of natural law *does* have a 'history', in the strict sense of the term. The present work is not, therefore, a contribution to an 'archaeology of knowledge' in Michel Foucault's sense of the term (Foucault, 1993 [1963], 1994 [1966], 1995 [1969]; also Burns, 2011a).

This reading of the intellectual relationship which exists between the views of Cicero and the Stoics, on the one hand, and Aristotle on the other, implies that the former were connected to the latter, and that the historical process by means of which they were connected was a slow, evolutionary one rather than one of rupture and discontinuity. Neither the Stoics nor Cicero initiated the ancient equivalent of Kant's 'Copernican revolution in ethics', although as we have seen some commentators appear to think so. This reading also implies that the ideas of both the Stoics and of Cicero were not as new or original as is sometimes thought. In the case of Cicero, in particular, W. A. Robson has argued with some plausibility that conceptually his writings have little to add to those of his Greek predecessors. They merely 'reflect the juridical and ethical theories of Greece expressed in the language of Rome' (Robson, 1935: 245). Robson also argues that Cicero merely 'used the phrase *lex naturae*' to convey the earlier Greek 'notion of natural law' (Robson, 1935: 245).

To summarize this brief excursus on the significance of the writings of Cicero for the history of the concept of natural law, it is a mistake to think that it was Cicero who first coined or gave birth to the concept. Moreover, even if we focus on the issue of terminology and consider, not the concept of natural law but the *term* or linguistic expression with which to designate it, even here Cicero's contribution was a limited one. For it is arguable that such a linguistic expression entered the history of political thought for the first time, not in the works of Cicero, but either as *physikon dikaion* in Aristotle's *Ethics*, or *nomos koinos* in the *Rhetoric*, or *nomos tes physeos* in Plato's *Gorgias* (the meaning of which was significantly altered by later Stoic thinkers in yet another early act of appropriation). It may be conjectured that it is one or the other of these Greek expressions which is translated into Latin in the writings of Cicero as *lex naturalis*.

In the case of the phrase *nomos physeos*, although they may disagree over the issue of possible sources, numerous commentators accept not only that this phrase can be found in the writings of the Greek Stoics, at least the later ones, but also that it was this particular linguistic expression which was used by them to designate the concept of natural law. Glenn Morrow, for example, refers to the expression *nomos physeos* as a 'Stoic phrase' (Morrow, 1948: 19), and Sir Frederick Pollock has claimed that 'the later Stoics at any rate spoke of *nomos physikos*', which, he alleges, 'Aristotelian usage would not allow' (Pollock, 1961b: 126). Similarly, Richard Horsley has maintained that natural law reasoning, or what he refers to as the 'natural law argument', was 'apparently standard and widespread' at the time when the Roman Stoics were writing and that 'it is evident that there was a well established tradition concerning the law of nature' and, by implication, the use of the expression φυσεος νομος (*physeos nomos*, natural law), upon which figures like Cicero could rely when compiling their popular accounts of Stoic beliefs regarding questions of ethics (Horsley, 1978: 39; see also Salmond, 1895: 124; Watson, 1966: 217–8). On the other hand, though, it must be conceded that it is surprisingly difficult to pin down a specific text written by any Greek thinker after Plato, even amongst the Stoics, which employs the expression *nomos physeos* in the appropriate way. Indeed, Ernest L. Fortin has gone so far as to claim that claim that 'the expression itself does not occur in *any* of the surviving fragments' (Fortin, 1982: 610; see also Kroger, 2004: 923–4; Koester, 1968: 529).

Given the lack of originality in Cicero's thinking, about which there does appear to be almost unanimous agreement, it might plausibly be suggested that Cicero's Latin expression *lex naturalis* was coined by him in order to translate into the Latin language some Greek expression or other which had been employed by his predecessors amongst the Stoic philosophers. With respect to this issue, Lloyd L. Weinreb has claimed that Cicero's writings 'contain the first clear statements of natural law as a distinct philosophical doctrine' (Weinreb, 1987: 39). It is arguable, however, that this overlooks the contribution made by Cicero's Greek predecessors, including Plato and Aristotle, as well as that of the Greek Stoics. So far as Aristotle in particular is concerned, Weinreb simply sets aside Aristotle's comments about the *nomos koinos* being the 'law of nature' in his *Rhetoric*. On the other hand though it is noteworthy that, despite making the remark just cited, Weinreb nonetheless also concedes that the concept of 'natural law in all its essentials was already there, waiting only' for Cicero 'to transcribe them into Latin'. It 'remained', he says, only 'for Cicero to give us the phrase', that is to say a linguistic expression in the Latin language by means of which this concept could be designated or expressed (Weinreb, 1987: 39).

On this view, then, Cicero is a figure of importance for the history of the concept of natural law, not because he actually originated the concept, and not even because he was the first person to think of coining a linguistic expression in any language as a name for it, but merely because he coined the phrase *lex naturalis* (the obvious equivalent for one or the other of the earlier Greek expressions) as a means of expressing this concept in Latin. Cicero was both a transmitter and an influential popularizer of the views of the Greek Stoic philosophers who preceded him. It is for this reason only that he is often rightly considered to be a central, if not *the* most decisive, figure in the history of the concept of natural law. As G. H. Sabine has noted, the political thought of Cicero is not important 'because of its originality' but rather because he gave 'the Stoic doctrine of natural law a statement' in which it became 'universally known throughout Western Europe from his own day down to the nineteenth century' (Sabine, 1973a: 159, 161; see also Bowle, 1961 [1947]: 76; Rommen, 1998 [1947]: 18; Watson, 1996: 218).

So far as the relationship between Aristotle's ethics and Stoicism is concerned, it is arguable that the views on natural law which Aristotle expresses (and criticizes) in his *Rhetoric* did have a significant impact upon those held by the Stoic philosophers who came after him. The three characteristic features which Aristotle associates with the idea of the 'law of nature' there, an idea which he claims was endorsed by Alcidamas, Empedocles and Sophocles, and which he himself rejected, are the same as those which are usually associated with the Stoic conception of natural law as adumbrated by Cicero, who also maintains that the principles of natural law are eternal, that they are universally valid, and that they constitute a higher standard of justice than that of the civil law. Indeed, Cicero might have had Aristotle's *Rhetoric* specifically in mind, especially the allusion there to the existence of a 'universal law' which is also the 'law of nature', when in his *De Officiis* he too characterizes 'natural law' as 'universal law' (*ius gentium*), contrasting this with the 'civil law' and asserting that this 'universal law *ought* also to be the civil law' (Cicero, 1956 [1916]: III, XVII, 69, 339–40).

This is a possibility which appears to have been overlooked in the literature which deals with Aristotle's relationship to the Stoics (Long, 1968; Sanbach, 1985; White, 1979). It is also a weakness in an otherwise excellent article by John R. Kroger dealing with the issue of the philosophical foundations of Roman law (Kroger, 2004). According to Kroger the divergent views about natural law expressed by the Roman jurists Gaius and Ulpian in the *Digest* of Justinian 'reflect a larger philosophical conflict in the ancient world between Aristotle and the Stoics about the classification of law, and scope and character of natural law' (Kroger, 2004: 906). Kroger maintains that 'the sharp differences between Gaius's and Ulpian's accounts of natural law are not accidental or haphazard, but are rooted in the philosophical debate between Aristotelians and Stoics over the character, origin and function of natural law' (Kroger, 2004: 938–39). By presenting a stark contrast between the beliefs of Aristotle and the Stoics in this way, Kroger overlooks the possibility that the Stoics themselves were indebted to Aristotle for at least some of their views. This oversight is a consequence of the fact that Kroger supposes, first, that there is a clear differentiation and opposition between the views expressed by Gaius and those of Ulpian; and second that Gaius drew his views on natural law from Aristotle whereas Ulpian relied on the writings of the Stoics. This line of reasoning more or less compels Kroger to maintain that the Stoics could have owed very little to Aristotle so far as their views on natural law are concerned. However, there are reasons for doubting this judgement.

In particular, it is not implausible to suggest that the Stoic belief that natural law might be used to criticize positive law and legal institutions was inherited ultimately from the writings of Aristotle. For example, we have already seen that Cicero's formulation of the Stoic view that positive law ought to 'copy' the law of nature appears to hint at the views expressed by Aristotle in his *Nicomachean Ethics*. And similar remarks might be made about what Aristotle says about the *nomos koinos* being the 'law of nature' in his *Rhetoric*. Indeed, E. R. Dodds has argued, referring to the expression 'natural law' (νομος φυσεος, *nomos physeos*), which Plato places in the mouth of his character Callicles in the *Gorgias*, that, although 'Callicles's coinage is not to be confused with "natural law" in the Stoic sense', nevertheless 'the term seems to be first used in *that* way', that is to say, as the Stoics were later to use it, 'by Aristotle' in his *Rhetoric* (Aristotle, 1995i: 1373b6, 2187; Dodds, 1959b: 268). According to Dodds, then, it might plausibly be suggested that these remarks about natural law or 'the law of nature' in Aristotle's *Rhetoric* was at least one of the sources of inspiration for the later Stoic conception of natural law. On this view, the Stoics simply took this argument from Aristotle and, wittingly or unwittingly, positively endorsed the notion of natural law which Aristotle himself had rejected. To employ a phrase which has often been used to characterize Marx's relation to Hegel, the Stoics might be said, therefore, to have in a sense 'inverted' the view of natural law which Aristotle puts forward in his *Rhetoric*. In so doing they continued the tradition of natural law speculation which Aristotle himself associated (rightly or wrongly) with the writings of his predecessors, Alcidamas, Empedocles and Sophocles.

That Aristotle might have directly or indirectly influenced later Stoic thinking about natural law is also evidenced by a striking passage in Book VIII of the *Nicomachean Ethics*, referred to earlier, which runs as follows:

> [W]here there is nothing common to ruler and ruled, there is not friendship either, since there is not justice; e.g. between craftsman and tool, soul and body, master and slave; the latter in each case is benefited by that which uses it, but there is no friendship nor justice towards lifeless things. But neither is there friendship towards a horse or an ox, nor to a slave qua slave. For there is nothing common to the two parties; the slave is a living tool and the tool a lifeless slave. *Qua* slave then, one cannot be friends with him. But *qua* human being one can; for there seems to be some justice between any human being and any other who can share in a system of law or be a party to an agreement; therefore there can also be friendship with him in so far as he is a man (Aristotle, 1995f: 1161a31–1161b7, 1835).

Although Aristotle does not say so explicitly, there is good reason to think that in this passage he is talking about what he refers to in the *Politics* as 'conventional' rather than 'natural' slavery. One of the striking things about this passage is the fact that within it Aristotle indicates quite clearly that he thinks of both masters and slaves as 'human beings' as well as being masters and slaves. This passage, considered in isolation, suggests that for Aristotle being either a master or a slave, or possessing a particular recognized identity of that kind, is a matter of social and legal convention only. It is not, therefore, something which might be said to be natural, or sanctioned by any principle of natural justice or law. In other words here at least for Aristotle, if only implicitly, by nature (or the 'law of nature') all human beings are equals, precisely in respect of their possession of those features which make them 'human'. Consequently, it is by law only, that is to say positive law, or what Aristotle refers to as conventional justice, that they *become* unequals, the one a master and the other a slave.

These remarks in the *Ethics* are quite astonishing because they appear to flatly contradict what Aristotle says elsewhere about slavery, especially in his defence of (natural) slavery in Book One of the *Politics*. Indeed when making them Aristotle appears to be implicitly agreeing, rather than disagreeing, with the views of the 'anonymous opponents of slavery' which he refers to there. Here then, if not in the *Politics*, Aristotle appears to endorse ideas which are usually associated, in the later history of political thought, with the Stoic conception of natural law. As in the case of the views which Aristotle expresses about natural law in the *Rhetoric*, it is not difficult to imagine how these ideas in the *Ethics* might be taken out of context and selectively interpreted or appropriated by later thinkers who, ignoring or even reversing Aristotle's intentions in his treatment of slavery generally, were set on putting them to a quite different use.

In his *Poetics*, Aristotle suggests that the two principal characteristics of Greek tragedy, especially as we find it in the writings of Sophocles, are the idea of *peripeteia* or 'reversal of intention' and the idea of 'discovery' or 'recognition'. Reversal of intention, he says, is 'a change by which the action veers round to its opposite'. Thus, for example, in Sophocles' *Oedipus*, 'the messenger comes to cheer Oedipus and free him from his alarms about his mother, but by revealing who he is, he produces the opposite effect' (Aristotle, 1902: 41, 1995i: 1452a23–1452b13, 2324). Recognition, as the name indicates, is a 'change from ignorance to knowledge, producing love or hate between the persons destined by the poet for good or bad fortune' (Aristotle, 1902: 41, 1995i: 1452a30–31, 2324). Aristotle observes that if these two principles operate together, when 'recognition is coincident with a reversal of intention', as in the *Oedipus*, then this will 'produce either pity or fear' in the audience. Aristotle defines the concept of tragedy as being a combination of such 'actions producing these effects'. It is this, he says, which 'by our definition, tragedy represents' (Aristotle, 1902: 41, 1995i: 1452a38–1452b2, 2324).

The concept of tragedy understood in this sense (particularly the notion of *peripeteia*) is especially relevant for any assessment of the natural law interpretation of the *Antigone* which Aristotle refers to in the *Rhetoric*. This is so for two reasons. In the first place, the natural law reading of the play involves a 'reversal of intention' in that it appears to deliberately misrepresent rather than simply misunderstand the basic political message of its author. In the second place, Aristotle introduces this reading of the *Antigone* whilst developing a critique of the concept of natural law, as this concept was used by his contemporaries, figures such as Euripides, Antiphon and Alcidamas. Aristotle's own intention when interpreting the play in the way that he does was, it may be conjectured, to persuade his readers that the concept of natural law employed in this radical sense is nothing more than an empty rhetorical device. However it might be argued that, just as in the case of Sophocles, so also (ironically) in that of Aristotle, the intentions of the author were either misunderstood or deliberately misrepresented by later generations of readers. Students of Aristotle in the later history of political thought came to take seriously the very concept which Aristotle himself sought to dismiss as rhetorical verbiage and which he had himself brought to their attention. Given Aristotle's political intentions, especially his hostility to the idea of natural law understood as a standard of justice which might be employed to critically evaluate existing social and political conditions, this is indeed ironic. The implications of this second 'reversal of intention' for our understanding of the history of the concept of natural law are plain to see. Despite Aristotle's efforts to prevent it, the concept of natural law did eventually, in the natural law theory of the Stoics, come to have the radical political implications to which he himself was always fundamentally opposed and which he actively sought to combat in his writings. The fact that *this* should be the final outcome of the later reception of the natural law reading of Sophocles' *Antigone* alluded to in the *Rhetoric* is something which itself lies within the best tradition of Sophoclean tragedy.

Bibliography

Abrams, M. H. (1991a [1989]), *Doing Things With Texts: Essays in Criticism and Critical Theory*. New York & London: W. W. Norton.

Abrams, M. H. (1991b [1989]), 'The deconstructive angel', in *Doing Things With Texts: Essays in Criticism and Critical Theory*, pp. 237–52.

Adams, J. L. (1945), 'The law of nature in Graeco-Roman thought', *The Journal of Religion*, 25, 2, 97–118.

Allen, C. K. (1951), *Law in the Making*. Oxford: Clarendon Press.

Allen, C. K. (1951), 'Equity', in *Law in the Making*, pp. 383–425.

Allen, J. W. (1960 [1928]), *A History of Political Thought in the Sixteenth Century*. London: Unwin.

Ambler, W. (1987), 'Aristotle on nature and politics: the case of slavery', *Political Theory*, 15, 3, 390–410.

Anderson, D. J. (1989), 'Deconstruction: critical strategy/strategic criticism', in Atkins and Morrow eds., *Contemporary Literary Theory*, pp. 137–57.

Annas, J. (1996), 'Aristotle on human nature and political virtue', *The Review of Metaphysics*, XLIX, 4, 731–53.

Annas, J. (1993a), *The Morality of Happiness*. New York & Oxford: Oxford University Press.

Annas, J. (1993b), 'Morality, ancient and modern', in *The Morality of Happiness*, pp. 439–55.

Appleton, R. B. (1927), *Euripides the Idealist*. New York.

Aquinas (2006 [1966–75]) *Summa Theologiae*, translated with Latin text, by the Dominican Fathers, in 60 volumes. London: Blackfriars.

Aquinas (2006 [1966]) *Summa Theologiae*, Vol. 28, *Law and Political Theory* (la2ae, QQ. 90–97), ed. T. Gilby. London: Blackfriars.

Aquinas (2006 [1969]) *Summa Theologiae*, Vol. 29, *The Old Law* (la2ae, QQ. 98–105), eds. D. Bourke and A. Littledale. London: Blackfriars.

Aquinas (2006 [1975a]) *Summa Theologiae*, Vol. 37, *Justice* (2a2ae, QQ. 57–62), ed. T. Gilby. London: Blackfriars.

Aquinas (2006 [1975b]) *Summa Theologiae*, Vol. 38, *Injustice* (2a2ae, QQ. 63–79), ed. M. Lefebure. London: Blackfriars.

Aquinas (2006 [1974]) *Summa Theologiae*, Vol. 36, *Prudence* (2a2ae, QQ. 47–56), ed. T. Gilby. London: Blackfriars.

Aquinas, T. (1964), *Commentary on the Ethics of Aristotle*, ed. C. I. Litzinger. Chicago.

Aristotle (2000), *Nicomachean Ethics*, ed. R. Crisp. Cambridge: Cambridge University Press.

Aristotle (1995a [1984]), *The Complete Works of Aristotle*, in two volumes, the revised Oxford translation, ed. J. Barnes. Princeton, NJ.

Aristotle (1995b), *Posterior Analytics*, trans. J. Barnes in *The Complete Works of Aristotle*, ed. J. Barnes, I, pp. 114–66.
Aristotle (1995c), *Topics*, trans. W. A. Pickard-Cambridge, in *The Complete Works of Aristotle*, I, pp. 167–277.
Aristotle (1995d), *On the Soul*, trans. J. A. Smith, in *The Complete Works of Aristotle*, I, pp. 641–92.
Aristotle (1995e), *Metaphysics*, trans. W. D. Ross, in *The Complete Works of Aristotle*, ed. J. Barnes, II, pp. 1552–1728.
Aristotle (1995f), *Nicomachean Ethics*, trans. W. D. Ross, revised J. O. Urmson, in *The Complete Works of Aristotle*, ed. J. Barnes, II, pp. 1729–1867.
Aristotle (1995g), *Eudemian Ethics*, trans. J. Solomon, revised J. O. Urmson, in *The Complete Works of Aristotle*, ed. J. Barnes, II, pp. 1922–1981.
Aristotle (1995h), *Politics*, trans. B. Jowett, in *The Complete Works of Aristotle*, ed. J. Barnes, II, pp. 1986–2129.
Aristotle (1995i), *Rhetoric*, trans. W. Rhys Roberts, in *The Complete Works of Aristotle*, ed. J. Barnes, II, pp. 2152–69.
Aristotle (1995j), *Poetics*, trans. I. Bywater, in *The Complete Works of Aristotle*, ed. J. Barnes, II, pp. 2316–40.
Aristotle (1970), *L'Éthique à Nicomaque*, eds. R. A. Gauthier and J. Y. Jolif in 4 volumes, 2nd ed. Louvain-Paris.
Aristotle (1969 [1946]), *The Politics of Aristotle*, trans. with intro., notes and appendices, by Ernest Barker. Oxford: Clarendon Press.
Aristotle (1966a), *De Poetica*, trans. I. Bywater, in *The Works of Aristotle*, ed. Sir David Ross, Vol. XI. Oxford.
Aristotle (1966b), *Rhetorica*, trans. W. Rhys Roberts, in *The Works of Aristotle*, ed. Sir David Ross, Vol. XI. Oxford: Clarendon Press.
Aristotle (1965), *The Ethics of Aristotle*, ed. J. A. K. Thompson. Harmondsworth: Penguin.
Aristotle (1902), *The Poetics of Aristotle: Edited with Critical Notes and a Translation by* S. H. Butcher . London.
Aristotle, (1900), *ΑΡΙΣΤΟΤΕΛΟΨΣ ΗΘΙΚΑ ΝΙΚΟΜΑΧΕΙΑ: The Ethics of Aristotle*, ed. J. Burnet. With introduction and notes. London: Methuen.
Aristotle (1881–1902), *Aristotle: The Politics*, in four volumes, ed. W. L. Newman. Oxford.
Aristotle (1879), *ΠΕΡΙ ΔΙΚΑΙΟΣΥΝΗΣ: The Fifth Book of the Nicomachean Ethics of Aristotle*, ed. H. Jackson. Cambridge: Cambridge University Press.
Aristotle (1865), *The Ethics of Aristotle: Illustrated with Essays and Notes*, ed. Sir Alexander Grant, in 2 volumes, 4th ed. London.
Aristotle (n. d.), *The Nicomachean Ethics of Aristotle*, ed. D. P. Chase. London.
Armstrong, R. A. (1966), *Primary and Secondary Precepts in Thomistic Natural Law Teaching*. The Hague: Martinus Nijhoff.
Arrington, R. L. (1989a), *Rationalism, Realism and Relativism: Perspectives in Contemporary Moral Epistemology*. Ithaca and London: Cornell University Press.
Arrington, R. L. (1989b), 'Moral realism', in *Rationalism, Realism and Relativism: Perspectives in Contemporary Moral Epistemology*, pp. 119–91.
Arthur, C. (1990) 'Hegel as lord and master', in S. Sayers and P. Osborne eds., *Socialism, Feminism and Philosophy*. London: Routledge, 27–45.

Atkins, G. D. (1983), *Reading Deconstruction: Deconstructive Reading*. Lexington, KT: University Press of Kentucky.
Atkins. G. D. and L. Morrow, eds. (1989), *Contemporary Literary Theory*. London: Macmillan.
Attilio Levi, M. (1965), *Political Power in the Ancient World*. New York: Mentor Books.
Aubenque, P. (1980), 'La loi selon Aristote', *Archives de philosophie de droit*, 147–57.
Avineri, S. (1979 [1972]), *Hegel's Theory of the Modern State*. Cambridge: Cambridge University Press.
Baier, K. (1966 [1958]), *The Moral Point of View: A Rational Basis of Ethics*. New York: Random House.
Baldry, H. C. (1965), *The Unity of Mankind in Greek Thought*. Cambridge: Cambridge University Press.
Ball, T. (1988), *Transforming Political Discourse: Political Theory and Critical Conceptual History*. Oxford: Oxford University Press.
Ball, T., J. Farr and L. Hanson, eds. (1995 [1989]), *Political Innovation and Conceptual Change*. Cambridge: Cambridge University Press.
Bambrough, R. (1970), 'Universals and family resemblances', in *Wittgenstein: The Philosophical Investigations*, ed. Pitcher, pp. 65–103.
Barker, E. (1969 [1946]), 'The vocabulary of the *Politics*', in Aristotle, *Politics*, trans. Ernest Barker. Oxford: Clarendon Press, pp. lxiii–lxxvi.
Barker, E. (1960a [1918]), *Greek Political Theory*. London: Methuen.
Barker, E. (1960b [1918]), 'The Antithesis of φυσις and μομος', in *Greek Political Theory: Plato and His Predecessors*, pp. 74–76.
Barker, E. (1959), *The Political Thought of Plato and Aristotle*. New York: Dover Publications.
Barker, E. (1948a) *Traditions of Civility*. Cambridge: Cambridge University Press.
Barker, E. (1948b) 'Natural law and the American Revolution', in *Traditions of Civility*, pp. 263–355.
Barker, E. (1945), *Essays on Government*. Oxford: Oxford University Press.
Barthes, R. (1977), *Image-Music-Text*, ed. S. Heath. London: Fontana Books.
Barthes, R. (1977), 'From work to text', in S. Heath ed., *Image-Music-Text*, pp. 155–64.
Bartlett, R. C. and S. D. Collins, eds. (1999), *Action and Contemplation: Studies in the Moral and Political Thought of Aristotle*. Albany: State University of New Press.
Battaglia, A. (1981), *Toward a Reformulation of Natural Law*. New York: Seabury Press.
Beardslee, J. W. (1918), *The Use of ΦΥΣΙΣ in Fifth Century Greek Literature*. Chicago: The University of Chicago Press.
Begin, R. F. (1959), *Natural Law and Positive Law*, Canon Law Studies 393. Washington, DC: Catholic University of America Press.
Benson, P. (1991–92), 'The basis of corrective justice and its relation to legal justice', *Iowa Law Review*, 77, 515–624.
Bentham, J. (1977a), *The Collected Works of Jeremy Bentham*, ed. J. H. Burns. London: Athlone Press.

Bentham, J. (1977b [1776]), *A Comment on the Commentaries*, in *A Comment on the Commentaries and A Fragment on Government*, eds. J. H. Burns and H. L. A. Hart, in *The Collected Works of Jeremy Bentham*.

Berki, R. N. (1984), *The History of Political Thought: A Short Introduction*. London: Dent.

Berlin, I. (1955–56), 'Equality', *Proceedings of the Aristotelian Society*, 56, 301–326.

Berman, H. J. (1993a), *Faith and Order: The Reconciliation of Law and Religion*. Grand Rapids, MI: Eerdmans.

Berman, H. J. (1993b), 'Towards an integrative juripsrudence: politics, morality, history', in *Faith and Order: The Reconciliation of Law and Religion*, pp. 289–312.

Berman, H. J. (1993–94), 'The origins of historical jurisprudence: Coke, Selden, Hale', *Yale Law Journal*, 103, 1651–1738.

Bernadete, S. (1975), 'A reading of Sophocles' *Antigone*', *Interpretation: A Journal of Political Philosophy*, V, 1–55.

Besselink, L. (1988), 'The impious hypothesis revisited'. *Grotiana*, 9 N.S., 3–63.

Bevir, M. ed. (2010), *Sage Encyclopaedia of Political Theory*. London: Sage Books.

Bevir, M. (2000), 'The logic of the history of ideas', *Rethinking History: The Journal of Theory and Practice*, 4, 3, 295–300.

Bevir, M. (1999). *The Logic of the History of Ideas*. Cambridge: Cambridge University Press.

Bevir, M. (1994), 'Are there perennial problems in political theory', *Political Studies*, 42, 662–75.

Blackledge, P. and K. Knight, eds. (2011), *Virtue and Politics: Alasdair MacIntyre's Revolutionary Aristotelianism*. Notre Dame: Notre Dame University Press.

Blackstone, W. T. (1967), 'On the meaning and justification of the equality principle', *Ethics*, 77, 4, 239–53.

Blake T., W and L. J. Bennett (1998), *Recapturing Sophocles' Antigone*. Rowman and Littlefield.

Bloch, E. (1986), *Natural Law and Human Dignity*, trans. Dennis J. Schmidt. Cambridge, MA: MIT Press.

Blundell, M. W. (1989) *Helping Friends and Harming Enemies: A Study in Sophocles and Greek Ethics*. Cambridge: Cambridge University Press.

Bodéüs, R. (1999), 'The natural foundation of right and Aristotelian philosophy', in Bartlett and Collins eds., *Action and Contemplation: Studies in the Moral and Political Thought of Aristotle*, pp. 69–106.

Bodéüs, R. (1989), 'Deux propositions aristotéliciennes sur le droit naturel chez continteaux d'Amérique', *Revue de metaphysique et de morale*, 94, 3, 369–89.

Boucher, D. (1985), *Texts in Context: Revisionist Methods for Studying the History of Ideas*, The Hague: Martinus Nijhoff.

Bowle, J. (1961 [1947]), *Western Political Thought: An Historical Introduction from the Origins to Rousseau*. London: Jonathan Cape.

Boyd, R. N. (1988), 'How to be a moral realist', in Sayre-McCord ed., *Essays on Moral Realism*, pp. 181–228.

Brennan, J. M. (1977), *The Open Texture of Moral Concepts*. London: Macmillan.

Brett, A. (2002), 'Natural right and civil community: the civil philosophy of Hugo Grotius', *The Historical Journal*, 45, 1, 31–51.

Brunt, P. A. (1993), 'Aristotle and slavery', in *Studies in Greek History and Thought.* Oxford, pp. 343–88.

Bryce, J. (1901), 'The law of nature', in *Studies in History and Jurisprudence,* in 2 volumes. London, Vol. 2, pp. 566–605.

Buckle, S. (2002), 'Aristotle's republic or, why Aristotle's ethics is not virtue ethics', *Philosophy* 77, 4, 565–595.

Bull, M. (1998), 'Slavery and the multiple self', *New Left Review,* 231, 94–131.

Burle, E. (1908), *Essai historique sur le developpement de la notion de droit naturel dans l'antiquite grecque.* Trevoux: Jeannin.

Burnet, J. (1897), 'Law and nature in Greek ethics', *International Journal of Ethics*; reprinted in *Essays and Addresses* (1929), pp. 23–8.

Burns, T. (2012), 'The politics of recognition in the ancient world? Aristotle, cosmopolitanism and slavery', in Burns and Thompson eds., *Global Justice and the Politics of Recognition.* Forthcoming.

Burns, T. (2011a), 'Conceptual history and the philosophy of the later Wittgenstein: A critique of Quentin Skinner's contextualism', *Journal of the Philosophy of History,* 5 (1), 54–83.

Burns, T. (2011b), 'Interpreting and appropriating texts in the history of political thought: Quentin Skinner and poststructuralism', *Contemporary Political Theory,* 10, 3, 313–31.

Burns, T. (2011c), 'Revolutionary Aristotelianism? The political thought of Aristotle, Marx and MacIntyre, in Blackledge & Knight eds., *Virtue and Politics,* pp. 35–53.

Burns, T. (2010a), 'Aristotelianism', in M. Bevir ed., *Sage Encyclopaedia of Political Theory,* Volume 1, pp. 71–7.

Burns, T. (2010b), 'Strauss on Aristotle and the idea of a "state of exception"', in Burns and Connelly eds., *The Legacy of Leo Strauss,* pp. 43–66.

Burns, T. (2010c), 'Capitalism, modernity and the nation state', *Capital & Class,* 235–55.

Burns, T. (2009 [2002]), 'Aristotle', in D. Boucher and P. Kelly eds., *Political Thinkers: A History of Western Political Thought,* 2nd ed. Oxford: Oxford University Press.

Burns, T. (2006), 'Hegel, identity politics and the problem of slavery', *Culture, Theory and Critique,* 47, 1, 81–98.

Burns, T. (2005a), 'Whose Aristotle, which Marx? ethics, law and justice in Aristotle and in Marx', *Imprints: Egalitarian Theory and Practice,* 8, 2, 125–55.

Burns, T. (2005b), 'Hegel', in T. Carver and J. Martin eds., *Palgrave Advances in Continental Political Thought,* London: Palgrave, pp. 45–58.

Burns, T. (2003) 'The tragedy of slavery: Aristotle's *Rhetoric* and the history of the concept of natural law', *History of Political Thought.* XXIV, 1, pp. 16–36.

Burns, T. (2002a), 'Sophocles' *Antigone* and the history of the concept of natural law', *Political Studies,* 50, 3, 545–57.

Burns, T. (2002b), 'Jospeh Dietzgen and the history of Marxism', *Science & Society,* 66, 2, 202–27.

Burns, T. (2002c), 'Hegel (1770–1831)', in A. Edwards and J. Townshend eds., *Interpreting Modern Political Philosophy from Machiavelli to Marx,* London: Macmillan. pp. 162–79.

Burns, T. (2000a), 'Aquinas's two doctrines of natural law', *Political Studies*, 48, 5, 929–46.
Burns, T. (2000b), 'The purloined Hegel: semiology in the thought of Saussure and Derrida', *The History of the Human Sciences*, 13, 4, 1–24.
Burns, T. (2000c), 'Materialism in ancient Greek philosophy and in the writings of the young Marx', *Historical Materialism: Research in Critical Marxist Theory*, 7, 3–40.
Burns, T. (1998a), 'Aristotle and natural law', *History of Political Thought*, 19, 2, 142–66.
Burns, T. (1998b), 'Metaphysics and politics in Aristotle and Hegel', in A. Dobson and G. Stanyer eds., *Contemporary Political Studies: 1998*, vol. 1, pp. 387–99. The Political Studies Association of Great Britain.
Burns, T. (1996a), *Natural Law and Political Ideology in the Philosophy of Hegel*. Avebury: Ashgate.
Burns, T. (1996b), 'Natural law theory', in *Natural Law and Political Ideology in the Philosophy of Hegel*, pp. 12–41.
Burns, T. (1996c), 'Conclusion', in *Natural Law and Political Ideology in the Philosophy of Hegel*, pp. 163–8.
Burns, T. (1995), 'Hegel and natural law theory', *Politics*, 15, 1, 27–32.
Burns, T. and J. Connelly, eds. (2010a), *The Legacy of Leo Strauss*. Imprint Academic.
Burns, T. and J. Connelly (2010b), 'Introduction: Straussian Voices', in *The Legacy of Leo Strauss*, pp. 1–26.
Burns, T. and S. Thompson, eds. (2012), *Global Justice and the Politics of Recognition*. London: Palgrave. Forthcoming.
Cambiano, G. (1987), 'Aristotle and the anonymous opponents of slavery', in Finley, ed., *Classical Slavery*, pp. 22–41.
Caputo, J. D. (1987), *Radical Hermeneutics: Repetition, Deconstruction and the Hermeneutic Project*. Indiana: Indiana University Press.
Carlyle, R. W. and J. Carlyle (1903–36), *The History of Medieval Political Theory in the West*, in 6 volumes. Edinburgh: Blackwood.
Carlyle, R. W. and J. Carlyle (1909), *The History of Medieval Political Theory in the West*, Vol. 2.
Cartledge, P. (1993), *The Greeks: A Portrait of Self and Others*. Oxford: Oxford University Press.
Cassirer, E. (1967) *The Myth of the State*. New Haven and London: Yale University Press.
Catlin, G. (2005 [1939]), *The Story of the Political Philosophers*. New York: Kessinger.
Charette, L. (1981), 'Droit naturel et droit positif chez Saint Thomas d'Aquin', *Philosophiques*, 8, 113–30.
Charles, D. (1995), 'Aristotle and modern realism', in Heineman, ed., *Aristotle and Moral Realism*, pp. 135–72.
Cherniss, H. (1935), *Aristotle's Criticisms of Presocratic Philosophy*. Baltimore: Johns Hopkins University press.
Cherniss, H. (1951), 'The Characteristics and effects of Presocratic philosophy', *Journal of the History of Ideas*, 12, 239–54.

Chroust, A. H. (1943), 'Hugo Grotius and the scholastic natural law tradition', *New Scholasticism*, 17, 2, 101–33.
Cicero (2001 [1927]), *Tusculan Disputations*, trans. J. E. King. Cambridge MA: Loeb Classical Library.
Cicero (1966 [1928]), *De Republica*, trans. C. W. Keyes. Cambridge MA: Loeb Classical Library.
Cicero (n. d.), *On the Commonwealth*, ed. and trans. G. H. Sabine and S. B. Smith. New York: Bobbs Merrill.
Cicero (1961 [1933]), *De Natura Deorum*, Cambridge, MA: Loeb Classical Library.
Cicero (1956 [1913]), *De Officiis* with an English translation by W. Miller. Cambridge, MA: Loeb Classical Library.
Classen, C. J. (1981), in Kerferd ed., 'Aristotle's picture of the Sophists', in *The Sophists and their Legacy*, pp. 7–24.
Coleman, J. (2000), *A History of Political Thought*, Vol. 2, *From the Middle Ages to the Renaissance*. Oxford: Oxford University Press.
Collins, S. (1999), 'The moral virtues in Aristotle's Nicomachean Ethics', in Bartlett and Collins eds., *Action and Contemplation: Studies in the Moral and Political Thought of Aristotle*, pp. 131–58.
Conacher, D. J. (1998), *Euripides and the Sophists: Some Dramatic Treatments of Philosophical Ideas*. London: Duckworth.
Conklin, W. E. (1997), 'Hegel, the author and authority in Sophocles' *Antigone*', in L. G. Rubin ed., *Justice v. Law in Greek Political Thought*. New York: Rowman & Littlefield, 129–51.
Copleston, F. (1963), *A History of Philosophy*, Vol. 3, *Late Medieval and Renaissance Philosophy*, Part II, *The Revival of Platonism to Suarez*. New York: Doubleday.
Copleston, F. (1962), *A History of Philosophy*, Vol. 2, *Medieval Philosophy*, II, *Albert the Great to Duns Scotus*. New York: Doubleday.
Corbett, R. J. (2009), 'The question of natural law in Aristotle', *History of Political Thought*, XXX, 2, 229–50.
Crisp, R. (2000), 'Introduction', in Aristotle, *Nicomachean Ethics*, pp. vii–xxxv.
Crisp, R. and M. Slote, eds. (1997), *Virtue Ethics*. Oxford: Oxford University Press.
Crowe, M. B. (1977), *The Changing Profile of Natural Law*. The Hague: Martinus Nijhoff.
Crowe, M. B. (1963) 'Human nature – mutable or immutable?', *Irish Theological Quarterly*, 30 (3), 204–31.
Darwall, S. ed. (2002), *Virtue Ethics*. Oxford: Blackwell.
Daube, D. (1972), *Civil Disobedience in Antiquity*. Edinburgh: Edinburgh University Press.
del Vecchio, G. (1952), *Justice*, ed. A. H. Campbell. Edinburgh.
del Vecchio, G. (1921 [1914]), *Philosophy of Law*, trans. J. Lisle. New York.
d'Entrèves, A. P. (1974), *Natural Law*, 2nd. ed. London; Hutchinson.
Derrida, J. (1982 [1972]), *Margins of Philosophy*. London: Harvester.
de Sainte Croix, G. E. M. (1983), *The Class Struggle in the Ancient Greek World: From the Archaic Age to the Arab Conquests*. London: Duckworth.
de Sainte Croix, G. E. M. (1981), 'The class struggle on the ideological plane,' in *The Class Struggle in the Ancient Greek World: From the Archaic Age to the Arab Conquests*, pp. 409–52.

Destrée, P. (2000), 'Aristote et la question du droit naturel, *Eth. Nic.*, V, 10, 1134b18–1135a5)', *Phronesis*, XLV, 3, 220–39.

de Wulf, M. (1909), *A History of Medieval Philosophy*, trans. P. Coffey. London: Longman Green.

Dherbey, G. M. (2002), 'La question du droit naturel (*Ethique a Nicomaque* V 10, 1134b19–1135a6)', in *L'Excellence de a Vie: Sur L'Ethique a Nicomaque*, pp. 125–37.

Dobbs, D. (1994), 'Natural right and the problem of Aristotle's defense of slavery', *The Journal of Politics*, 56, 1, 69–94.

Dodds, E. R. (1973a), *The Ancient Concept of Progress and Other Essays on Greek Literature*, London: Oxford University Press.

Dodds, E. R. (1973b), 'The ancient concept of progress', in *The Ancient Concept of Progress and Other Essays*, pp 1–25.

Dodds, E. R. (1973c), 'The Sophistic movement and the failure of Greek liberalism', in *The Ancient Concept of Progress and Other Essays*, pp. 92–105.

Dodds, E. R. (1959a), 'Introduction' to Plato, *Gorgias*, ed. Dodds, pp. 1–68.

Dodds, E. R. (1959b), 'Commentary', in Plato, *Gorgias*, ed. Dodds, pp. 188–386.

Dodds, E. R. (1959c), 'Appendix: Socrates, Callicles and Nietzsche', in Plato, *Gorgias*, ed. Dodds, pp. 387–91.

Doyle, P. (1966), *A History of Political Thought*. London: Jonathan Cape.

Dworkin, R. (1978a), *Taking Rights Seriously*. London: Duckworth.

Dworkin, R. (1978b), 'Hard cases', in *Taking Rights Seriously*, pp. 81–130.

Eagleton, T. (1994a [1983]), *Literary Theory: An Introduction*. Oxford: Blackwell.

Eagleton, T. (1994b [1983]), 'Psychoanalysis', in *Literary Theory: An Introduction*, pp. 151–93.

Eccleshall, R. (1978), *Order and Reason in Politics: Theories of Absolute and Limited Monarchy in Early Modern England*. Oxford: Oxford University Press.

Edwards, C. (1970), 'The law of nature in the thought of Hugo Grotius', *The Journal of Politics*, 32, 4, 784–807.

Ehrenberg, V. (1954a), *Sophocles and Pericles*. Oxford: Basil Blackwell.

Ehrenberg, V. (1954b), 'Unwritten laws', in *Sophocles and Pericles*, pp. 22–50.

Engstrom, S. and J. Whiting, eds. (1998), *Aristotle, Kant and the Stoics: Rethinking Happiness and Duty*. Cambridge: Cambridge University Press.

Euripides (1972), *Phoenician Women*, in *Orestes and Other Plays*, trans P. Vellacott, Harmondsworth: Penguin, pp. 233–96.

Euripides (1967), *Ion*, in *The Bacchae and Other Plays*, trans. P. Vellaccott. Harmondsworth: Penguin, pp. 35–82.

Evans, I. ed. (1965), *Light on the Natural Law*. London: Burns and Oates.

Farr, J. (1995 [1989]), 'Understanding conceptual change politically', in Ball, Farr and Hanson eds., *Political Innovation and Conceptual Change*, pp. 24–49.

Fears, R. T. (2000), 'Natural law: the legacy of Greece and Rome', in Edward P. McLean ed., *Common Truths: New Perspectives on Natural Law*. Wilmington Delaware: IS Books, pp. 19–71.

Feinberg, J. ed. (1969), *Moral Concepts*. Oxford: Oxford University Press.

Ferguson, J. (1972), *A Companion to Greek Tragedy*. London: University of Texas Press.

Fideler, D. (1988), 'Introduction' to Guthrie ed., *The Pythagorean Sourcebook and Library: An Anthology of Ancient Writings which Relate to Pythagoras and Pythagorean Philosophy*, pp. 19–56.

Field, G. C. (1930), *Plato and his Contemporaries: A Study in Fourth Century Life and Thought*. London: Methuen.

Finley, M. ed. (1987), *Classical Slavery*. London: Routledge.

Finley, M. (1983), *Ancient Slavery and Modern Ideology*. Harmondsworth: Penguin.

Finley, M. (1981), 'Was Greek civilization based on slave labour?', in *Economy and Society in Ancient Greece*, eds. M. I. Saller & R. P. Shaw. London: Chatto & Windus, pp. 97–115.

Finley, M. ed. (1968), *Slavery in Classical Antiquity*. Cambridge: Heffer.

Finnis, J. (1991), *Moral Absolutes: Tradition, Revision and Truth*. Washington DC: Catholic University of America Press.

Finnis, J. (1980), *Natural Law and Natural Rights*. Oxford: Clarendon Press.

Foot, P. (1994), 'Nietzsche's immoralism', in R. Schact ed., *Nietzsche, Genealogy, Morality: Essays on Nietzsche's The Genealogy of Morals*. Berkeley and Los Angeles: University of California Press, pp. 3–34.

Foot, P. (2003), *Moral Dilemmas: And Other Topics in Moral Philosophy*. Oxford: Oxford University Press.

Foriers, P. and Ch. Perelman (1973), 'Natural law and natural rights', *Dictionary of the History of Ideas*, ed. P. Wiener Vol. 3. New York: Macmillan, pp. 13–27.

Fortenbaugh, W. W. (1991), 'Aristotle on slaves and women', in D. Keyt and F. D. Miller eds., *A Companion to Aristotle's Politics*, pp. 135–58.

Fortenbaugh, W. W. ed. (1983), *On Stoic and Peripatetic Ethics. The Work of Arius Didymus*. New Jersey: Transaction.

Fortin, E. L. (1982), 'The new rights theory and the natural law', *The Review of Politics*, 44(3), 590–612.

Foucault, M. (1995 [1969]), *The Archaelology of Knowledge*. London: Routledge.

Foucault, M. (1994 [1966]), *The Order of Things: An Archaeology of the Human Sciences*. London: Routledge.

Foucault, M. (1993 [1963]), *The Birth of the Clinic: An Archeology of Medical Perception*. London: Routledge.

Frankena, W. (1980), *Thinking About Morality*. Ann Arbor: University of Michigan Press.

Fraser, N. and A. Honneth (2001), *Redistribution or Recognition? A Political-Philosophical Exchange*. London: Verso.

Fraser, N. (2001a), 'Social justice in the age of identity politics', in *Redistribution or Recognition*, pp. 7–109.

Fraser, N. (2001b), 'Distorted beyond all recognition: a reply to Axel Honneth', in *Redistribution or Recognition*, pp. 198–236.

Fraser, N. and A. Honneth (2001), 'Introduction: redistribution or recognition?', in *Redistribution or Recognition*, pp. 1–6.

Freeden, M. (2003a), *Ideology: A Very Short Introduction*. Oxford: Oxford University Press.

Freeden, M. (2003a), 'The Struggle over political language', in *Ideology: A Very Short Introduction*, pp. 45–66.

Freeden, M. (1996a), *Ideologies and Political Theory: A Conceptual Approach*. Oxford: Clarendon Press.

Freeden, M. (1996b), 'Assembling: from concepts to ideologies', in *Ideologies and Political Theory: A Conceptual Approach*, pp. 47–95.

Frege, G. (1977), 'On sense and reference', in *Translations from the Philosophical Writings of Gottlob Frege,* trans. P. Geach and M. Black. Oxford: Blackwell, pp. 56–78.

Friedmann, W. (1967), *Legal Theory,* 5th ed. London: Stevens Co.

Friedrich, C. J. (1963 [1958]), *The Philosophy of Law in Historical Perspective,* 2nd ed. Revised and enlarged. Chicago, IL: University of Chicago Press.

Friedrich, C. J. (1955), 'Two philosophical interpretations of natural law', *Diogenes,* 10, 98–112.

Furley, D. J. (1981), 'Antiphon's case against justice,' in G. B. Kerferd ed., *The Sophists and Their Legacy.* Franz Steiner Verlag: Wiesbaden, pp. 81–91.

Gadamer, H. G. (1975a), *Truth and Method,* 2nd revised ed., trans. J. Weinsheimer and D. G. Marshall. London: Sheed & Ward.

Gadamer, H. G. (1975b). 'The hermeneutic relevance of Aristotle', in *Truth and Method,* pp. 312–24.

Gagarin, M. (2002), *Antiphon the Athenian: Oratory, Law and Justice in the Age of the Sophists.* Austin: University of Texas Press.

Gagarin, M. and P. Woodruff, eds. (1995), *Early Greek Political Thought from Homer to the Sophists.* Cambridge: Cambridge University Press.

Gardiner, S. ed. (2005), *Virtue Ethics: Old and New.* Ithaca, NY and London: Cornell University Press.

Garnsey, P. (1999 [1996]), *Ideas of Slavery from Aristotle to Augustine.* Cambridge: Cambridge University Press.

Gewirth, A. (1979), *Reason and Morality.* Chicago: University of Chicago press.

Gierke, O. (1958), *Political Theories of the Middle Age,* trans. and intro. F. W. Maitland. Boston, MA: Beacon Press.

Ginsberg, M. (1971a), *On Justice in Society.* Harmondsworth: Penguin.

Ginsberg, M. (1971b), 'The concept of justice', in *On Justice in Society,* pp. 50–73.

Goheen, R. F. (1951), *The Imagery of Sophocles' Antigone.* Princeton: Princeton University Press.

Gough, G. W. (1967), *The Social Contract: A Critical Study of its Development,* 2nd ed. Oxford: Clarendon Press.

Gouldner, A. W. (1965), *Enter Plato: Classical Greece and the Origins of Social Theory.* London: Routledge & Kegan Paul.

Greene, W. C. (1948), *Moira: Fate, Good and Evil in Greek Thought.* Cambridge, MA: Harvard University Press.

Greenleaf, W. (1968), 'Idealism, modern philosophy and politics', in *Politics and Experience: Essays Presented to Professor Michael Oakeshott on the Occasion of His Retirement,* eds. Preston King and Bhiku Parekh. Cambridge: Cambridge University Press, pp. 107–24.

Grene, M. (1998 [1963]), *A Portrait of Aristotle.* Bristol: Thoemmes Press.

Grotius, H. (2005), *The Rights of War and Peace,* Book I, ed. & intro. R. Tuck. Indianapolis: Liberty Fund.

Gunnell, J. G. (1998), 'Time and interpretation: understanding concepts and conceptual change', *History of Political Thought,* 19, 4, 641–58.

Guthrie, K. S. ed. & trans. (1988 [1920]), *The Pythagorean Sourcebook and Library: An Anthology of Ancient Writings which Relate to Pythagoras and Pythagorean Philosophy,* intro. D. Fideler, foreword by J. Godwin, with additional translations by T. Taylor and A. Fairbanks jnr. Grand Rapids. Mi.: Phanes Press.

Guthrie, W. K. C. (1971), *The Sophists, A History of Greek Philosophy*, Vol. 3, Part I. Cambridge: Cambridge University Press.
Guthrie, W. K. C. (1971a), 'The "*Nomos*"–"*Physis*" Antithesis in Morals and Politics', in *The Sophists, A History of Greek Philosophy*, pp. 55–134.
Guthrie, W. K. C. (1970 [1956]), 'Introduction' to Plato, *Protagoras*, trans. W. K. C. Guthrie, Penguin: Harmondsworth, pp. 7–25.
Guthrie, W. K. C. (1957), 'Aristotle as a historian of philosophy: some preliminaries', *Journal of Hellenic Studies*, 77, pp. 35–41.
Haakonssen, K. (1985), 'Hugo Grotius and the history of political thought', *Political Theory*, 13, 2, 239–65.
Haddock, B. (1974), 'The history of ideas and the study of politics', *Political Theory*, 2, 420–31.
Hamburger, M. (1951), *Morals and Law: The Growth of Aristotle's Legal Theory*. New Haven: Yale University press.
Hamilton, B. (1965), 'Some arguments against natural law theories', in Illtud Evans, ed. *Light on Natural Law*. London: Burns & Oates, p 38.
Hamilton, W. (1975 [1960]), 'Introduction', to Plato, *Gorgias*, trans. Walter Hamilton, Harmondsworth: Penguin Books, pp. 7–18.
Hare, R. M. (1963 [1952]), *The Language of Morals*. Oxford: Oxford University Press.
Hare, R. M. (1963), *Descriptivism*. Oxford: Oxford University Press.
Harris, J. W. (1980), *Legal Philosophies*. London: Butterworths.
Hart, H. L. A. (1961a), *The Concept of Law*. Oxford: Clarendon Press.
Hart, H. L. A. (1961b), 'Formalism and rule scepticism', in *The Concept of Law*, pp. 120–50.
Hart, H. L. A. (1961c), 'Laws and morals', in *The Concept of Law*, pp. 181–207.
Hastings, G. ed. (1914), *The Encyclopaedia of Religion and Ethics*, vol. 6. New York: Charles Scribner & Sons.
Havelock, E. A. (1964 [1957]), *The Liberal Temper in Greek Politics*. New Haven, CT: Yale University Press.
Havelock, E. A. (1964 [1957]), 'Antiphon', in *The Liberal Temper in Greek Politics*. New Haven, CT: Yale University Press, pp. 255–94.
Hearnshaw, F. J. C. ed. (1925), *The Social and Poltiical Ideas of Some Great Thinkers of the Renaissance and Reformation*. London: Harrap.
Hegel, G. W. F. (1991 [1817]), *Elements of the Philosophy of Right*, ed. A. Wood. Cambridge: Cambridge University Press.
Hegel, G. W. F. (1979), *Philosophy of Right*, trans. T. M. Knox. Oxford: Oxford University Press.
Hegel, G. W. F. (1977 [1807], *Phenomenology of Spirit*, trans. A. V. Miller, Foreword J. N. Findlay. Oxford: Oxford University Press.
Hegel, G. W. F. (1975), *Hegel's Logic: Being Part One of the Encyclopaedia of the Philosophical Sciences* (1830), trans. W. Wallace, Intro. J. N. Findlay. Oxford: Clarendon Press.
Hegel, G. W. F. (1970), *Philosophy of Right*, ed. T. M. Knox. Oxford: Oxford University Press.
Hegel, G. W. F. (1968 [1892]), *Hegel's Lectures on the History of Philosophy*, Vol. 1, trans. E. S. Haldane and F. H. Simson. London: Routledge.

Heidegger, M. (1987 [1927]), *Being and Time.* Trans. John Macquarrie & Edward Robinson. Oxford: Blackwell.

Heinaman, R. ed. (1995), *Aristotle and Moral Realism.* Boulder, CO: Westview Press.

Heinimann, F. (1945), *Nomos und Physis: Herkunft und Bedeutung Einer Antithese im Greichischen Denken des 5 Jahrhunderts.* Darmstadt: Wissenschaftlich Buchgesellschaft.

Hertzler, J. O. (1934), 'On golden rules', *International Journal of Ethics* , 44, 4, 418–36.

Hester, D. A. (1971), 'Sophocles the unphilosophical: a study in the *Antigone*', *Mnemosyne,* XXIV, 1–59.

Heyman, S. J. (1991–92), 'Aristotle on Political Justice', *Iowa Law Review,* 77, 851–63.

Hirsch Jr., E. D. (1976), *The Aims of Interpretation.* Chicago, IL: University of Chicago Press.

Hittinger, R. (1994), 'Natural law and virtue: theories at cross purposes', in George ed., *Natural Law Theory: Contemporary Essays.* Oxford: Clarendon, pp. 42–70.

Hittinger, R. (1989), 'After MacIntyre: natural law theory, virtue ethics and eudaimonia', *International Philosophical Quarterly,* 29. 4, 449– 461.

Hobbes, T. (1998 [1642]), *On the Citizen,* trans R. Silverthorne, ed. R. Tuck. Cambridge: Cambridge University Press.

Hobbes, T. (1991 [1651]), *Leviathan,* ed. R. Tuck. Cambridge: Cambridge University Press.

Hobbes, T. (1839–45a), *The English Works of Thomas Hobbes,* in 11 volumes, ed. W. Molesworth. London: Bohn.

Hobbes, T. (1839–45b), *Philosophical Rudiments Concerning Government and Society,* in *The English Works of Thomas Hobbes,* Volume 2.

Hobbes, T. (1839–45b), *The Whole Art of Rhetoric,* in *The English Works of Thomas Hobbes,* Volume VI, pp. 423–510.

Hobbs, A. (2000), 'Why should I be good? Callicles, Thrasymachus and the Egoist Challenge', in *Plato and the Hero: Courage, Manliness and the Impersonal Good.* Cambridge University Press, pp. 137–74.

Honneth, A. (2001), 'Redistribution as Recognition: A Response to Nancy Fraser', in Frasewr and Honneth, eds. *Redistribution or Recognition: A Political-Philosophical Exchange,* pp. 110–97.

Hooker, B. and M. Little eds. (2000), *Moral Particularism.* Oxford: Clarendon Press.

Hooker, R. (1836 [1593]), *Of the Laws of Ecclesiastical Polity,* in *The Works of Richard Hooker,* ed. I. Walton, rev. J. Keble. Oxford: Oxford University Press.

Horsley, R. A. (1978), 'The law of nature in Philo and Cicero', *Harvard Theological Review,* 71, 1/2, 35–9.

Hudson, W. M. ed. (1969a), *The Is/Ought Question: A Collection of Papers on the Central Problem in Moral Philosophy.* London: Macmillan.

Hudson, W. M. ed. (1969b), 'Description and evaluation', in *The Is/Ought Question: A Collection of Papers on the Central Problem in Moral Philosophy,* pp. 175–258.

Hudson, W. M. (1970a), *Modern Moral Philosophy.* London: Macmillan.

Hudson, W. M. (1970b), 'Descriptivism', in *Modern Moral Philosophy,* pp. 249–330.

Hursthouse, R. (1999), *On Virtue Ethics.* Oxford: Oxford University Press.

Irwin, T. (2008), *The Development of Ethics,* Vol. 2, *From Suarez to Rousseau.* Oxford: Oxford University Press.

Irwin, T. (2000), 'Ethics as an inexact science: Aristotle's ambitions for moral theory', in Hooker & Little eds., *Moral Particularism*, pp. 100–29.
Irwin, T. (1996), 'Ethics in the Rhetoric and in the Ethics', in Rorty ed. *Essays on Arisottle's Rhetoric*, pp. 142–74.
Jackson, M. (2001), 'Designed by theorists: Aristotle on utopia', *Utopian Studies*, 12, 2, 1–12.
Jaeger, W. (1939–45), *Paideia: The Ideals of Greek Culture*, in 3 vols. Oxford: Oxford: University Press.
Jefferson, A. and D. Robey eds. (1995 [1982]), *Modern Literary Theory: A Comparative Introduction*, 2nd ed. London: Batsford.
Joachim, H. H. (1951), *Aristotle, The Nicomachean Ethics: A Commentary*. Oxford: Clarendon Press.
Jost, L. A. (1979), 'A descriptivist reading of Aristotle's treatment of virtue terms', *Apeiron*, 13, 41–8.
Kant, I. (1993), *Grounding for the Metaphysics of Morals*, trans. J. W. Ellington. Indianapolis: Hackett.
Kelsen, H. (1973a), *Essays in Legal and Moral Philosophy*, ed. O. Weinberger. Dordrecht: Reidel.
Kelsen, H. (1973b), 'The idea of natural law', in *Essays in Legal and Moral Philosophy*, pp. 27–60.
Kelsen, H. (1973c), 'The foundations of the theory of natural law', in *Essays in Legal and Moral Philosophy*, ed. O. Weinberger. Dordrecht: Reidel, pp. 122–46.
Kelsen, H. (1972a[1961]), *A General Theory of Law and the State*. New York: Russell and Russell.
Kelsen, H. (1972b[1961]), 'Natural law doctrine and legal positivism', in *A General Theory of Law and the State*, pp. 439–40.
Kelsen, H. (1957a), *What is Justice? Justice, Law and Politics in the Mirror of Science: Collected Essays by Hans Kelsen*. Berkeley and Los Angeles: University of California Press.
Kelsen, H. (1957b), 'Aristotle's doctrine of justice', in *What is Justice?*, pp. 125–36.
Kelsen, H. (1957c) 'The natural law doctrine before the tribunal of science', in *What is Justice? Justice, Law and Politics in the Mirror of Science*, pp. 137–73.
Kerferd, G. B. (1981a), *The Sophists and their Legacy*. Wiesbaden: Franz Steiner Verlag.
Kerferd, G. B. (1981b), *The Sophistic Movement*. Cambridge: Cambridge University Press.
Kerferd, G. B. (1981c), 'The *Nomos–Physis* Controversy', in *The Sophistic Movement*. Cambridge: Cambridge University Press, pp. 11–30.
Keyt, D and F. D. Miller Jr. eds. (1991), *A Companion to Aristotle's "Politics"*. Oxford: Blackwell.
Kitto, H. D. F. (1977 [1956]), *Form and Meaning in Drama*. London: Methuen.
Knox, B. M. W. (1983), *The Heroic Temper: Studies in Sophoclean Tragedy*. Berkeley: University of California Press.
Koester, H. (1968), '*ΝΟΜΟΣ ΦΥΣΕΩΣ*: The Concept of Natural Law in Greek Thought', in Neusner ed., *Religions in Antiquity: Essays in Memory of Erwin Ramsdell Goodenough*, pp. 521–40.
Konvitz, M. R. and A. E. Murphy, eds. (1948), *Essays in Political Theory*. New York: Cornell University Press.

Koselleck, R. (1996), 'A response to comments on the *Geschictliche Grundbegriffe*', in Lehmann and Richter eds., *The Meaning of Historical Terms and Concepts: New Studies on Begriffsgeschicte*, pp. 59–70.

Kovesi, J. (1967), *Moral Notions*. London: Routledge.

Kraut, R. (2005), *Aristotle's Politics: Critical Essays*. Lanham, MD.: Rowman & Littlefield.

Kraut, R. (2002), *Aristotle: Political Philosophy*. Oxford: Oxford University Press.

Kripke, S. (1988 [1972]), *Naming and Necessity*. Oxford: Oxford University Press.

Kroger, J. R. (2004), 'The philosophical foundations of Roman law: Aristotle, the Stoics, and Roman theorists of natural law', *Wisconsin Law Review*, 905–44.

Kuhn, T. S. (1970 [1962]), *The Structure of Scientific Revolutions*, 2nd ed. Chicago, IL: University of Chicago Press.

Kuttner, S. (1936), 'Sur les origines du terme droit positif', *Revue historique de droit français et étranger*, 15, 728–740.

Kymlicka, W. (2000), *Contemporary Political Philosophy: An Introduction*, 2nd ed. Oxford: Oxford University Press.

Lane, W. J. and A. M. Lane (1986), 'The politics of *Antigone*', in J. P. Euben ed. *Greek Tragedy and Political Theory*. Berkeley and Los Angeles: University of California Press), pp 162–82.

Laversin, M. J. (1933), 'Droit naturel et droit positif d'après Saint Thomas, *Revue Thomiste*, 38, 3–49, 177–216.

Lefebvre, C. (1963), 'Natural equity and canonical equity', *Natural Law Forum*, 8, 122–36.

Lefebvre, C. (1951), 'Le role de l'équité en droit canonique', *Ephemerides Iuris Canonici*, 7, 137–53.

Lehmann, H and M. Richter eds., *The Meaning of Historical Terms and Concepts: New Studies on Begriffsgeschicte*. Washington D.C.: German Historical Institute.

Lerner, L. ed. (1983), *Reconstructing Literature*. Oxford: Blackwell.

Lesky, A. (1978), *Greek Tragedy*, 3rd ed., ed. and trans. H. Frankfort. London: Ernest Benn.

Levinson, R. B. (1953a), *In Defense of Plato*. Cambridge, MA: Harvard University Press, pp. 139–244.

Levinson, R. B. (1953b), 'Plato and humanitariansm', in *In Defense of Plato*. Cambridge MA: Harvard University Press, pp. 139–244.

Lewis, E. K. (1954), *Medieval Political Ideas*. New York and London: Routledge and Kegan Paul.

Lewis, E. K. (1946) 'Natural law and expediency in medieval political theory', *Ethics*, 50, 144–63.

Lisska, A. J. (1997), *Aquinas's Theory of Natural Law: An Analytic Reconstruction*. Oxford: Clarendon Press.

Lloyd, D. (1972), *The Idea of Law*. Harmondsworth: Penguin.

Lloyd, D. (1959), *Introduction to Jurisprudence*. London: Stevens and Sons.

Lockyer, A. (1979),' "Traditions" as context in the history of political theory', *Political Studies*, 27, 201–17.

Long, A. A. (2005), 'Law and nature in Greek thought', in M. Gagarin and D. Cohen eds., *The Cambridge Companion to Ancient Greek Law*. Cambridge: Cambridge University Press, pp. 412–30.

Long, A. A. (1975–76), 'Heraclitus and Stoicism', *Philosophia*, 5–6, 133–56.

Long, A. A. (1968), 'Aristotle's legacy to Stoic ethics', *Bulletin of the Institute of Classical Studies* 15, 72–85.

Long, A. A. and D. N. Sedley (1987a), *The Hellenistic Philosophers*, Vol. I, *Greek and Latin Texts with Notes and Bibliography*. Cambridge: Cambridge University Press.

Long, A. A. and D. N. Sedley (1987b), *The Hellenistic Philosophers*, Vol. II, *Greek and Latin Texts with Notes and Bibliography*. Cambridge: Cambridge University Press.

Long, R. T. (1996), 'Aristotle's conception of freedom', *The Review of Metaphysics*, XLIX, 4, 776–802.

Louden, R. B. (1997a), 'On some vices of virtue ethics', in Statman ed., *Virtue Ethics: A Critical Reader*, pp. 180–93.

Louden, R. B. (1997b), 'Kant's virtue ethics', in Statman ed., *Virtue Ethics: A Critical Reader*, pp. 286–99.

Lovejoy, A. O. (1960 [1936]), *The Great Chain of Being: A Study of the History of an Idea*. New York: Harper & Row.

Lowes-Dickinson, G. (1960), *The Greek View of Life*. London: Methuen.

Luria, S. (1926), 'On the anarchism of Antiphon,' *Hermes*, 61, 343–8.

MacIntyre, A. (2006a [1999]), *Dependent Rational Animals: Why Human Beings Need the Virtues*. Chicago & Lasalle, IL: Open Court.

MacIntyre, A. (2006b), *Ethics and Politics, Selected Essays*, Volume 2. Cambridge: Cambridge University Press.

MacIntyre, A. (2006c), 'Rival Aristotles: Aristotle against some modern Aristotelians', in *Ethics and Politics, Selected Essays*, Volume 2, pp. 22–40.

MacIntyre, A. (2000 [1981]), *After Virtue: A Study in Moral Theory*, 2nd ed. London: Duckworth.

MacIntyre, A. (1990), *Three Rival Versions of Moral Enquiry: Encyclopaedia, Genealogy and Tradition*. London: Duckworth.

MacIntyre, A. (1988), *Whose Justice? Which Rationality?* London: Duckworth.

MacIntyre, A. (1967), *A Short History of Ethics: A History of Moral Philosophy from the Homeric Age to the Twentieth Century*. London: Routledge.

MacKay, L. A. (1962), 'Antigone, Coriolanus and Hegel', *Transactions of the American Philological Association*, 193, 166–74.

Mackie, J. L. (1988), 'The subjectivity of values', in Geoffrey Sayre-McCord ed., *Essays on Moral Realism*. Ithaca: Cornell University Press.

Maguire, G. P. (1947), 'Plato's theory of natural law', *Yale Classical Studies*, X, 151–78.

Maine, H. (1965a), *Ancient Law*, ed. J. H. Morgan. London.

Maine, H. (1965b), 'Law of nature and equity', in *Ancient Law*, pp. 26–42.

Maitland, F. W. (1936), *Equity: A Course of Lectures*. New York: Macmillan & Co.

Marcus Aurelius (1984), *Meditations*, trans. with an introduction by M. Staniforth. Harmondsworth: Penguin.

Marc-Wogau, K. (1967a), *Philosophical Essays: History of Philosophy, Perception, Historical Explanation*. Library of Theoria, No. XI. Skara: Vastergotlands.

Marc-Wogau, K. (1967b), 'Aristotle's theory of corrective justice and reciprocity', in *Philosophical Essays: History of Philosophy, Perception, Historical Explanation*, pp. 21–40.

Maritain, J. (1942), *The Rights of Man and the Natural Law*. London: Geoffery Bles.

Maritain, J. (1958), *Man and the State.* Chicago, IL: University of Chicago Press.
McCormick, N. (1994), *Legal Reasoning and Legal Theory.* Oxford: Clarendon Press.
McDowell, J. (1998a), *Mind, Value and Reality.* Cambridge, MA.: Harvard University Press.
McDowell, J. (1998b), 'Some issues in Aristotle's moral psychology', in *Mind, Value and Reality*, pp. 23–49.
McDowell, J. (1998c), 'Virtue and reason', in *Mind, Value and Reality*, pp. 50–73.
McDowell, J. (1995), 'Eudaimonism and realism in Aristotle's ethics', in Heineman, ed. *Aristotle and Moral Realism*, pp. 201–18.
McIlwain, C. H. (1932), *The Growth of Political Thought in the West: From the Greeks to the End of the Middle Ages.* New York: Macmillan.
McKay, L. A. (1962) 'Antigone, Coriolanus and Hegel', *Transactions of the American Philological Association*, 193, 166–74.
McKirahan, R. (1994), *Philosophy Before Socrates.* Indianapolis: Hackett.
McLean, E. P. ed. (2004), *Common Truths: New Perspectives on Natural Law.* Wilmington Delaware: IS Books.
Meiksins-Wood, E. and N. Wood (1978), *Class Ideology and Ancient Poltiical Theory: Socrates, Plato and Arisottle in Social Context.* Oxford: Blackwell.
Merlan, P. (1950), 'Alexander the Great or Antiphon the Sophist?', *Classical Philology*, 45, 161–66.
Michelfelder, D. P. and R. E. Palmer (1989), *Dialogue and Deconstruction: The Gadamer-Derrida Debate.* Albany, NY: SUNY Press.
Miller Jr. F. and Carrie-Ann Biondi, eds. (2007), *A Treatise of Legal Philosophy and General Jurisprudence*, Vol. 6, *History of the Philosophy of Law From the Ancient Greeks to the Scholastics.* Dordrecht: Kluwer.
Miller Jr. F. (2007), 'Aristotle's philosophy of law', in *History of the Philosophy of Law From the Ancient Greeks to the Scholastics*, pp. 79–110.
Miller Jr. F. (2000), 'Naturalism', in Rowe and Schofield eds., *The Cambridge History of Greek and Roman Political Thought*, pp. 321–43.
Miller Jr. F. (1997), *Nature, Justice and Rights in Aristotle's Politics.* Oxford: Oxford University Press.
Miller Jr. F. (1991), 'Aristotle on natural law and justice', in Keyt and Miller eds., *A Companion to Aristotle's Politics*, pp. 279–306.
Miller Jr. F. (1989), 'Aristotle's political naturalism,' in Penner and Kraut eds., *Nature, Knowledge and Virtue: Essays in Memory of Joan Kung*, pp. 195–218.
Moffatt, A. ed. (1984), *Maistor: Classical, Byzantine and Renaissance Studies for Robert Browning.* Canberra: Australian Association for Byzantine Studies.
Morrall, J. B. (1977), *Aristotle.* London: Routledge.
Morrall, J. B. (1958), *Medieval Political Thought.* New York: Harper Torchbooks.
Morrow, G. R. (1948), 'Plato and the law of nature', in R. Konvitz and A. E. Murphy eds., *Essays in Political Theory*, pp. 17–26.
Moulton, C. (1972), 'Antiphon the Sophist, *On Truth*', *Transactions and Proceedings of the American Philological Association*, 103, 329–66.
Mulgan, R. G. (1977), *Aristotle's Political Theory: An Introduction for Students of Political Thought.* Oxford: Clarendon Press.
Murphy, J. B. and R. O. Brooks, eds. (2003), *Aristotle and Modern Law.* London: Ashgate Dartmouth.

Murray, G. (1913), *Euripides and His Age*. London: Williams & Norgate.
Myres, J. L. (1975 [1927]), *The Political Ideas of the Greeks: With Special Reference to Early Notions about Law, Authority, and Natural Order in Relation to Human Ordinance*. New York: Augustus M. Kelley.
Nelson, D. M. (1992), *The Priority of Prudence: Virtue and Natural Law in Thomas Aquinas and the Implications for Modern Ethics*. Pennsylvania: Pennsylvania State University Press.
Neumann, F. (1957), 'Types of natural law', in *The Democratic and the Authoritarian State: Essays in Political and Legal Theory*. Chicago: University of Chicago Press, pp. 73–83.
Neusner, J. ed. (1968), *Religions in Antiquity: Essays in Memory of Erwin Ramsdell Goodenough*. Leiden: Brill.
Newman, R. ed. (1973), *Equity in the World's Legal Systems: A Comparative Study*. Brussels: Bruylant.
Newman, W. L. ed. (1881–1902), *Aristotle: The Politics*, in four volumes. Oxford: Oxford University Press.
Nietzsche, F. (1968), *The Will to Power*, trans. W. Kaufmann and R. J. Hollingdale. New York: Vintage Books.
Nill, M. (1985), *Morality and Self-Interest in Protagoras, Antiphon and Democritus*. Leiden: Brill.
Norman, R. (1990 [1983]), *The Moral Philosophers: An Introduction to Ethics*. Oxford: Clarendon Press.
North, H. F. ed. (1977), *Interpretations of Plato*. Leiden: Brill.
Ober, J. (1995), 'Law and political theory'. in Gagarin and Cohen eds., *The Cambridge Companion to Ancient Greek Law*, pp. 394–411.
Ostwald, M. (1990), '*Nomos* and *Phusis* in Antiphon's Περι Αληθεια, in M. Griffith and D. J. Mastronarde, eds., *Cabinet of the Muses: Essays on Classical and Comparative Literature in Honour of Thomas G. Rosenmeyer*. Atlanta, pp. 293–306.
Ostwald, M. (1977), 'Plato on law and nature', in H. F. North ed., *Interpretations of Plato*, pp. 41–63.
Ostwald, M. (1973),'Was there a concept of νομos φυσεos in Classical Greece', in E. N. Lee ed., *Exegesis and Argument: Studies in Greek Philosophy Presented to Gregory Vlastos*. Assen: Van Gorcum, pp. 70–104.
Palonen, K. (2003a), *Quentin Skinner: History, Politics, Rhetoric*. Cambridge: Polity Press.
Palonen, K. (2003b), 'Conceptual change through rhetorical redescription', in *Quentin Skinner: History, Politics, Rhetoric*, pp. 161–8.
Palonen, K. (2000), 'Logic or rhetoric in the history of political thought? Comments on Mark Bevir', *Rethinking History: The Journal of Theory and Practice*, 4. 3, 301–10.
Palonen, K. (1999), 'Rhetorical and temporal perspectives on conceptual change', *Finnish Yearbook of Political Thought*, 3, 41–9.
Palonen, K. (1997), 'Quentin Skinner's rhetoric of conceptual change', *History of the Human Sciences*, 10, 2, 61–80.
Pangle, T. L. and P. J. Ahrensdorf (1999), *Justice Among Nations: On the Moral Basis of Power and Peace*. Lawrence: University Press of Kansas.
Parry, G. (2003), *Political Thinkers: Aristotle*. London: Routledge.
Parry, G. (2004), *Political Thinkers: From Aristotle to Marx*. London: Routledge.

Patterson, D. M. ed. (2004), *Wittgenstein and Law*. Aldershot: Ashgate.
Patterson, D. M. ed. (1992), *Wittgenstein and Legal Theory*. Boulder, CO: Westview Press.
Patzig, G. ed. (1990), *Aristoteles' "Politik": Akten des XI Symposium Aristotelicum*. Gottingen: Vandenhoeck.
Pendrick G. J. ed. (2002), *Antiphon of Athens: The Fragments/Antiphon the Sophist*, with introduction, translation and commentary. Cambridge: Cambridge University Press.
Penner, T. and R. Kraut eds. (1989), *Nature, Knowledge and Virtue: Essays in Memory of Joan Kung*. Edmonton.
Perelman, Ch. (1980), *Justice, Law and Argument: Essays on Legal and Moral Reasoning*. Dordrecht: Kluwer.
Perelman, Ch. (1980), 'Equity and the rule of justice', in *Justice, Law and Argument*, pp. 34–43.
Perelman, Ch. (1967a), *Justice*. New York: Random House.
Perelman, Ch. (1967b), 'Justice and its problems', in *Justice*, pp. 3–17.
Perelman, Ch. (1967c), 'Equity and the rule of justice', in *Justice*, pp. 18–34.
Perelman, Ch. (1963), *The Idea of Justice and the Problem of Argument*. London.
Plato (1996 [1925]), *Gorgias*, trans. W. R. M. Lamb. Cambridge MA: Harvard University Press. Loeb Classical Library.
Plato (1994), *Gorgias*, ed. and trans. R. Waterfield. Oxford: Oxford University Press.
Plato (1981 [1926]), *Laws*, trans. R. G. Bury. Cambridge, MA: Harvard University Press.
Plato (1959), *Gorgias*, ed. and trans E. R. Dodds. Oxford.
Plato (1952 [1924]), *Protagoras*, trans. W. R. M. Lamb. Cambridge, MA: Harvard University Press. Loeb Classical Library.
Platts, M. (1988), 'Moral reality', in Sayre-McCord ed. *Essays on Moral Realism*, pp. 282–300.
Pollock, F. (1961a). *Jurisprudence and Legal Essays*, intro. A. L. Goodhart. London: Macmillan.
Pollock, F. (1961b), 'The history of the law of nature', in *Jurisprudence and Legal Essays*, pp. 124–56.
Pomeroy, A. J. ed. (1999), *Arius Didymus. Epitome of Stoic Ethics*. Atlanta, GA: Society of Biblical Literature.
Ponton, L. (1987), 'Eric Weil: Le droit naturel aristotélicien et les droits de l'homme', *Laval Theologique et Philosophique*, 43, 49–65.
Popper, K. R. (1969a), *The Open Society and its Enemies*, Vol. I, *The Spell of Plato*. London: Routledge.
Popper, K. R. (1969b) *The Open Society and its Enemies*, Vol. II, *The High Tide of Prophecy: Hegel, Marx and the Aftermath*. London: Routledge.
Putnam, R. (1993), 'Aristotle after Wittgenstein', in Sharples, ed. *Modern Thinkers and Ancient Thinkers*, pp. 117–37.
Raphael, D. D. (1970), *Problems of Political Philosophy*. London: Macmillan.
Raphael, D. D. (1946), 'Equality and equity', *Philosophy*, 21, pp. 118–32.
Rawls, J. (1999 [1972]), *A Theory of Justice*, rev. ed. Oxford: Oxford University Press.
Rawls, J. (1978 [1972]), *A Theory of Justice*. Oxford: Oxford University Press.
Raz, J. (1994), 'Formalism and the rule of law', in George ed., *Natural Law Theory: Contemporary Essays*, pp. 309–40.

Reesor, M. E. (1987), 'The *Truth* of Antiphon the Sophist', *Apeiron*, 20, 203–18.

Reesor, M. E. (1951), *The Political Theory of the Old and Middle Stoa*. New York: Augustin.

Reid, T. (1991 [1788]), *Essays on the Active Powers of Man*, in Raphael ed., British Moralists: 1650–1800, Vol. II, pp. 273–6.

Remow, G. (2008), 'Aristotle, Antigone and natural justice, *History of Political Thought*, XXIX, 4, 585–600.

Renault, A. (1991), 'Aristote et le droit naturel', in A. Renault and L. Sosoe eds., *Philosophie du Droit, Philosophie du Droit*. Paris: Presses Universitaires de France, pp. 233–55.

Renault, A. and L. Sosoe eds. (1991), *Philosophie du Droit*. Paris: Presses Universitaires de France.

Richter, M. (1995), *The History of Political and Social Concepts: A Critical Introduction*. Oxford: Oxford University Press.

Ricoeur, P. (1983a), *Hermeneutics and the Human Sciences: Essays on Language, Action and Interpretation*, ed. J. B. Thompson. New York: Cambridge University Press.

Ricoeur, P. (1983b), 'Appropriation', in *Hermeneutics and the Human Sciences: Essays on Language, Action and Interpretation*, pp. 182–93.

Ricoeur, P. (1976), *Interpretation Theory: Discourse and the Surplus of Meaning*. Fort Worth, TX: The Texas Christian University Press.

Riley, J. (1948), *The History, Nature and Uses of Epieikeia in Moral Theology*. Washington, DC.: Catholic University of America Press.

Riley, J. (1948), 'A conspectus of the meaning of "epieikeia" and "aequitas" in history', in *The History, Nature and Uses of Epieikeia in Moral Theology*, pp. 10–18.

Risser, J. (1997), *Hermeneutics and the Voice of the Other: Re-Reading Gadamer's Philosophical Hermeneutics*. New York: SUNY Press.

Ritchie, D. G. (1916 [1894]), *Natural Rights: A Criticism of Some Political and Ethical Conceptions*, 3rd ed. London: Macmillan.

Ritchie, D. G. (1916 [1894]), 'On the history of the idea of "nature" in law and politics', in *Natural Rights*, pp. 20–47.

Ritchie, D. G. (1894), 'Aristotle's subdivisions of particular justice', *Classical Review*, VIII, 185–92.

Ritter, J. (1969), 'Le droit naturel chez Aristote: contribution au renouveau du droit naturel', *Archives de Philosophie*, 32, 416–57.

Roberts, J. (2005 [2000]), 'Natural and conventional justice', in C. Rowe and M. Schofield eds., *The Cambridge History of Greek and Roman Political Thought*. Cambridge: Cambridge University Press, pp. 345–50.

Robson, W. A. (1935), *Civilization and the Growth of Law: A Study of the Relations Between Men's Ideas About the Universe and the Institutions of Law and Government*. London: Macmillan.

Rommen, H. (1998 [1947]), *The Natural Law: A Study in Legal and Social History and Philosophy*. Indianapolis: Liberty Fund.

Rorty, A. S. ed. (1996), *Essays on Aristotle's Rhetoric*. Berkely and Los Angeles: University of California Press.

Rosen, S. (2003a [1990]), *Hermeneutics as Politics*, 2nd ed., with a foreword by Robert B. Pippin. New Haven, CT: Yale University Press.

Rosen, S. (2003b), 'Hermeneutics as politics', in *Hermeneutics as Politics*, pp. 87–140.

Ross, A. (2007a [1959]), *On Law and Justice*. Harmondsworth: Penguin.

Ross, A. (2007b [1959]), 'The idea of justice', in *On Law and Justice*, pp. 268–88.
Ross, W. D. (1964), *Aristotle*. London: Methuen.
Rowbotham, S. (1973), *Hidden From History: Rediscovering Women in History From the Seventeenth Century to the Present*. Harmondsworth: Penguin.
Rowe, C. and M. Schofield eds., (2000), *The Cambridge History of Greek and Roman Political Thought*. Cambridge: Cambridge University Press.
Ryan, C. (1965) 'The traditional concept of natural law', in I. Evans ed., *Light on the Natural Law*, pp. 13–18.
Sabine, G. H. (1973a), *A History of Political Theory*, 4th ed. Hinsdale, IL: Holt Saunders.
Sabine, G. H. (1973b), 'Nature and convention', in *A History of Political Theory*, 4th ed., pp. 42–5.
Sabine, G. H. and S. Barney Smith (n.d. [1929]), 'The political theory of the Stoics', in Cicero, *On the Commonwealth*, trans. and intro. G. H. Sabine and Stanley Barney Smith. Indianapolis: Bobbs-Merrill, pp. 7–38.
Saller, R. P. and B. D. Shaw eds. (1981), *Economy and Society in Ancient Greece*. London.
Salmond, J. W. (1895), 'The law of nature', *The Law Quarterly Review*, 42, 121–43.
Salomon Shellens, M. (1959), 'Aristotle on natural law', *Natural Law Forum*, 4, 1, 72–100.
Salomon, M. (1937), 'Le droit natural chez Aristote', *Archives de philosophie de droit et de sociologie juridique*, 7, 120–27.
Sanbach, F. H. (1985), *Aristotle and the Stoics*. Cambridge: Cambridge Philological Society.
Santas, G. X. (1997), 'Does Aristotle have a virtue ethics?' in Statman ed. *Virtue Ethics: A Critical Reader*, pp. 260–85.
Santirocco, M. (1980) 'Justice in Sophocles' *Antigone*', *Philosophy and Literature*, IV, 180–198.
Saunders, T. J. (1984), 'The controversy about slavery reported in Aristotle, *Politics* I vi, 1255 a 4ff', in Moffatt ed., *Maistor: Classical, Byzantine and Renaissance Studies for Robert Browning*, pp. 25–36.
Saunders, T. J. (1977–78), 'Antiphon the Sophist on Natural Laws (B44DK)', *Proceedings of the Aristotelian Society*, 7, 215–35.
Sayre-McCord, G. (1988a), *Essays on Moral Realism*. Ithaca and London: Cornell University Press.
Sayre-McCord, G. (1988b), 'Introduction: the many moral realisms', in *Essays on Moral Realism*, pp. 1–26.
Schlaifer, R. (1968 [1936]), 'Greek theories of slavery from Homer to Aristotle', in M. Finley ed., *Slavery in Classical Antiquity*. Cambridge: Heffer, pp. 165–204.
Schneewind, J. B. (1998), *The Invention of Autonomy: A History of Modern Moral Philosophy*. Cambridge: Cambridge University Press.
Schneewind, J. B. (1998a), 'Natural law restated: Suarez and Grotius', in *The Invention of Autonomy: A History of Modern Moral Philosophy*, pp. 58–81.
Schofield, M. S. (1990), 'Ideology and philosophy in Aristotle's theory of slavery' in G. Patzig ed., *Aristoteles' "Politik": Akten des XI Symposium Aristotelicum*, pp. 1–27.
Schofield, M. S. (1996), 'Sharing in the constitution', *The Review of Metaphysics*, XLIX, 4, 831–58.
Schrift, A. D. (1990), *Nietzsche and the Question of Interpretation; Between Hermeneutics and Deconstruction*. London: Routledge.

Schroeder, D. N. (1981), 'Aristotle on law', *Polis*, 4, 17–31.
Scruton, R. (1983), 'Public text and common reader', in Lerner ed., *Reconstructing Literature*, pp. 36–59.
Segal, C. P. (1964), 'Sophocles' praise of man and the conflicts of the *Antigone*', *Arion*, 3, 44–66.
Selsam, H. (1947), *Socialism and Ethics*. London: Lawrence and Wishart.
Selznick, P. (1961), 'Sociology and natural law', *Natural Law Forum*, 6, 84–108.
Sharples, R. W. ed. (1993), *Modern Thinkers and Ancient Thinkers*. Boulder, CO: Westview Press.
Shephard, J. (1947), *The Wisdom of Sophocles*. London: Allen and Unwin.
Sherman, N. (1997a), *Making a Necessity of Virtue: Aristotle and Kant on Virtue*. Cambridge: Cambridge University Press.
Sherman, N. (1997b), 'Aristotelian particularism', in *Making a Necessity of Virtue: Aristotle and Kant on Virtue*, pp. 239–75.
Shiner, R. A. (1994), 'Aristotle's theory of equity', *Loyola of Los Angeles Law Review*, 27, 4, 1245–64.
Shorey, P. (1933), *What Plato Said: A Resume of the Entire Body of the Platonic Writings*, Chicago, IL: University of Chicago Press.
Sigmund, P. E. (1971), *Natural Law in Political Thought*. Cambridge, MA: Winthrop.
Silverman, H. J. (1994), *Textualities: Between Hermeneutics and Deconstruction*. London: Routledge.
Silverman, H. J. and D. Ihde eds. (1985), *Hermeneutics and Deconstruction*. Albany, NY: SUNY Press.
Simpson, P. (1997), 'Contemporary virtue ethics and Aristotle', in Statman ed., *Virtue Ethics: A Critical Reader*, pp. 245–59.
Sinclair, T. A. (1959 [1951]), *A History of Greek Political Thought*. London: Routledge.
Skinner, Q. (2002a), *Regarding Method, Visions of Politics*, Vol. I. Cambridge: Cambridge University Press.
Skinner, Q. (2002b), 'Retrospect: studying rhetoric and conceptual change,' in *Visions of Politics*, Vol. 1, 175–87.
Skinner, Q. (2002c), *Hobbes and Civil Science, Visions of Politics*, Vol. III. Cambridge: Cambridge University Press.
Skinner, Q. (2002d), 'Hobbes on rhetoric and the construction of morality', in *Hobbes and Civil Science, Visions of Politics*, 87–142.
Skinner, Q. (1999), 'Rhetoric and conceptual change', *Finnish Yearbook of Political Thought*, 3, 60–73.
Skinner, Q. (1996), *Reason and Rhetoric in the Philosophy of Hobbes*. Cambridge: Cambridge University Press.
Skinner, Q. (1995 [1989]), 'Language and political change', in T. Ball, J. Farr and L. Hanson eds., *Political Innovation and Conceptual Change*, pp. 6–23.
Skinner, Q. (1985), *The Return of Grand Theory in the Human Sciences*. Cambridge: Cambridge University Press.
Skinner, Q. (1985a), 'Introduction: The Return of Grand Theory', in *The Return of Grand Theory in the Human Sciences*, pp. 1–20.
Slote, M. (1992), *From Morality to Virtue*. New York: Oxford University Press.
Smith, M. (1991), 'Aristotle's theory of natural slavery', in Keyt and Miller eds., *A Companion to Aristotle's Politics*, pp. 142–55.
Smith, S. B. (1991), *Hegel's Critique of Liberalism: Rights in Context*. Chicago, IL: University of Chicago Press.

Snell, E. H. T. (1915), *The Principles of Equity*, 17th. ed. London: Sweet and Maxwell.
Snyder, R. N. (1973), 'Natural law and equity', in Newman ed., *Equity in the World's Legal Systems*, pp. 33–43.
Sophocles (1987), *Sophocles' Antigone*, ed. and trans., Andrew. L. Brown. Warminster: Aris & Phillips.
Sophocles (1970), *Sophocles: the Theban Plays*, trans. E. F. Watling. Harmondsworth: Penguin.
Spooner, W. A. (1914), 'Golden rule', in Hastings ed., *The Encyclopaedia of Religion and Ethics*, vol. 6.
St. German, C. (1974), *Doctor and Student*, eds. T. F. T. Plunckett and J. L. Barton. London: The Selden Society.
St. Leger, J. (1962), *The Etiamsi Daremus of Hugo Grotius: A Study in the Origins of International Law*. Rome: Pontificium Athenaeum Internationale.
Stammler, R. (1969 [1925]), *The Theory of Justice*. New Jersey: Lawbook Exchange.
Statman, D. ed. (1997a), *Virtue Ethics: A Critical Reader*. Edinburgh: Edinburgh University Press.
Statman, D. (1997b), 'Introduction to virtue ethics', in *Virtue Ethics: A Critical Reader*, pp. 1–41.
Steiner, G. (1984), *Antigones: The Antigone Myth in Western Literature, Art and Thought*. Oxford: Clarendon Press.
Stevenson, J. G. (1974), 'Aristotle as historian of philosophy', *Journal of Hellenic Studies*, 94, 138–43.
Stewart, J. (1996), *The Hegel Myths and Legends*. Evanston, IL: Northwestern University Press.
Stewart, J. A. (1892), *Notes on the Nicomachean Ethics of Aristotle*, in 2 volumes. Oxford.
Strauss, L. (1983a), *Studies in Platonic Political Philosophy*. Chicago, IL: University of Chicago Press.
Strauss, L. (1983b [1968]), 'On natural law', in *Studies in Platonic Political Philosophy*, pp. 237–46.
Strauss, L. (1974 [1953]), *Natural Right and History*. Chicago, IL: University of Chicago Press.
Strauss, L. (1973 [1936]), *The Political Philosophy of Hobbes: Its Basis and Its Genesis*, Chicago, IL: University of Chicago Press.
Strauss, L. (1969 [1958]), *Thoughts on Machiavelli*. Seattle and London: University of Washington Press.
Strauss, L. (1968a [1959]), *Liberalism: Ancient and Modern*. New York: Clarendon Press.
Strauss, L. (1968b [1959]), 'The liberalism of classical political philosophy', in *Liberalism: Ancient and Modern*, pp. 26–64.
Striker, G. (1996), 'Origins of the concept of natural law', in *Essays on Hellenistic Epistemology and Ethics*. Cambridge: Cambridge University Press, pp. 209–20.
Striker, G. (1987) 'Origins of the concept of natural law', *Proceedings of the Boston Area Colloquium in Ancient Philosophy*, 2, 79–94.
Strong, T. B. (2000 [1975]), *Friedrich Nietzsche and the Politics of Transfiguration*. Urbana: University of Illinois Press.
Stuurman, S. (2000), 'On intellectual innovation and the methodology of the history of ideas', *Rethinking History: The Journal of Theory and Practice*, 4(3), 311–19.

Suarez, F. (1995a [1612]), *Selections from Three Works*, trans. L. Wlliams, A. Brown and J. Waldron, revised H. Davis, intro J. B. Scott. New York: Hein & Co.
Suarez, F. (1995b), *De Legibus ac deo Legislatore*, in *Selections from Three Works*, pp. 1–646.
Swanson, J. (1999), 'Aristotle on nature, human nature, and justice', in Bartlett and Collins eds., *Action and Contemplation: Studies in the Moral and Political Thought of, Aristotle*, pp. 225–47.
Synodinou, K. (1977), *On the Concept of Slavery in Euripides*. Ioannina: University of Ioannina Press.
Taylor, A. E. (1955), *Aristotle*. New York: Dover Publications.
Taylor, A. E. (1949 [1908]), *Plato: The Man and His Work*. London: Methuen.
Tessitore, A. ed. (2002), *Aristotle and Modern Politics: The Persistence of Political Philosophy*. University of Notre Dame Press.
Thompson, E. P. (1975), *The Making of the English Working Class*. Harmondsworth: Penguin.
Thucydides (1952), *History of the Peloponnesian War, in four volumes*, Vol. III *Books V and VI*, with an English translation by C. Foster Smith. Cambridge, MA: Harvard University Press. Loeb Classical Library.
Tierney, B. (1997), *The Idea of Natural Rights: Studies on Natural Rights, Natural Law and Church Law: 1150–1625*. Grand Rapids, MI: William Eerdman.
Torrance, R. M. (1965) 'Sophocles: some bearings', *Harvard Studies in Classical Philology*, 619, 269–327.
Trianosky, G. (1990), 'What is virtue ethics all about?' *American Philosophical Quarterly*, 27, 335–44.
Tuck, R. (1979), *Natural Rights Theories: Their Origin and Development*. Cambridge: Cambridge University Press.
Twining, W. and D. Miers (1986a [1976]), *How to Do Things with Rules*, 2nd ed. London: Weidenfield & Nicolson.
Twining, W. and D. Miers (1986b [1976]), 'Interpretation and application', in *How to Do Things with Rules*, pp. 165–88.
Ullmann, W. (1975), *Law and Politics in the Middle Ages*. London: Hodder & Stoughton.
Untersteiner, M. (1954), *The Sophists*, trans. K. Freeman. Oxford: Basil Blackwell.
Van den Eynde, D. (1949), 'The terms *ius positivum* and *signum positivum* in Twelfth Century scholasticism', *Franciscan Studies*, 9, 41–9.
Vinogradoff, P. (1943), *Common Sense in Law*. London: Oxford University Press.
Vinogradoff, P. (1923), *Historical Jurisprudence*. Oxford: Oxford University Press.
Vinogradoff, P. (1908), 'Reason and conscience in sixteenth century Jurisprudence', *The Law Quarterly Review*, 96, 373–74.
Vogel, J. (1996), 'The tragedy of history', *New Left Review*, 220, 36–61.
Vogt, J. (1974a), *Ancient Slavery and the Ideal of Man*. Oxford: Basil Blackwell.
Vogt, J. (1974b), 'Slavery and the ideal of man in classical Greece', in *Ancient Slavery and the Ideal of Man*, pp. 1–25.
von Leyden, W. (1985), *Aristotle on Equality and Justice: His Political Argument*. London.
Waismann, F. (1978), 'On verifiability', in *The Theory of Meaning*, ed. G. H. R. Parkinson Oxford: Oxford University Press, pp. 35–60.
Warnock, G. J. (1971), *The Object of Morality*. London: Methuen.
Waterfield, R. (2000), *The First Philosophers: The Presocratics and the Sophists*. Oxford: Oxford University Press.

Watson, G. (1996), 'The natural law and Stoicism', in A. A. Long ed., *Problems in Stoicism*. London: Athlone Press, pp. 217–36.

Watson, G. (1966) 'The early history of natural law', *Irish Theological Quarterly*, 33, 65–74.

Weinreb, L. L. (1994), 'Natural law and rights', in George ed., *Natural Law Theory: Contemporary Essays*, pp. 278–308.

Weinreb, L. L. (1987), *Natural Law and Justice*. Cambridge, MA: Harvard University Press.

Weinreb, L. L. (1978), 'Law as order', *Harvard Law Review*, 91, 909–59.

Weinrib, E. (1994), 'Why legal formalism?' in George ed., *Natural Law Theory: Contemporary Essays*, pp. 341–64.

Weinrib, E. J. (1991–92), 'Corrective justice', *Iowa Law Review*, 77, 404–24.

Weinrib, E. J. (1987), 'Legal formalism: on the immanent rationality of law', *Yale Law Journal*, 97, 949–84.

Weldon, T. D. (1953), *The Vocabulary of Politics*. Harmondsworth: Penguin.

Westphal, J. (1996), *Justice*. Indianapolis: Hackett.

White, N. P. (1979), 'The basis of Stoic ethics', *Harvard Studies in Classical Philology*, 83, 143–78.

Whitman, C. H. (1951), *Sophocles: A Study in Heroic Humanism*. Cambridge, MA: Harvard University Press.

Wild, J. (1953), *Plato's Modern Enemies and the Theory of Natural Law*. Chicago: University of Chicago Press.

Willey, B. (1965), *The English Moralists*. London: Methuen.

Williams, B. (1967), 'The idea of equality', in P. Laslett and W. G. Runciman, eds., *Philosophy, Politics and Society*, second series, pp. 110–31.

Winnington-Ingram, R. P. (1980), *Sophocles: An Interpretation*. Cambridge: Cambridge University Press.

Winthrop, D. (1978), ' Aristotle and theories of justice', *American Political Science Review*, 72(4), 1201–16.

Wittgenstein, L. (1972), *Philosophical Investigations*, trans. G. E. M. Anscombe. Oxford: Blackwell.

Wittgenstein, L. (1969), *The Blue and Brown Books: Preliminary Studies For the Philosophical Investigations*. Oxford: Blackwell.

Wolin, S. (2004a [1964]), *Politics and Vision*, expanded second edition. Princeton, NJ: Princeton University Press.

Wolin, S. (2004b [1964]), 'Tradition and innovation', in *Politics and Vision*, pp. 23–26.

Wollheim, R. (1967), 'Natural law', *The Encyclopaedia of Philosophy*, ed. Paul Edwards, New York: Macmillan, 5, 450–54.

Wormuth, F. D. (1948), 'Aristotle on law', in Konvitz and Murphy eds., *Essays in Political Theory*, pp. 45–61.

Wright, E. (1995 [1982]), 'Modern psychoanalytic criticism', in Jefferson and Robey eds., *Modern Literary Theory*, pp. 145–65.

Yack, B. (1993), *The Problems of a Political Animal: Community, Justice and Conflict in Aristotelian Political Thought*. Berkeley: University of California Press.

Yack, B. (1990), 'Natural right and Aristotle's understanding of justice', *Political Theory*, 18, 2, 216–37.

Zeller, E. (1997 [1883]), *Outlines of the History of Greek Philosophy*. Bristol: Thoemmes Press.

Index

www.ingramcontent.com/pod-product-compliance
Ingram Content Group UK Ltd.
Pitfield, Milton Keynes, MK11 3LW, UK
UKHW020141290926
15471UKWH00004B/623

9 781472 506603